"As a reporter, Browning reveals himself as sensitive, honest, and wryly unillusioned, an appealing character. His approach is always thoughtful, sometimes engaged, sometimes detached. A central, unifying image or metaphor is the image of desire; elusive, spent, and self-renewing, desire that he embodies in autobiographical, journalistic and poetic terms to unify his book and bring it home."
—*Boston Globe*

"Portraying the best and the worst of gay culture [and] covering a wide variety of races and professions, *The Culture of Desire* juxtaposes drag queens and tobacco farmers, corporate accountants and triathletes, radical faeries and seminarians, liberal gay rabbis and the Sisters of Perpetual Indulgence, a venerable Bay Area sect of unspeakably obscene, transvestite 'nuns.'"
—*Los Angeles Times Book Review*

"Browning has traveled the lush archipelago of American gay life and brought back a spellbinding piece of anthropological reportage."
—*Boston Phoenix Literary Section*

"Ambitious . . . one is always engaged by Browning's thinking and conclusions. *The Culture of Desire* manages to provoke and tantalize. Browning's inquiries seem vibrant. . . . He is deeply engaged in and committed to examining and understanding gay male life."
—*Advocate*

"Provocative."
—*Philadelphia Daily News*

"*The Culture of Desire* is a valuable contribution to understanding [gay] culture."
—*Lambda Book Report*

Frank Browning

The Culture of Desire

Frank Browning has reported for National Public Radio since 1983 and has covered issues ranging from the rise of neo-Nazi movements to the Iran–contra scandal to the social impact of the AIDS epidemic. The coauthor of *The American Way of Crime,* he is a recipient of the Alicia Patterson Fellowship. He lives in New York and Kentucky.

The Culture of Desire

**Paradox
and
Perversity
in
Gay
Lives
Today**

Frank Browning

Vintage Books
A Division of Random House, Inc.
New York

First Vintage Books Edition, April 1994

Library of Congress Cataloging-in-Publication Data
Browning, Frank.
The culture of desire : paradox and perversity in gay lives today
/ Frank Browning.—1st Vintage Books ed.
p.   cm.
Includes bibliographical references and index.
ISBN 0-679-75030-4
1. Gay men—United States.   2. Life-style—United States.
3. Subculture.   I. Title.
HQ76.U5B745   1994
306.76′62—dc20   93-42430
CIP

Author photograph © Marc Geller

Manufactured in the United States of America

10 9 8 7 6 5 4 3

Contents

Acknowledgments

Attempting to acknowledge all those who have made a book possible is almost always an unrealizable endeavor—all the more so when the work has been a journey of self-clarification. In this case, the list would include those who have been supportive and those who have been revolted by any mention of homosexuality. Formally, the interviewing for and writing of this book took two years, but the events, relationships, and remembrances that propelled me toward it have occupied the better part of a lifetime.

For thoughts, suggestions, and creative argument, I am indebted to many friends and colleagues, homo and hetero, among them David Bank, William Beeman, Kai Bird, Adam Block, Joseph Blum, Eleanor Burkett, Judith Coburn, Andrea Eagan, Richard Eagan, Doug Foster, Marc Geller, Fred Hersch, Fred Hertz, Beth Horowitz, Deborah Johnson, Robert Johnston, Michael Kazin, Gali Kronenberg, Eric Marcus, Danny Matherly, Andrew

Mellen, Andrew Moss, Barry Owen, Raul Ramirez, Eric Rofes, Steven Rosenberg, Dan Share, Sophie Fierro-Share, Sharon Silva, Tom Stoddard, Bob Thompson, David Tuller, Victor Zonana, Robert Weingarten, and Ron Zuckerman.

Others who also read portions of the manuscript and gave valuable criticism include Jeffrey Escoffier, John Dinges, Linda Hunt, Lynn Meyer, Brenda Wilson, and Frank Viviano. At National Public Radio, senior science editor Anne Gudenkauf provided smart and inspirational guidance during my two years there as an "AIDS reporter," a stint that in many ways led to my writing this book.

In addition, I would like to thank Arthur Kretchmer and Playboy Enterprises for financial support, and Margaret Engel of the Alicia Patterson Foundation, which awarded me a fellowship in 1991.

I owe enormous gratitude to a remarkable editor, David Groff, who offered guidance to my research and singular skill in untangling too many knotted sentences. And finally, for the remembrance of C, whose presence and devotion made life seem sweeter.

Introduction

◆

Tradition. Memory. Convention. Life-style. Culture.

In the year since the hardcover edition of *The Culture of Desire* appeared, these are the terms of conversation that have arisen as I have traveled the post-publication reading and interview circuit. This seems to be an apt moment to reflect on how those discussions have affected my own perceptions about the shifting nature of "gay culture" in America.

I am writing in a small, chilly apartment set along the Rio di San Girolamo, a small canal in Venice. Each morning motorized barges chug along the *fondamento* below the windows, picking up trash, loading large panes of window glass, hauling heavy cargos of lumber and masonry, delivering fresh crates of cheese, yogurt, pomegranates, persimmons, oranges, and fennel—the relentless opera of sustenance, construction, and repair that have preserved this impossible carnival of a city for more than a thousand years.

Here the layered landscape of "culture" bears down with all the weight of ancient, crumbling marble.

Venice is a living museum of cultural memory, where the very movements of the men loading the barges have gone unchanged for centuries upon centuries—which, oddly enough, turns my reflections to a high-tech designer bar and restaurant on the eastern end of Sunset Boulevard in Los Angeles. There, on the hip, mostly gay periphery of Hollywood, "history" and "cultural memory" are concepts that stretch back about as far as the heyday of Rock Hudson's film career with Doris Day. I am there on the final leg of my promotional tour, at a benefit reading for the gay chapter of the ACLU. The crowd is divided into two parts: older ladies, once bohemian, now mostly widowed, regular supporters of civil liberties' causes; and gay men of middle age, most of them professionals in the entertainment, public relations, and fashion industries—the stalwarts of America's "urban gay culture."

The reading goes well, followed by a half hour of discussion on the usual topics: How will the question of gays in the military resolve itself? How big a threat do the right-wing fundamentalist gay bashers pose? What about domestic partnership campaigns? Will we survive AIDS? The gay bashers, the military, even the epidemic: these, I answer, are the forces that have worked to codify and strengthen the social phenomenon that has come to be called American gay culture. Tragedy and hostility are, for the short term at least, the ramparts of cultural identity. They intensify our sense of solidarity and inform the quality of memory.

Fortunately, however, I am snapped back from the comfort of my own bromides by a younger man—about twenty-seven—representing a new L.A. 'zine called *Spunk*.

"I haven't read your book," he admits quickly, "but I'm not sure what this 'gay culture' is." More to the point, he doesn't call himself "gay." He is not in the least bit closeted; he prefers "queer." (As we talk later, I wonder if he even finds "queer" too confining.) He has grown tired of the gay ghetto of bars and restaurants in West Hollywood, packed with all its hairless hunks angling for a weekend with a powerful producer in Palm Springs. He has grown sick of the organized "gay culture" represented by the gay men at this reading.

"You know who reads *Spunk*?" he asks me. "Not the gym queens and the attitude boys on San Vicente Boulevard. Our biggest drops are in the skate shops out in the Valley."

"There are gay skateboard shops in the Valley, San Fernando Valley?" I ask, nonplussed.

"No. Regular skate shops."

Where seventeen-, eighteen-, and nineteen-year-olds go to buy boards, bearings, straps, and the rest.

Spunk, he explains, is not a gay paper. Maybe it's not even a "queer" paper (though it has a lot of ads from discos where gay *and* straight guys go and a lot of listings for homo sex clubs). Maybe, he says, it's a post-queer paper. "A lot of our readers would never think of going to the bars in West Hollywood. They don't want to live in any gay ghetto. They don't need those labels."

Spunk and other papers like it are at the forward edge of young queer life in America's largest cities. They are written and read by young men—and, unlike most of the older gay weeklies, women—who take homosexual desire for granted. Generally, they have not gone through the long years of denial and furtive lovemaking that marked the members of the middle-aged "gay establishment" who run most of the social and commercial centers of the "gay ghettos." Their hallmarks are irony, distance, *and* passion. Their style is self-consciously radical. Yet they are absolute in their determination to participate in the whole of America, refusing to retreat into the old, stereotypical gay careers and neighborhoods. To wit, one of the feistiest groups comes from California's Silicon Valley and calls itself Digital Queers. Curiously enough, this book seems to have found a special resonance with these fiercely independent cultural queers, perhaps because, like them, I share a profound ambivalence toward the whole process of "culture making."

More than the nastiness of the homo-haters, more even than

the grotesque horrors of the AIDS epidemic, the newest twist in the story of gay Americans poses a fundamental challenge to the idea of a "gay culture." For at root, the gentleman from *Spunk* asks of us the most disturbing questions about cultural identity: How do we know one another? How do we remember one another? Like every other sub-population in American history, gay people of the last quarter century have staked out their geographical turf—specific districts in New York and San Francisco, Houston and Chicago and Los Angeles. We have built businesses and churches and shops and social clubs and launched political campaigns. And, like Italians and Jews and Poles and Chinese, we have taken the artifacts of our personal lives—food, furniture, fashion, dance—and decorated our neighborhoods to demonstrate our pride in location. We have made ourselves up, in short, like all the other Americans determined to establish their own cultural identity. But also like all those other lonely, immigrant Americans, we are addicted to the ideology of continual self-reinvention. As Americans, we try desperately to convince ourselves that we can invent our own traditions, communities, families, faiths, and value systems out of nothing more than willpower. Then we assess the resilience and vitality of our efforts by measuring the rapidity with which we alter our shared dreams and identities.

The fabricators of a specifically gay culture dream could hardly be any different. If, however, we are free to find our own culture through nothing more than the force of collective self-assertion, through naming and renaming, forming and reforming ourselves until memory has no possibility of meaning, it may also be that we are condemned to dwell in the solitude of our self-invention, in which the culture of desire turns out to be nothing more than the loneliest of American longings, the simple desire for culture.

—Frank Browning
December 1993

Prologue

"Can I

Meet People? . . .

Is It

Dying?"

This book is an inquiry into the faiths, practices, structure, and meanings of gay life in America, an exploration of the unwinding and reformulation of gender, the dissolution and reconstruction of family, the impulse toward community, the passage of generations, and an emerging reconciliation with death. It is both a personal investigation and a cultural exploration. It is a reporter's journey through contemporary history, inspired by scores of private lives that, intentionally or not, became the stuff of a social movement. Throughout, I have been driven by one critical question: Do the subculture and life-style of urban gay life in America (though homosexuality is everywhere, gayness has been and remains mostly an urban phenomenon) constitute an actual culture comparable to other ethnic and racial cultures—black, Jewish, Latin, Asian—that make up the heterogeneity of modern American life?

1

Behind that question lie several more questions. If gay men in the late twentieth century have established their own culture, can it survive AIDS? Even if a sufficient number of gay men do survive the epidemic, is there any evidence that their values and behavioral styles will be transmitted to younger generations of gay people? If ethnic cultures classically arrange for their own preservation through the rites of passage from infancy into adulthood—baptisms, bar mitzvahs, confirmations, weddings, and other communal dances, all of them public and collective—what experience of common bonding do homosexual men have?

The genesis of this book came in early March 1988, when I was on assignment for National Public Radio. I had finished five years of reporting on a broad array of issues—the finances of the Miami-based cocaine trade, the rise of midwestern Christian neo-Nazi movements during the farm crisis, the labyrinthine world of Washington's Iran-contra conspirators, and the devastation wrought by illegal Appalachian strip-mining. I'd also had some droll diversions into American consumer obsessions: the antics of the buddy boys Steven Spielberg and George Lucas as they pressed their handprints into wet cement at Mann's Chinese in Hollywood, the fanciful literary labels and newsletters of a California boutique wine maker, the anxieties of the mega-wealthy at Kentucky's annual Bluegrass Yearling Sales. Along the way, I had reported occasionally on gay concerns and AIDS issues, and although NPR had distinguished itself with superb scientific reportage of the AIDS epidemic, increasingly it seemed to me that the textured lives of gay men were appearing only through medical gauze. How they/we were maintaining the new gay world that had been so hard won only a few years earlier—*that* was an elusive story. My assignment in March 1988 was to go to the gay Mecca, to the heart of gay San Francisco, and to report back on how the living were contending with the specter of death.

The night I arrived in San Francisco, I stayed not in the city but in Marin County, in a pleasant, simple hillside house a few minutes' walk from the ocean. My hosts were a gay doctor and his longtime boyfriend, a health-care planner who helped manage his lover's practice. Their home was a refuge for them from the ravages of city life. Most of the doctor's patients were dying of AIDS or were HIV infected; he saw no prospect that the devastation would abate anytime soon. They both told me that the city's gay Castro district felt like a war zone, and that many if not most gay men they knew had descended into a state of sexual shock—so exhausted with death, with the care of the dying, with fear of becoming the dying, that they had gone numb. Indeed, one man they introduced me to said he hadn't experienced orgasm with a partner for more than five years.

Two days later, after I had come into San Francisco, I walked down the steep slope from Twin Peaks (sometimes called the Swish Alps) to take breakfast in the Castro; I expected the worst. Halfway there, I passed a middle-aged man shuffling slowly with a cane. A block farther on, I passed the storefront office of the Names Project, producers of the traveling quilt commemorating the AIDS dead. I looked into the faces of passersby, searching for the "aura of death" that my hosts had warned me suffused the district.

At the corner of Noe and Market streets, I stepped into an open, airy café guarded by clumps of bamboo and windbreaking glass walls. In the 1970s, when I'd first lived in San Francisco, the Cafe Flore had been one of the city's many semibohemian polyglot haunts for hippies, arty types, and agitators gay and straight; I'd never been able to figure out what lines of work enabled so many people to while away their days over espresso and herb tea. In 1988, the Cafe Flore was full at nine-thirty in the morning, but not with the people I expected. Now it seemed completely gay—or queer, as I would learn to say in the next few months. The air crackled with intensity, not at all the laid-back yet dyspeptic cool style I remembered. The clientele was young—midtwenties to early thirties, most of them. It took only a few moments for me to overhear some table-conversation references to AIDS, and the mood was angry, fierce, exuberant. If my hosts had seen only death on Castro Street, here in the Cafe Flore I saw a gay resurgence that found in the shattered world of the old Castro the fuel of rebellion.

Over the next three weeks, I gathered nearly thirty hours of tape that became the basis of NPR's most detailed look at the shape of gay life in the midst of the epidemic. I spoke with a Buddhist priest who had once been a female impersonator performing as "Tommy Dee—The Boy as Cute as the Girl Next Door"; now he was called Issan and was opening an AIDS hospice. I spoke to a ten-year-old who had made a quilt panel at the Names Project for his gay dad's lost lover; he said he wasn't old enough to know whether he would be gay or straight. I went to a community meeting where AIDS activists discussed in sophisticated biochemical language the merits and possible importation of new drugs being produced in Germany and Japan. I went to a country-western bar where lanky men in Levi's, boots, and cowboy hats danced the San Antonio Stroll and the Slap Leather. I spoke to an ex–Catholic seminarian who teaches men how to give one another nonorgasmic erotic massages; to the rabbi of the city's gay synagogue; to the mayor's powerful adviser on gay concerns; and to a twenty-two-year-old named Paul Herman who had moved to San Francisco from Iowa to find out for himself if there was still a gay Mecca in America.

When he and I first spoke, Paul was not quite a year out of college, and was clerking in a bookstore. We sat beside a fountain at Opera Plaza during his midafternoon break. Being gay had never troubled him, he told me; he had not suffered the coming-out traumas that had driven legions of seventies gays to flee home-towns in Michigan or Kentucky or Kansas. Early in his adolescence, Paul had simply realized he was attracted to men instead of women and had therefore concluded that he was gay. Though he did have sexuality-related anxieties, they concerned not individual identity but the question of a collective cultural identity.

Paul's selection of words was halting and tentative. "When I decided to move here," he said, "my mother was against it because of AIDS. But I wanted to be in the middle of that. I wanted to be in the worst spot." He fixed his eyes hard on mine. "I wanted to be where it was hitting the most, to feel like I was in a town where people were facing the disease rather than . . . rather than running from it."

More than any experience I can recall, this conversation with a twenty-two-year-old San Francisco immigrant shattered my comfortable notion of sexuality as an essentially private right. Slogans, parades, sit-ins, lawsuits, political campaigns: All these I had understood as tactics in a struggle for diverse but essentially *personal* freedoms. Something had always seemed not quite right to me—somehow overdramatic, or self-indulgent—when my gay activist friends spoke of "our people," as though we were like African Americans or Jews or Armenians whose common cultural memory draws them together more powerfully than their individuality drives them apart. To my skeptical, rationalist mind, that gay men could fabricate their own culture seemed a shaky proposition. Yet here beside me sat a man who questioned not his sexuality but how he could engage with the culture of his own "people." Like the bright, angry, and optimistic young men and women who had marched with Martin Luther King, Jr., and had closed ranks in Birmingham at just the moment that Bull Connor turned on the fire hoses, Paul Herman seemed to know that his personal and cultural identities could be fused only through collective action. If being gay had been a matter of life-style rights to most members of my generation, it seemed an existential question to his.

"I had two questions when I came here," he told me. "Can I meet people? And is it, like . . . dying?"

Back at Grinnell College in Iowa, Paul said, his gay friends felt immune from the disease that was devastating their brothers in the cities. That attitude struck him as stupid and self-absorbed, lacking any sense of either past or future. If the culture in the place where his people seemed to be was dying, then where and how could he live? The question was not abstract to a young man whose sexual and emotional life was just beginning. Who do— who *can*—you sleep with in a community where half the people you meet are infected with a deadly virus? Do you take up with a man who has been diagnosed with AIDS? With a man who is infected but still asymptomatic? Do you form close friendships with the infected but have sex with only the healthy? What does it mean to say, as many do, "I only date 'negatives,' " those whose blood is free of infection with HIV? What are the social and psychological consequences within a culture when its young construct categories of intimate inclusion and rejection, categories with life-and-death consequences?

Here was a young man who had grown up with distinct images of a gay culture that would provide him an identifiable place in America, a place where aberrance was normalcy, where the intimacies of personal life were not at war with the impulse toward public ambition. But as an adult, he worried that the emerging gay cultural system was being erased by AIDS. And here was I, a middle-aged man who had achieved a measure of career success in American political journalism, who had lived a discontinuous life for twenty years in which my sexual identity had been neither hidden nor open, but was instead an incidental matter, private, effectively separated from my public life. Though I appreciated and defended the political and civil rights institutions that the gay movement had built, I regarded them as ephemeral, and valuable only as refuges and bulwarks against bigotry.

I remain unsure that the special world built by gay men and lesbians in America in the late twentieth century can or should claim a cultural power anything like that of a true ethnic, racial, or linguistic people with centuries (or millennia) of history. First, the gay movement is much too young: As an organized, public way of living, it has lasted a scant quarter century (though its identifiable roots in language, style, and mateship may run back a hundred years to the heyday of Oscar Wilde). Second, and more problematic, "gay" intersects with and transcends all cultures: Gay people are also black people and Cuban people and Polynesian people and Arab people, and the face of sexual identity varies enormously within and among those older and more established human collectivities.

Despite my uncertainties, however, Paul Herman's disarming readiness to face the question of cultural survival led me into this journey of social inquiry. For just at the very moment when many gay men feared that AIDS would dispatch the movement into the same oblivion that had swallowed up the Beats, hippies, and other social rebels, there appeared a new generation of intense, often angry, young homosexuals who were determined to salvage the movement and press it forward into new and as yet unimagined territories. And that, at a minimum—the passage of ritual, belief, and behavior from one generation to the next—is the basic material of cultural regeneration.

The meditative, journalistic explorations that make up this book are my attempt to address both Paul Herman's and my own personal concerns. To look at the homosexual world that Paul saw himself entering has required that I examine the one that my generation and those before us constructed—even if before the advent of the AIDS epidemic I considered myself at most a sometime sojourner in it. If a young man not yet seared by the experience of collective death could propel himself toward the center of the destructive blaze, where, I found myself asking, did *I* stand? Even within the safe psychological frame of the journalistic observer, what were my duties as witness? How could I possibly comprehend how Paul and his generation were remaking the gay world without also examining—if not resolving—my own role as a participant in it? The book that has emerged, then, is a journey of internal and external witnessing, an examination of the culture gay men have constructed and a monologue about my own relationship to it.

It is a voyage into a social terrain filled with contradictions, inconsistencies, and ambiguities. One of the most vexing of the ambiguities concerns language and its connection to gender. Does the word *gay,* for example, refer to homosexual men alone, or to homosexual men and lesbians, or, as some once argued, to all sexual dissidents? I've found that in the center of the country and in the South, lesbians and homosexual men alike—if they are over thirty—tend to embrace the word. On the coasts, lesbians tend to see *gay* as a male term. And throughout the country, many women *and* men under the age of twenty-five embrace *queer* as less male-oriented. Debates over language reflect more than oversensitive linguistic petulance. Throughout the 1970s and 1980s, "gay" publications, "gay" bars, "gay" baths, and "gay" bookstores ministered almost exclusively to men—and lesbians were only occasionally acknowledged, usually at political rallies. To the extent that a gay culture emerged in those years, it was an unmistakably male one, which only after the advent of AIDS began to enter into aggressive coalition with lesbians. As the nineties began, the youngest "queer" men began to spend more social time with lesbians, but as of this writing there is only scant indication that lesbians and gay men might someday share an integrated life: Coalitions and alliances do not make a culture. Consequently, this book is an inquiry into an avowedly and unmistakably male world undertaken by a man who has always found such social exclusiveness troubling and self-limiting.

My decision to focus on gay men is not meant to diminish the vitality or the complexity of lesbian life in America. Through its relation to the feminist movement and because lesbians have experienced different stigmas from those of gay men, the lesbian social sphere seems both more and less separate from heterosexual American life than gay culture is. Lesbians, for example, are regularly attacked for dividing the feminist movement, while gay men are seldom even associated with the new, pop "men's movement." Women, especially lesbian women, have played important if subordinated roles in gay male social life. Gradually lesbians have forced gay men to relinquish some power in social, political, and community organizations—and sometimes even in the operation of co-sexual sex clubs. Thus to examine gay culture is to look at a men's world where women make intermittent but vital appearances. (Lamentably, I fear that a parallel inquiry into lesbian life would reveal little if any male contribution.)

Unlike any accepted culture, gaydom is a social world that none of us has inherited from our parents or families. Because the part of identity that is "gay" emerges from the most powerful and universal of human drives—the imperative of desire—it is inextricably bound to the torments and the delicacies of taboo. Unavoidably, gayness is a tangle of dreams, ambitions, deceits, and contradictions, the examination of which may tell us as much about the portion of America that isn't gay as about the portion that is. For those gay men whose greatest dream is assimilation—to be viewed in their relationships as "just like everyone else"—the gay male "culture" that currently exists is only a transitional arrangement of refuge against the hatred of the majority culture; when that hostility dissolves, so too will the otherness projected upon those of us who copulate and mate with members of our own gender. For others, the invention of *any* gay "culture" is emblematic of a broader dilemma, in which postmodern man, shorn of family, place, and tradition, floats alone from freeway to shopping mall to suburb and constructs a succession of temporary, self-conscious cultures of his own desire.

As the most "other" of all "others," historically excluded as unnatural even by *other* excluded peoples, self-conscious gay men have settled along the perimeters of conventional culture: in real estate, as gentrifiers; in fashion, as recyclers of discarded elegance; in art, as subversive documentarians. To live in the gay demimonde has been to snatch up the fragments of other people's artifacts and transform them into a living aesthetic, an aesthetic that assembles the disintegrating garments of the old order into a new, high-style wardrobe of ironic kitsch and brings camp into the practice of daily life (and, indeed, claims that all contemporary life is a prolonged exercise in camp). Going even further, some feel that being gay intimates not so much an aesthetic or a culture of identities as an entrée into a world of forbidden, transgressive desire, a manner of living that challenges overtly the heterosexual conventions of marriage and procreation in favor of a radical, collaborative exploration of pleasure and spirituality.

What began for me as a tour of the state of gay "culture" under the profound stress of AIDS has, along the way, turned into an odyssey of personal and communal desire—desire not only in its limited physical sense, but desire for community, identity, and moral purpose. At root, Paul Herman's central questions—"Can I meet people?" and "Is it dying?"—are the same questions Americans have asked for centuries as they set out to reinvent themselves in new territories and new communities. His questions recall the venerable American anxieties over the pursuit of individual destiny, the yearning for solidarity, and the fear of losing both. In this land of immigrants and outsiders, it should come as little surprise that those who have long been society's consummate outsiders have finally found themselves at the center of this nation's deepest debates over the roles of morality and personal destiny in the quest for community.

one

Mystery, Plot, and Remembrance

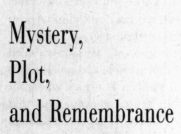

A Boy on the Dock and Other Intimations of Desire

Since early childhood I have been fascinated with the edge of difference. Although my parents were well educated—my father was a Yalie who went on to study Middle High German in Weimar Berlin—I started first grade in a one-room schoolhouse located on a ridge in eastern Kentucky, then moved on for the balance of my elementary-school years to a two-room building heated by a potbelly stove. We were, to say the least, a family of exotics, well respected socially but living, as far as our neighbors were concerned, beyond the pale of godliness. Even the family business—an apple orchard—marked us. Our prime sales day was the Sabbath.

The closest point of contact between the world of my schooling and the interior world of my family was when my classmates' parents came to buy our apples on those Sunday afternoons in autumn. The men would sit on turned-up wooden-slatted crates, peeling the fruit with finely honed jackknives while yellow jackets hovered around the dangling spirals of apple skin about to fall into the dirt. The faces of the men, pink melon faces of fourth- or fifth-generation Germans, or hard, rawboned, whisker-stubbled faces of Scotch-Irish descent, were impenetrable and undecipherable. They were faces of men with swollen knuckles who shot squirrels, grew tobacco, and went to church in wool suits that never conformed to the shape of their bodies. They never seemed to sweat. Except for the sun-reddened triangle that rode between the top shirt button and the chin, their bodies were as shrouded as the thoughts behind their eyes. Sure, the young men, in August, at tobacco-cutting time, would work shirtless in the fields. But they weren't the ones who came to buy apples. Our customers were older men with wives and children (or sometimes a bachelor uncle) who had long ago covered their bodies from the eyes of God and strangers. It was they who filled our yard on Sundays with their cars and pickup trucks, carting off the harvest.

They told tales, often as exotic as my father's Berlin stories. They told about moonshiners and mountain girls. They talked about the Salt Lake City woman who was brought to town by the carnival in an oversize fish tank, the woman who'd been dead for ten (twenty? thirty? forty?) years, drowned (murdered?) out in the Great Salt Lake, whose flesh had gone soft and crinkly but had never rotted because of the salt water, and whose beautiful red hair and pretty nails continued to grow. Old men with few teeth who spoke in a hillbilly twang and called young men "honey" would fold up their pocketknives, drop their apple cores, and tell dirty jokes about balls and hammers I couldn't quite understand. Or they'd crack out, leering, "Nanners, nanners, my nanner's still bigger'n yourn."

I never doubted that these men had sex, though they may have talked about it a lot more than they did it. They came from families of eight or ten or a dozen children, and it was neither surprising nor scandalous to find out that somebody's baby brother or sister was really a nephew or a niece. The overt language of sex, however, like the open display of the body, was always absent.

Two events from that time have recurred to me over the years, memories that have been little more than tight-focused images:

One image rises from a strawberry field. Two teenage boys are bent down between the rows, boasting to a third, much-younger boy about what they'd got and whom they'd got it from. The younger boy, eager to keep the talk going, hungry to make it more explicit (and to expand his own secret library of masturbatory fantasies), plies them with dumb questions about body parts and places.

"You just find the hardest place on you and the softest place on her, and then . . . you know," the older braggart says.

"Like your big toe?" the little boy ventures.

"Hain't your daddy learned you nothing with all them books?" the big boy snorts, reaching down through the bushy strawberry vines to grope himself. "This here's all you gotta know," he says, laughing with his buddy.

The mystery of what "this here" was also took in the fantastic and delectable notion that if you really knew what to do with *it,* you would magically discover who *you* were. You would discover that you and your body were not simply two things inhabiting the same place but were in fact one whole being. You would discover that the growing adolescent physicalness of your body was not disconnected from the self that hid within that strange gangling thing—and then, privy to the mystery, you would enter into the brotherhood of the knowing, the brotherhood of men who knew, men (boys?) whose solidarity with one another had guided and released them into the natural bodies of women (girls?)—released them from the terror of their aloneness. All that from a grope and a dirty joke. Because inside the dirt of a dirty joke, behind the cheap popular slang for sex organs and sex couplings, I supposed there were people who lived in a coherent world, where sights, sounds, symbols, speech, and daily behavior were all interconnected, where people knew, without asking, their place in the world.

The second image is of the foot and ankle of a nineteen-year-old, a natural country athlete whose sweetness and seemingly unconscious virility disarmed everyone. I, at age twelve, was never aware of feeling any overt sexual urge for him. Instead, what he presented was the vision of nearly ideal flesh integrated with, inseparable from, the spirit within him, a unity that revealed itself in the glistening black hairs that dusted his ankle as he stood one summer afternoon on a wooden lakeside dock, ready to dive into the water. Knee, calf, ankle, toe knuckle: All were as thoroughly and elegantly knit into the whole of him as all my appendages seemed disconnected, unrelated, and inept. In those days, boys like me (not straight, not gay, just unformed) would pass evenings in overstuffed chairs watching cowboy hunks and Zorro, glancing down from time to time to peer at the flesh in which we resided, all elbows and rib cages and feet, ramshackle bodily bungalows. Somehow, in the mystery of heterosex—that mystery of knowing that we thought we would all, soon enough (don't rush it), come to experience—we would be delivered from the divisions within us that built up walls of division among us. Just as each ebony hair on the nineteen-year-old's ankle, like the tail feathers of a lark, seemed to guide him through a graceful arc into the water, so, sometime, we would glide, whole, complete, fully formed, into the waters of a natural mateship, leaving behind the disjointedness of self and body.

No one I knew actually spoke of such things, neither among the churchgoing families whose kids knew quite well that only God could make a tree, nor in my liberal-intellectual family, sequestered in a reconstructed cabin lined with books. The realm of the senses lay within the lyric poetry of Edna St. Vincent Millay or in color reproductions of Renaissance paintings, material presented for the stimulation of the mind, bound in books with black covers and faded spines. As sensually evocative as the works themselves were, their burial in old, dehydrated books left them nearly as shrouded as the buttoned-up bodies of the Sunday apple customers. The books' contents were as delicious as a diver's ankle, and just as distant.

Cut off from any context, that ankle became a kind of pornography, an image of my desire, not for the actual boy, with whom I could hardly speak—older, powerful, charming, he was beyond my possibility—but for some chimera of lust. It wasn't exactly sexual pornography. On the afternoon I'd watched him dive, I'd also caught momentary sight of shiny pubic curls as he adjusted the drawstring on his trunks, but I had no longing for the organs inside. No, I would violate his body more thoroughly: penetrate the whole of his flesh, dive in and consume the meat of him—celebrate a forbidden Communion that found in the image of his flesh the release from my growing disunion. (And we were the godless family not raised on church.)

I had no language or labels to interpret the sight of his ankle or the conversation in the strawberry patch. When the strawberry picker grabbed his crotch, declaring, "This here's all you gotta know," a whole family of perverse mysteries was born: There were the mystery images in his mind of penetrating rapture articulated in schoolyard talk of pussies and peters and cherries that somehow made him know that he was his own boss in the chain of fruitful reproduction. And he stirred in me curious images of his (not her) excited flesh (forearms and hamstrings and pectorals and testicles) writhing about in the reproductive dance. But there was a double mystery, too, of whether and why our images of desire, as we knelt there sweating in the strawberry field, were different.

The strawberry picker could unravel the mystery of his sexual nature more easily than I could; he had a context. But what I had to untangle was less mystery than premystery, because my story lacked form. This was a time and place where the notion of growing up gay was simply unimaginable, not because it seemed bad or sick in the way that homosexuals were seen to be bad, sick people, but because there was at large no idea or model of what a gay life might be.

Of course, nearly all modern adolescents, gay or straight, face sexual anxieties, but the library of heterosexual plots is full—from the gynecological to the mythic-archetypal—and readily available on the paperback-romance racks of every corner drugstore. Any adolescent can find the landmarks by which to plot the points of a heterosexual journey, because the culture has already charted the basic route. But there was available in my youth no equivalent queer plot—and I mean *queer* not only in the schoolyard-epithet sense, but *queer* in its standard sense, as in "What a queer story you tell." There is an unmistakable queerness in realizing that the emerging story of your internal desires has little in common with the tales of straightforward desire recounted in dime-store novels. By its very absence, the queer plot tantalizes. Because we do not recognize ourselves in the available popular plots, we are drawn—liking it or not—to probe further mysteries of fate and flesh. The peculiarity of our inquiries, we find, propels us onto the journey of difference. Because we persist in asking queer questions, we find that we have become queer people. Midway through my second year in high school, I got into a spat in French class with a new student, a cheerleader, who had arrived from Cincinnati. I have long ago forgotten the content of the argument, but her final rejoinder remains as clear as the image of her bobbed strawberry-blond hair and sharp-chinned, sallow face.

"Well," she said, picking up her books, "everybody knows you're queer."

"What?" I remember thinking, and maybe saying, feeling not angry or offended but completely confused. How could "everybody" know the answer to the mystery that had so thoroughly eluded the person inside my body? Still, for years I tried to puzzle out what she was saying. (For it wasn't until much later that I'd taken the first male into my body, or even imagined wrapping myself around one.) What she knew, however, was something far simpler: Whatever plot of animal response I was deciphering in no way included her and her drugstore-romance world. I was not queer because of what I had done—she knew nothing of what I'd done; I'd done nothing—but because my story's plot showed no sign of connection to any of the plots other young men were following. On the surface, her word meant *faggot,* a guy who goes down on other guys, but her retort implied that everything about me was queer. If I had knocked up the school's star cheerleader, it would have appeared only as a desperate effort to camouflage the queerness that differentiated me from regular people. For the issue was not really who was having what kind of sex with whom. As rural high school sophomores, almost none of us were having sex with anybody. What all of us were doing was sorting through the rush of sensual responses our bodies were offering up, calling on all the available plots of family, church, television, and paperback novels to enable us to savor some and discard others. The codes we created emerged not from what we had done but from which images we acknowledged and then, voluntarily or involuntarily, shared with one another—not always in explicit speech but by letting ourselves be observed watching one another. We might be caught resting our eyes on the semi-aroused nipple beneath the cheerleader's blouse or, far more dangerously, on the quarter-back's muscled stomach when his jersey separated from his pants or on the skin and fur of a foot as it springs off the board of a lakeside dock. By what we said, and by what we contrived to be overheard saying, we learned (or didn't) whether we were explor-ing the same mysteries, whether we were inhabiting common plots.

Not long ago, only a few months before this book was completed, two prominent, liberal-minded Washington correspondents came across a review I'd written of *Coming Out Under Fire,* Allan Berube's history of gay men and lesbians during World War II. The review included some of my own childhood recollections, and the journalists were deeply offended. As recounted to me later, the brief dialogue went more or less as follows:

"Oh, this is disgusting!" says one of them, quoting a few words.

The co-worker, sitting at the adjacent desk, picks up the magazine, scans the article, and agrees, adding, "Really, I don't care what they do. I don't care what anybody does. But why do they have to put it in my face?"

The revulsion expressed by these two liberal journalists, noted for their commitment to civil liberties, fascinated me. If the offending material had been raunchy pornography, the outrage might not have seemed strange. But in fact the cited line read simply, "To a child who had no words to articulate the stirring of his own secret drives . . ." What in the phrase had so disgusted them? That unarticulated desire actually exists in children? Or that a writer who has been granted the privilege of working in the presumably unqueer world of Washington political journalism should expose his queerness in touchable, intimate terms? Both, perhaps, but it seemed to me more probable that like the high school cheerleader, the reporters objected not to the fact of sex itself but to open discussion of the queer condition of being. Their plea not to have it put in their face amounted to nothing more—or less—than a demand that queer people conduct their lives in silence.

It is not that such otherwise tolerant people dislike gay people. Frequently, they include among their friends national leaders who are gay. Occasionally, they invite gay people to dinner or even to intimate afternoon barbecues in their backyards. But gay people are admitted only to the degree that they sequester their difference and conduct a sexless public life that offers no model, no quarter, no inspiration, to others—child or adult—who would explore all that is queer about themselves. To those who would examine in public the queer mysteries of life, the sympathetic liberals raise an eyebrow, lower their voices, and say impatiently, "Don't you think you're becoming a Johnny One-Note?"—their belittlement in effect reformulating the cheerleader's rejoinder, "Everybody knows you're a queer."

In the thirty years between the cheerleader's retort and the correspondent's disdain, people who were called and now call themselves queer have stolen back the language of their own denigration. They have set about constructing neighborhoods, communities, even cities, of their own, forging out of their formerly wordless desire a cultural system that at once celebrates queerness and agitates for the collective security of being queer. Despite the assaultive disgust of both cheerleaders and commentators, and despite a massive and deadly epidemic, that project has persisted through one generation and into the next. Having spent years standing on sidewalks in movie lines watching straight couples nuzzling and embracing, same-sex couples now refuse to deny themselves demonstrative intimacy. Bombarded with straight adolescent romance films in their own youth, they have begun to film their own romance stories. With breadth and irony, they are creating and communicating their own queer plots.

These queer stories, tragic and exuberant, at last transformed into images and words, have proved distressing to straight people at large and to many of my colleagues particularly. During the summer of 1990, one of NPR's most prominent reporters marched into a producer's office and complained, "You're running far too much about gays." Over the previous twelve months, fewer than a dozen full-length stories, not counting AIDS stories, had aired about gay people. During the same period, the *New York Times* had published several dozen pieces on non-AIDS-related elements of gay and lesbian life. Even the *Washington Post,* whose editor was widely known to react with disgust to almost any homosexual reference, had covered far more stories about gay political and social issues than NPR had. Yet to this prize-winning journalist, all the AIDS reports we had run had, I presume, felt like gay stories—or, worse, stories in the service of the gay agenda.

To some degree, of course, the unhappy reporter was right. When science correspondents at NPR began filing pieces on AIDS in the early 1980s, they ran smack into one of the sternest barriers against the public discussion of homosexuality: the taboo of anal sex. It was clear from the start that whatever caused AIDS was most easily spread through anal intercourse because abrasions of the thin tissues of the rectal walls permitted transmission of the disease from the spray of semen during ejaculation. It was all very simple, very clinical, and very critical. Avoid anal intercourse, or keep the potentially virus-infected semen inside a condom, and the man or woman being penetrated would not be infected. These were details, however, that could not be discussed in 1984, on the radio or in most newspapers. To discuss them would be to dangle the means of male homosexual ecstasy before the faces of heterosexual editors who could not bear to hear what precisely *they* really do. Eventually, reporters won the battle to discuss anal sex. It just wasn't possible to talk about epidemiology, safe-sex campaigns, or condom use without referring to anal intercourse. However discomforting these details were for editors and producers, they were still the facts of medicine and disease and had to be reported.

The reintroduction of medical language surrounding the subject of homosexual union reawakened bitter tensions between science and gay people. Since the mid-1970s, it had come to be politically unacceptable for enlightened, liberal-minded straight people to see or discuss homosexual people as diseased. Generally, it had even become unacceptable for them to use *homosexual* as a noun: *Gay* was the correct term. (That the *New York Times* declined to use *gay* until 1986 was regarded as an archaic embarrassment.) Then anal sex talk turned everything upside down. The presumed pièce de résistance of homosexual acts came again under the medical umbrella. Reviled by straight people as the next thing to castration in the unmanning of real men, anal penetration was remedicalized as the antithesis of healthy behavior, indeed as behavior that could cause death. Science had again provided prima facie evidence of the inherently diseased nature of homosexuality, and certified it this time not in psychiatric language but in the irrefutable terminology of microbial and cellular biology. Couched in the discourse of disease—where abstinence was equated with responsibility, and promiscuity with homicidal negligence—gay men were given a new place in the vocabulary of the media. We were, infected or not, medical victims: not simply HIV/AIDS victims but, as a class of human beings, victims of unhealthy practices through which any of us could become the willing victim of the virus. Across the nation, stories surfaced of landlords and employers rejecting gay men—and lesbians—on the basis of AIDS panic, fear of contamination through casual contact with diseased people. And in the newsrooms, right-thinking editors and reporters shook their heads in dismay at such ignorant bigotry. Still, if the journalists understood enough biology not to succumb to the hysteria, the concept of homos as sick people regained a measure of discreet currency.

If gay men had been willing to walk the respectable path of sad victims into that grisly good night, the editors and reporters might have rested comfortably. But in 1987, gay men revolted. Raging against a national complacency that saw only pathos (and that was the most charitable reaction) in the likely deaths of a million homosexual men, a corps of activists found allies—gay and straight—in the press whom they conscripted to tell the full stories of the lives that were being lost, and not just stories of gaunt, hollow-faced men in hospital gowns. These activists were not so much interested in winning sympathy as in commanding public acknowledgment of their existence and the facts of government inertia and the lack of AIDS-fighting drugs. They stormed federal bureaucracies, disrupted the New York Stock Exchange, and gave the TV cameramen tight shots of French kissing on the Capitol steps. Their aim was not to moisten the eyes of straight viewers, but to project an image of themselves as fierce fighters who would not relinquish their fate to pharmaceutical companies, government agencies, and academic researchers. If in the first years of the epidemic many gay men found that they could win greater social acceptance by presenting themselves as people who *had* a disease rather than people who *were* homosexual and thus suffered *from* a disease, by the end of the eighties a new generation of gay men came to insist upon and celebrate the fact of their queerness—whether they had HIV or not. They demanded attention to the emotional, sexual, and familial dimensions of their daily lives; they insisted upon bringing home to straight America the queer plot that surrounds AIDS. They were unwilling to have their stories transformed into the jargon of science.

One night in 1983, three months after I had begun working at National Public Radio, I was in a sleeping car aboard the Silver

Meteor, the overnight train from New York to Miami. I was preparing an investigative series on the finances of the Florida cocaine trade. Dinner was over; the club car was closed. Piled up beside me on my roomette bed were several magazines, newspapers, and reports. On top was an issue of *Newsweek,* its first to showcase AIDS on the cover. I meant to thumb through it quickly and move on to researching cocaine, but there on the first page of the AIDS cover story, in full color, was Tommy Biscotto, kneeling beside the wolf-size German shepherd of his I'd come to know on my visits with Tommy in Chicago.

To describe Tommy as a lover of mine would not be quite right, though there was no shortage of passion in our periodic visits. Our affair was more like one of those recurring trysts between distant cousins in nineteenth-century England. Although we came together no more than once or twice a year, we had between us an animal electricity unlike anything I'd ever experienced. When our relationship began, Tommy was a stage manager at Chicago's Goodman Theatre and I was an itinerant magazine writer and part-time furniture maker.

Sometimes it seems inevitable that two distant lives must cross each other's tracks. If I had moved to Chicago in the mid-seventies, as I almost did, Tommy and I would surely have encountered each other through the political-theatrical-journalistic milieu around Lincoln Park. Or we might have met in the theater. Or on a softball team. As it happened, we met on a street, one night just before midnight, outside a not-really-raunchy denim-and-leather bar in an industrial warehouse district. Neither of us had found anyone interesting *in* the bar, and both of us had decided to go home. I was walking across a parking lot when in the periphery of my vision I spotted a bushy-haired, black-bearded man sitting in an alley on an upended cement building block. We spoke only a few minutes, ambling down the alley, but we quickly realized we had more in common than horniness.

Hardly any of my colleagues over the years could quite have imagined that sort of encounter, a mixture of trash and grace, wantonness and repartee, foolhardy risk and thorough trust, that could come of two strangers wandering into each other late at night in a shadowy city alley. But that chanciness is part of the lasting magic of gay life, a sort of radical plot twist that characterizes queer life and sets aside so many conventions of social judgment, class, race, and attitude, supplanting them with a direct and naïve faith that bonds of great value can be forged on nothing more than instinct.

Not that such bonds always occur (more often than not, these brief encounters are merely tiring and banal). But there is a genuine spiritual affirmation in discovering how often magic can arise between strangers—magic that in most of our waking moments we train ourselves not to see. The love of strangers, or the love of loving strangers, teaches us that one man can touch the soul of another before he knows the size of his companion's shoes or paycheck. From the fragmentary details one man shares with his stranger-friend—the private glades of a morning stroll, the suppressed angers of a family feud—from these random glimpses of identity a window can open between the souls of unconnected people, a window framed only by intuitive readiness and undimmed by a lifetime's accumulated judgments. Led on by nothing more than the broken line of a shoulder's scar or the wrinkle of a closed eyelid, strangers reveal themselves in confessions that more careful lovers may take years to express.

Tommy and I became intimates. We realized from the beginning that we would not become a couple, but we knew that as occasional as our assignations would be, we were of value to each other. We were friends and fuckbuddies, two men who discovered delight in each other's presence. We could talk easily about the conundrums of integrating work and passion and identity—in part because we lived far apart, free of the usual daily obligations that define mateship. Other more regular partners might enter our lives, stay awhile, and pass on, but over time we came to our own peculiar mutual reliance.

That night on the train when I found his picture in *Newsweek,* Tommy Biscotto was not dead yet, though AIDS had sapped his strength and chemotherapy had taken away most of his hair. A few days later I called him, and a few months after that, during a period when his health seemed restored, we met in Chicago and made love. By that time, autumn 1983, he had become one of the first AIDS poster boys, a regular interviewee for newspaper writers and television talk-show hosts. That role made him uncomfortable. He feared that press reports on AIDS would turn into Presbyterian lectures on abstinence. He worried that waves of recrimination would envelop gay enclaves, killing for others the spirit in which we two had found our validation.

About a year later, Tommy Biscotto died. Since then, the death and suffering have been far deeper, far broader, than any of us could have predicted in 1983 or 1984. To those who have not experienced it, the intensity of caring for the sick, worrying about the well, and planning and attending funerals every month for friends and mates who were at the prime of their lives—all the while knowing that soon, you too may be cared for and memorialized—is utterly unimaginable. Yet we do more than imagine it: We recreate it, incorporate it into the ongoing plot of being queer, just as others have, just as Tommy himself did. By 1988, when I began the formal interviews for this book, I could operate on the premise that gay people *would* persevere, adding more elements to our plots, integrating the facts of AIDS and death into our mysteries. Despite the mounting death toll, the cultural system that gay men and, increasingly, lesbians have been constructing has released far more passion and diversity and even play than ever existed in the bar-and-bathhouse gay world before AIDS. And just as queer plots have changed, so have straight ones. As AIDS has changed us, the entire society has been asking fundamental questions about what constitutes identity and what motivates desire, what it means to be male or female (or both). And that discourse has itself become intertwined with broad American debates about the longing for community and the search for individual purpose.

For gay people especially, collisions constantly occur between the pursuit of community and the exploration of desire. Those gay men who pursue a radical, transgressive sexuality don't coexist easily with those who want to assimilate into conventional, middle-class, coupled communities—and a wrenching psychological dissonance can arise when those two urges exist in the same person. Superannuated iconic imagery of masculinity—gym boys on the Nautilus racks—contests the androgyny of long-haired Radical Faeries. Bacchanalian boy orgies on Fire Island compete with (and often supplement) evenings in which stockbrokers and lawyers reinvent the codes of masculinity and learn to be caregiving nurses. Lesbians who once denounced macho-clone sidewalk cruisers as abject physicalists have generated their own movement of radical porn, and now both males and females find themselves dancing in the same all-night discos. And the youngest queer generation has developed a radical direct-action movement among men and women who are no longer interested in dwelling only within the safe ghettos of gaydom.

Rich, raucous, passionate, sometimes self-absorbed, often petulant, the builders of the new gay social terrain in this country have, at the very least, challenged the way Americans think about desire in ordinary life. From the deepest hollows of Appalachia to the flattest prairies of Nebraska, there is not a high school football captain or cheerleader alive who does not know that there are other human plots than the ones taught in Sunday school or sold on the paperback racks at Rexall. Most of these kids know that many of the great icons of movie romance, the Rock Hudsons and Monty Cliffs and James Deans, satisfied their lust with other men (in Kentucky, we even knew which former college athlete Rock Hudson seduced and then launched into Hollywood fame). Increasingly, Americans are unwilling to leave the living icons alone in their secrecy, even as they press the Hollywood image industry to move further and further into the formerly forbidden scenarios of perverse desire. By and by, all of us, homo and hetero, male and female, queer and conventional, are brought along onto journeys of rage and irony and sadness and revelation that neither the queer insurgents nor their pinched and prudish antagonists could have foreseen even a few years ago.

Queer
Rage

◆

I t was on one of the few hot July afternoons in San Francisco, 1990, that I first saw the queer manifesto, reproduced on twelve-by-eighteen-inch folio sheets. The title, written in inch-high letters, was: "I HATE STRAIGHTS." The man who passed the leaflet to me, samizdat-style, having retrieved it from a sheaf of copies in the trunk of his car, was also a journalist, a reporter for a national daily. He told me I'd be upset by it, but that it was an important document we all had to read.

"I HATE STRAIGHTS," one of several anonymous essays in a newsprint tabloid flier headed *Queers Read This,* had surfaced a few weeks earlier in New York's annual gay pride parade. The piece's tone reflected its title: bitter, fed up, inflammatory, and *separatist*.

"I have friends. Some of them are straight," the author began. "Year after year, I see my straight friends. I want to see them,

26

to see how they are doing, to add newness to our long and complicated histories, to experience some continuity.

"Year after year, I continue to realize that the facts of my life are irrelevant to them and that I am only half listened to, that I am an appendage to the doings of a greater world, a world of power and privilege, to the laws of installation, a world of exclusion. . . .

"They've taught us that good queers don't get mad," it continued. "They've taught us so well that we not only hide our anger from them, we hide it from each other. WE EVEN HIDE IT FROM OURSELVES. We hide it with substance abuse and suicide and overachieving in the hope of proving our worth. They bash us and stab us and shoot us and bomb us in ever-increasing numbers and still we freak out when angry queers carry banners or signs that say, BASH BACK. . . . LET YOURSELF BE ANGRY. Let yourself be angry that the price of our visibility is the constant threat of violence, anti-queer violence to which practically every segment of this society contributes. Let yourself feel angry that THERE IS NO PLACE IN THIS COUNTRY WHERE WE ARE SAFE, no place where we are not targeted for hatred and attack, the self-hatred, the suicide—of the closet."

And then the gauntlet is thrown down.

"The next time some straight person comes down on you for being angry, tell them that until things change, you don't need any more evidence that the world turns at your expense. You don't need to see only hetero couples grocery shopping on your TV. . . . You don't want any more baby pictures shoved in your face until you can have or keep your own. No more weddings, showers, anniversaries, please, unless they are our own brothers and sisters celebrating. And tell them not to dismiss you by saying, 'You have rights,' 'You have privileges,' 'You're overreacting,' or 'You have a victim's mentality.' Tell them, 'GO AWAY FROM ME, until YOU can change.' "

Most gay people I know publicly rejected the essay as crazy, as little more than a naïve, simplistic, self-indulgent tantrum parading as a political manifesto. And yet secretly, a surprising number loved it and rejoiced over it. So did I. For in ways that few other treatises, slogans, or manifestos had ever done, "I HATE STRAIGHTS" caught the pure rage most of us had learned to swallow. I didn't realize how deeply the essay resonated within me until a few months later, during a dinner in Louisville with Tony,* a man I'd known for almost twenty years.

Tony has always had grand ambitions, and he has carefully marshaled the patience and persistence to make them real. Long ago, he set his sights on the federal bench, or at least a seat in Congress. Tony is also, unashamedly, a liberal: an education reformer, a civil rights campaigner, a pro-choice Democrat. He is reticent, respectful, gentlemanly. He lives in a single-story Federal brick house, decorated in clean Deco lines and subdued, creamy colors. He is the sort of gay guy about whom women, dear friends, sigh, "Ah . . . Such a waste," and then shake their heads.

"Rage? Do I feel rage? Of course I feel rage. How can you be a gay man and not feel rage?" Tony was answering a question I'd put to him about the upsurge of the new, militant queer movement. I was, frankly, stunned by his vehemence. Bashfully polite, Tony had hardly uttered an even caustic remark in all the years we had known each other. He was too good-looking, too well spoken, too poised, I had supposed, to harbor rage. But there it was, and I came to understand it fully only by working though the history of our friendship.

When we first met on a hot, sticky afternoon in 1973, in the doorway of a suburban house outside Murfreesboro, Tennessee, neither of us knew how queer the other was. I had just finished a three-hour drive from Paradise, a charming little river town in western Kentucky that had been strip-mined into a moonscape by the Peabody Coal Company. I was in the area on assignment for *Penthouse,* which had hired investigative reporters to lend itself the patina of serious political purpose, and I had come to spend the weekend with my old friends Liz and Bert.

* Throughout, I have changed names or places to protect the identity of people whose exposure would put their lives or careers at risk.

I was on the way out the door of their house to retrieve luggage from my car, and Tony was on his way in: white shorts, sneakers, no shirt, a squared-off, clean collarbone, and waves of dark hair glistening over his chest and stomach. He carried a regulation soccer ball, and behind him were Liz and Bert's two boys; the three had just returned from a match. Tony, recently graduated from law school, was their coach. He was my fantasy.

Fantasies, of course, can remain perfect only as long as they remain fantasies, and much of my Tony fantasy lay in how untouchable he was. I assumed he was straight, though my reflexive search for a wedding band gave reassurance that he wasn't yet taken. And keeping company with my assumption of his straightness was a self-denigrating assumption that so much perfection couldn't also take in homosexuality. So it was that I never mentioned my fantasy to my hosts, even though I knew that Liz had a gay brother and a number of gay friends. It was completely clear in my mind that if I told her of my attraction to Tony, she would hear it only as a predatory intended assault on his inherent decency. He was, remember, not only her slightly younger friend; he was the mentor and coach to her sons. To mention even the notion of my touching his perfect body (and to suggest even the possibility that he might respond) would cast a shadow of lechery and pederasty over all our relations, rupture her trust in him, smear his image of mentor to the boys, and cast me, as lascivious instigator, out into the street. It could not be done.

In later years, during phone calls and occasional visits with Liz and Bert, I would ask after Tony's progress: attorney, political strategist, judge, I was told; his profile in the community had grown increasingly prominent. Occasionally, he and I would see each other at a party or a dinner, though only if it were at an event our mutual friends had arranged. After a half dozen years had passed, and Tony had taken on the actual flesh of a real human being, he had also lost the fantasy flesh of lust. The memory of our first meeting in the summer doorway never disappeared, but gradually its atomic charge receded. Only after a decade had passed and Liz and Bert had announced that they were moving to Texas was I forced to revisit the twisted contortions of the fantasy Tony.

The moment of revelation came after a political reception—to this day, we seem to encounter each other only through drinking and eating—of which Tony was the host. Afterward, Liz and Bert and I went out to eat.

"So when's he going to run for Congress?" I asked, somewhat too simply.

They seemed more cautious in their responses than usual.

I went on.

"He's perfect. Looks, grace, a foreigner's family name [Portuguese-French], and just enough southern accent. A wife would help, probably, but . . ."

The more I babbled on, the more Liz and Bert shuffled between silence and discomfort.

"Look, you're a reporter, and this is not for the public," Bert began.

He and Liz didn't have to say any more, but they did. "Why do you think there were so many gay people at the reception?" Liz asked me. I hadn't noticed. I hadn't let myself notice. If Tony had entered my life as an impossible fantasy, and then gradually settled in my mind into ordinary heterosexual reality, it had still been impossible for me to see all the obvious signs of the truth of his life: his ongoing "bachelor" status, the other men at the reception without wedding rings or girlfriends or wives, his strange hesitance to run for prominent public office.

Tony's existence as my fantasy had rendered the actuality of his friends invisible to me and had, apparently, turned me invisible to them. Tony and I had unwittingly invented a banal interaction that had left us mute. Divided and unable to speak about what was queer about ourselves, we had passed a decade of superficial acquaintance without ever expressing what was at once vital and ordinary and shared. But now we could experience together something I had never known: We could be two southern gay friends trying to make our way in the world, two people who had chosen different routes but retained vital things in common, not least a profound sense of place and its value.

During my Louisville dinner with Tony in 1990, we spoke about the divisions, the denials, the invisibilities that breed anger: all the years he had to make polite comments about not yet having found the right woman to marry; all the years of not speaking directly and openly about his friends who were dying in midlife; all the years of sitting quietly by while liberals denounced nigger jokes in one breath and made fag jokes in another; all the years of not being "out" as a gay man even as he fought to secure rights and protections for gay people.

Tony, whose perfect image in the screen door years ago had snatched me from my preoccupations and left me faint with impossible admiration, had once again turned my perception of queerness inside out, forcing me to touch the raw tissue of rage that connected us far more completely than the ephemeral fantasy of lust. No matter that he spent his days in courtrooms and his evenings jawboning with party hacks while the young queer activists stomped through city streets and shopping malls in combat boots, sack dresses, and black leather motorcycle jackets, chanting, "Fag Power! Dyke Power! Qu-e-e-e-r Nation!" He shared their anger. It was there underneath the starched oxford cloth, the silk tie, the herringbone jacket, the black robes. Better than I had, Tony had learned to contain rage, to direct it, to draw on it as fuel to carry him through the cocktail parties and Democratic party meetings: to press for statements, positions, legislation, to watch for juridical opportunities that could affirm the rights and existence of gay people. Unlike many successful gay lawyers, doctors, and producers in New York and Los Angeles and San Francisco who saw radical queer punks as embarrassments, Tony saw himself as their comrade in another costume: as an eager participant in a genuine conspiracy of the spirit that conservative homosexual-haters have long railed against.

My first Queer Nation event starts in front of the Federal Building at San Francisco's Civic Center. Jonathan Katz is scurrying around the plaza clutching a white bullhorn in his right hand. He wears the black Doc Marten boots no hip young queer activist would be without this summer, and a white T-shirt emblazoned with the words QUEER NATION in bold black, underscored with a straight black bar. On this day in August, fog lurks overhead, shielding us from the sun, and the ocean wind is raw. He has to be colder than I, I think; despite four layers of cotton I'm shivering too much to stand still. Yet for activists on the line, adrenaline is often enough to drive away the chill.

"If you've not been selected for a homeroom, could you raise your hands?" His hard, thin, amplified voice cracks the fog like an old Chevy backfiring through a glasspack muffler or, perhaps, like some officious assistant principal's voice barking through the school PA system.

The motif for the upcoming Saturday-afternoon action is back-to-school prep; we're going on a queer shop-in to the sub-urban Sunbird Mall in Concord, twenty-five miles east of San Francisco, beyond the Berkeley hills. Jonathan, as head cheer-leader–coach–principal agitator, lays out the plan. Each person will be assigned to a "homeroom" (a code word for "affinity group," which is itself a code term for the small self-contained units that AIDS activists in ACT UP use to organize their civil-disobedience demonstrations). Each homeroom is to select its own name and homeroom teacher. Each homeroom also has a proctor, or legal observer. Other people, called hall monitors, walk the mall, keeping an eye out for potential violence or conflicts with shopkeepers.

"Thanks, everybody, for coming," Jonathan says.

"No, that was only heavy breathing," someone answers. The crowd groans.

"We're going to be at the mall for Back-to-School Days, and the reason we're going to be at the shopping mall is because it's the cultural center of suburbia." Pause for short laugh. Then Jonathan outlines this demo's logistics: It will begin with fifty or so queers, fags, and dykes taking over the head car of the BART commuter/subway train that will whisk them out to Concord. Once on board, they will transform the car into a "queer space," redecorating it with ropes of lavender crêpe streamers, confetti, and sparklers. But Jonathan offers an admonition: "We should greet all the people who come on [the train] with Queer Nation friendliness." The strategy for all these actions is to be playfully provocative, never hostile. His second admonition, however, leaves no doubt that a hostile response is expected from BART riders, shoppers, or mere passersby: "Don't go anywhere alone. We are deep behind enemy lines, in enemy territory. We don't know what could happen. So, please, go everywhere with at least one other person!"

Mall actions are a mainstay of the Queer Nation, whether the malls are in suburban San Francisco, Chicago, or Union City, New Jersey. Gay men and lesbians, usually in a three-to-one male-to-female ratio, mount "queer visibility" expeditions, walking hand in hand into stores, shopping a lot, buying a little, and engaging in exaggerated mimicry of the straights who surround them. Occasionally, there is a kiss-in. The look is punk, drag, leather, bleached hair, dyed hair, earrings, ear cuffs, nipple rings, nose pins, scarves, streamers, and balloons. It's demonstration as picnic, picnic as political action.

And always, there is "literature." For the Concord Back-to-School Day, the packet is called *Queer Studies 101—readin', 'ritin', 'rithmetic*. Under "readin' " is a list of books and pamphlets on coming out. The " 'ritin' " section includes quotes by and about queer people. Sample: "Love him . . . love him and let him love you. Do you think anything else under heaven really matters?" (*Giovanni's Room* by James Baldwin). " 'rithmetic" includes statistics on homosexuality in America and a section of "problem solving." Sample: "Scientists estimate that at least 10% of the population is queer. Solve the following question: The soccer team has 16 players. How many are queer? (Round up to the nearest whole player.)" The packet also includes safe-sex fliers (for gay and straight people alike), pages of PROMOTE HOMOSEXUALITY, FAG POWER, and DYKE POWER stickers, as well as "queer calling cards" listing phone numbers of gay community services: mental-health counselors, switchboards, AIDS advice lines, rap groups, coming-out groups. And, of course, there are pocketsful of condoms to be handed out to everyone.

"Remember," Katz tells the crowd before they head to the subway, "we're there for Back-to-School Days, and we're specifically there to recruit the kids."

"Ooooh," the crowd intones in mock shock.

Very camp, very clever, very playful, it is all a variation on a general theme: Queers Have More Fun. Steal back all the hateful epithets thrown at gay people over the decades, turn them inside out, and celebrate them. If homophobes and fundamentalist preachers rant on about homosexuals recruiting the young because it's the only way to replenish their unholy ranks, then steal that language back. Yes, queer people want to recruit the young, not by kidnapping young men as Chicago serial killer John Wayne Gacy did, but by being mentors and role models who would show gay and lesbian adolescents that they are not alone, that they are not freaks, that they need not continue committing suicide at three times the rate of straight teenagers.

Reclaiming the slurs and epithets of hatred is hardly unique to the new queer activists. Black people have done it for decades, and not only within their own neighborhoods. Lines like "Hey, nigga, who you think you are?" or "Look at this boy here, got a brand new car!" tossed between two black people on a city sidewalk are privileged statements, taken back from white racists of the not-so-distant segregationist South. My friend Brenda, a black journalist with a teenage son, has become fascinated with Queer Nation politics, its provocative separateness, and, especially, its language. She raises the parallel with black language style. "For a teenage kid to use that ["nigga"] language in a white setting is a kind of aggression. They know that white people are afraid of them, and they use that fear," she says. Brenda never uses the word "nigger," just as most middle-aged gay men I know do not use "queer." But she acknowledges that there is a mischievous demon inside her that loves the effect. "It's like you just say these outrageous things to the liberals and roll with laughter because you've scared the bejesus out of them." And she's right. If my black colleagues in the mostly white offices of NPR were using the N-word among themselves, it would tell me instantly that they, normally outsiders in a majority-white place, were deliberately employing language to exclude me. It would be language whose exact meaning I might not know and that I certainly have no permission to speak. Black teenagers using the N-word in front of me on a bus in an inner-city neighborhood have even more power. Not only am I isolated, but I'm frightened, because I'm in a place that rumor and the media tell me is unsafe and because the same rumor/media sources tell me these teenagers are likely armed and angry. The already aggressive, exclusive words become doubly threatening.

On the way to Concord, the language also sounds aggressive, though in a far more obviously orchestrated manner than on any given inner-city bus. I plant myself by the forward doors, clutching my tape recorder and microphone. As the train rolls along, its seats and handrails now bedecked in pink-and-lavender crêpe, the Queer Nationals hand out fliers on AIDS, safe sex, and gay rights to the presumably straight people boarding. There are queer versions of old campfire songs: "If you're queer and you know it, clap your hands: [Clap! Clap!]; If you're queer and you know it, stomp your feet: [Stomp! Stomp!]; If you're queer and you know it, shake your ass:[. . . ! . . . !]" Then there's the theme chant for the day: "We're here! We're queer! And we are going shopping! We're here! We're queer! Get used to it!"

I can never fully escape my reporter's engrained reticence to participate, and I am thankful to have the excuse that because I'm recording, I must keep my mouth shut. The fact, of course, is that the tape recorder is mostly a ruse. Even as a student draft evader during the Vietnam War, I always felt uncomfortable chanting and screaming, letting go of my role as committed observer.

A few chants later, I'm doubly thankful I haven't let myself break through the reportorial curtain. Out of some spontaneous inspiration, someone comes up with, "We're here in suburbia. Thank God it's not for eternia! We're here in suburbia. Thank God it's not eternia!" Halfway through the chant, a rather more reflective soul shouts, "That's awful! That's insulting the people who live out here, and it's a dumb way to change people." After a few moments of confusion and uncertainty, everyone agrees; the chant dies. Soon, the train pulls into the Concord station, end of the line, and it's back to the basic refrain: "Fag Power, Dyke Power, Qu-e-e-e-r Nation!"

A subdued undertow of anxiety surfaces now and then. Irwin, a slight, bespectacled lawyer who is Jonathan's longtime boyfriend, whistles "Stormy Weather." Others pull ballpoint pens from their pockets to scrawl emergency phone numbers on their palms in case they are arrested. And then, as the crowd leaves the BART train and waits for a local bus to haul everyone to the mall, a truly strange song emerges, the theme from the seventies sitcom *The Brady Bunch*. It is as though activist-politics-as-picnic has imploded into self-conscious nostalgia. This expedition to heighten queer visibility is not only a picnic, but also a sort of queer homecoming parade.

Homecoming parades, of course, offer a vastly different sort of reminiscence from the hindsight of sexual awakening that so marks gay men in their forties and fifties, who often look back to bus- and train-station lavatories as the places where they came of age. Gay men who first ventured into the forbidden zones of furtive homosexuality in the 1960s or before find genuine nostalgia in the imagery of the public-toilet stall: the tawdriness, the stench of urine, the glory hole between stalls through which priapic cocks became engulfed by unknown mouths—all this certified a radical release from the progammatic backseat heterosex that seemed to so excite other adolescents. For many of these men, toilet stalls were the stage sets where fantasy met identity. Little wonder that such a powerful memory should have been replicated in the dark mazes of the bathhouses that became the erotic temples of the gay seventies.

The men (and a few women) of the Brady Bunch generation, however, are the first to look back—six, eight, ten years—to shopping malls as the sites of their adolescent sexual anxieties, as the hangouts where they began to learn who they were and who they were not. Mall life, however, is not like bus-station toilet-stall action, and the nostalgia it can evoke is not a journey back to a darkly magic moment long past, but a rowdy commuter ride to the territory of the instant replay. Reared in families that were supposed to embrace the semi-hip, happy values of the Brady Bunch, these Queer Nationals are picnicking on their old turf to announce a new ersatz family, the Queer Bunch. If there is playful singing and chanting, funny-colored hair, and dresses on top of combat boots, little wonder there is also in this collision of family images a strong current of aggression and a not-so-deeply-disguised tone of contempt. Here is a man from Memphis who first heard of gays by watching Phil Donahue, and then proudly announced to his mother that he must be one. Here is a farm boy from central Missouri who every June watched the nightly news closely for shots of the annual gay pride parade in San Francisco, and counted the days until he could catch a bus and move there. Given to believe that gay was normal, never believing that it was criminally sick, they had marched through adolescence expecting to reach Camelot, only to learn that by the late 1980s more gay people were being beaten and maimed with baseball bats than ever before—and that many, their age and older, were dying. Freed from an earlier generation's fear of bar raids and sodomy prosecutions, they still chafe under the television rule of near homo invisibility, growing even angrier than their predecessors at the feeble gay characterizations in the new versions of *The Brady Bunch* on network prime time.

That's the purpose of the political gay visibility of this march on the mall, the big-Q Queer homecoming-parade side of the event articulated in the chant, "We're Here! We're Queer! Get Used to It!" But also tangled up in the repertoire of songs and chants is a love/hate scream at everything that a mall seems to represent to an adolescent: a cold, overlighted space, safe and antiseptic, fully secured, a place of commerce devoid of any ab-errance or idiosyncracy, indistinguishable from Concord to Dade-land to Yonkers. It is the world of Malls R Us. Not only are queers invisible within it, but the funky heart of difference, the force that makes each of us distinctively human, is nowhere visible. And so, contempt lurks behind the warning that this queer expedition is moving "deep behind enemy lines." Contempt in the spontaneous chant, "We're here in suburbia. Thank God it's not eternia!" Contempt even in the defining of these actions as instructive expeditions intended to enlighten the ill-educated bigots presumed to populate malls. Precisely because most of the Queer Nationals have come from Mall America, arriving in the cities to find not secret toilet stalls but a sort of high-energy middle-class bohemia, there is in this outreach the feel of a moralizing lecture to the benighted souls who haven't yet escaped.

Once the band of queer pranksters reach the Concord mall, they fan out according to plan, adding jaunty merriment to an otherwise dull Saturday afternoon of shopping. By far the most colorful of them is Sister Sadie the Rabbi Lady (one of the original Sisters of Perpetual Indulgence, a group that for a decade bounced around San Francisco wearing beards and nuns' habits, poking fun at homophobes and contributing to the city's general tone of studied eccentricity). Sadie (née Gil Block), who might politely be described as zaftig, sports makeup nearly as thick as her padded cleavage (her eyebrows alone take a half hour to paint), tends toward garish, swirling designs in orange, black, or pink, and performs juiced-up versions of Rodgers and Hammerstein at the slightest sight of a mike.

Her mall lyrics for the day run as follows:

> *I'm just a girl who can't say no,*
> *Shopping is my way of life.*
> *Didn't your mother tell you so?*
> *Makes you a wonderful wife.*
> *When a store has got a super sale*
> *I catch a cab to make sure I'm not late.*
> *When it comes to satin souvenirs*
> *I buy an extra dozen just in case.*
> *Even if I don't need a thing—*

Bargains I cannot resist.
Coupons I got by the fist.
How else you think I exist?
I can't say no-o-o-o. [Giggle.]

As Sadie and her entourage stroll down the corridors in troubadour drag, most of the rest wander about in twos and threes. Nowhere does anyone draw a slur or an epithet. Most other shoppers pay little attention: They take a flier or a leaflet, read it briefly, then toss it into the trash.

When Jonathan Katz and his boyfriend, Irwin, enter an ear-piercing shop, the owner, whose name is Rita, draws them into her own banter.

"You can have any kind of stud you want," she tells Irwin without a flicker of a smile. "Then choose the stone to match. We have colored studs for colored folks, and the man-made diamond for the high-class folks."

"I think something solid gold," Jonathan suggests.

"This is your man-made diamond, mounted on zirconium," Rita goes on. "This is the most popular because it does not lose luster or shine, like your birthstone designer stones. It costs ten dollars."

Irwin says he likes pearls, but Rita warns him that they will lose their gloss quickly.

"Yeah, well, dull might be better, because I have to go back to work in a couple of weeks, and I'll have to take it out."

"No. No. You can't take it out," Rita tells him.

Irwin agrees and presents his ear.

"Okay," she instructs, "three times a day you gotta clean your stud. Gotta keep it clean. Nothing worse than a dirty stud." She shows him a bottle of clear liquid. "This contains your cleaning fluid," she explains, somehow slipping into a Flatbush accent, though, I later discover, she's a native Californian.

"Do you pierce other body parts?" one of the accompanying queers asks.

"Nothin' below the ear," she answers. "Well, we pierce noses all the time. We make sure the hole is big enough so your boy-friend can lead you around with a chain."

Just as the piercing gun is mounted at Irwin's ear, he asks if guys come in asking which ear is for gays and which for straights.

"They do. We get football players and stuff," Rita says. "They want to know which is the right ear to put it in and which is the wrong one."

"Yeah, but a lot of football players are gay," Irwin says in a friendly challenge.

"That's true. A lot of them are."

"So what's the difference between left and right? What do you tell them?"

"Well, left is right, and right is, well, conservative. No. No. It's . . . it's . . ." Suddenly, she is as lost in the iconography of identity as a Mormon missionary in an S&M bordello. Then, recovering, she says, "Left is either way, and right is . . . is het-erosexual. But then, you know, that doesn't work either, because people from other parts of the country say different things. And then some guys want both ears pierced. So what do you say to that?"

Jonathan and Irwin are now trying to work their way out of the shop. There's a rally due to start at 1:30, and the plan is to launch a Queer Nation banner, to be carried aloft by a hundred helium-filled pink-and-black balloons, in the atrium. But Rita wants to keep talking, and asks for QN fliers.

"I had a gay guy work for me once at my other shop," she explains. "He worked for me for a couple of years. He was good with the customers. Probably more conscientious than a strait-laced guy would be. His name was Michael. I don't know if you know him. Do you?"

"No," Irwin says. "There are a lot of us."

Down at the far end of the mall corridor, near the atrium, the chanting has already started: "Two! Four! Six! Eight! How do you know your kids are straight?" And the new old reliable: "Fag Power! Dyke Power! Qu-e-e-e-r Nation!!"

* * *

In the spring of 1991, several months after the Sunbird Mall action, at a San Francisco Queer Nation meeting of about a hundred people, a young woman identifying herself as Laura stands up during the announcement period. (The consensus style of QN meetings is highly ordered, allotting a set number of minutes for each of the sub, or focus, groups to speak about its activities. Women have become steadily more vocal, and real effort is made to reserve time for Asians, blacks, and Latinos to speak. If any person feels seriously insulted by a comment, he or she is urged to yell "Ouch!" and a "facilitator" will come to talk with the offended person and may even stop the meeting to discuss the aspersion. This active concern is part of the Queer Nation commitment to creating a collective "safe space," a queer town meeting where the whole array of queer people will feel "empowered" to speak.)

Laura, a woman in her mid-twenties with long dirty-blond hair, tells how she and her girlfriend were denied service and assaulted a few days earlier at an Italian restaurant in San Francisco's North Beach district. A little later, during the midmeeting break period, when each focus group gathers to plan upcoming work, the "Laura Action" focus group forms. Fifteen to twenty people gather around the complainant as she recounts in detail how she and her partner, identified only as a "woman of color," had gone to Martinelli's restaurant to have a celebratory dessert in honor of their first year together. They asked to be seated by the window and were told that those tables were reserved for people taking full meals. After pointing out the number of empty tables in the restaurant and how special the evening was, Laura and her girlfriend were given window seats. Once they were seated, the waiter, whom Laura identified as "an Iranian with an unpronounceable name" who went by "Marco," refused to serve them. Laura says that she and her friend left, and that the waiter chased them down the street, grabbed them, threw them up against a plate-glass window, and yelled, "We don't serve lesbian bitches here." The whole restaurant was full, Laura now says, and the diners could see what was happening.

The police, with whom Laura filed a complaint, were unable to find corroborating witnesses and, she says, were unwilling to report the incident as a hate-crime offense. If anything is to be done, it seems, Queer Nation will have to do it: Stage a demonstration. Organize a boycott. Fill the restaurant's reservation list, then disrupt the dinner hour. After twenty minutes' talk, the decision is to do all three, and to do them three days later, on Saturday night.

"So have they tried and convicted the restaurant owner yet?" a friend asks me when I rejoin him for the full meeting. Though he is a steadfast supporter of Queer Nation's doctrine and most of its political actions, he feels (as I do) a measure of skepticism and some genuine discomfort over elements of the politics of rage as they're being expressed here tonight. Nagging questions persist in our minds. How, for example, in such a brief and convulsive episode could Laura have known the intricacies of Marco's name and identity? And how could the restaurant have been so empty when the couple entered that many of the tables were free, and so full a few moments later that there were tables packed with witnesses to the assault?

There must be answers to these questions, but no one in the Queer Nation focus group or general meeting is raising them; they're already planning the upcoming demonstration.

Around eight o'clock Saturday night, the QN diners begin to arrive at Martinelli's, most distinctive among them Sister Sadie the Rabbi Lady, her fluffy blond wig all aglow atop a black-and-white-curlicue dinner dress. For a half hour, nothing much happens. The queer diners request water and menus, then ask innumerable questions about the menu. A few order drinks. Sadie takes some soup, but keeps finding flies in it. Almost half the restaurant's tables are occupied by Queer Nationals. At 8:45—only fifteen minutes off schedule—a crowd of pickets and whistle blowers can be seen marching up to the restaurant's floor-to-ceiling plate-glass windows, waving signs and fists and raising enough ruckus to stop street traffic. Simultaneous with the demonstration outside, queer diners blow their whistles and then read, in unison, from a leaflet entitled, "THE LAURA ACTION: Lashing-out At Unacceptable Restaurant Aggression."

"We encourage all queers and non-queer supporters to boycott Martinelli's and voice their concerns over this monstrosity," they declaim loud and clear.

"We demand that Martinelli's dismiss Marco immediately. . . ."

"We demand that the district attorney's office try this case."

The manager, a tall, striking blond woman, gradually loses her composure. The louder the whistles blow, the more she stokes the formerly soft dining music, which at the peak of the cacophony turns out to be Frank Sinatra crooning "High Hopes" followed by "Nice 'n' Easy."

Soon enough, nice and easy doesn't do it. The manager, who has already called the police, approaches a seated foursome.

"Something wrong with you?" she yells at a Queer Nation woman reading the Laura leaflet. A plump, well-dressed man at the table pushes back his chair and stands up to face the manager. She slaps him. He cocks his arm to counterstrike, but thinks better of it as a cop approaches. Faced with arrest, the activists file out, but not before one QN man, who has earlier taken an emetic, begins retching, spewing a thirty-foot trail of vomit across the floor and tables to a rear rest room.

Outside, more activists have arrived with whistles and picket signs. They are beating their fists against the windows so fiercely it seems the glass will shatter at any moment.

A friend of mine and I are sitting at the bar through it all, sipping cappuccino and watching carefully. The bartender, a dark-haired woman of about thirty, is utterly unflustered.

"So what really happened?" we ask.

"Just what it says on that leaflet." One of the activists has left a Laura leaflet on the bar, and the bartender has it propped up on the espresso machine.

"Did the waiter really rough the women up?"

"I don't know that. I didn't see it." She pauses a moment, collecting our cups. "But he's the kind who would have."

By the end of the next week, Marco is no longer working at Martinelli's.

At neither Martinelli's nor the Sunbird Mall in Concord was fairness the central issue, though both actions were born of the reasonable belief that gays are treated unfairly. At the mall, nearly everyone—shoppers and shopkeepers alike—reacted supportively and with tolerance, and when queried endorsed fair treatment of gay people. At the restaurant, the offending waiter was sacked, with no attempt by Queer Nation to pursue an inquiry to assure that *his* rights weren't being sacrificed.

"I just don't really feel our actions are about fairness or social responsibility so much as about power and the projection of power," Jonathan Katz tells me in a long interview.

Jonathan knows how to use provocative language with precision. Actually, everything about him appears précise, even the way he arranges chairs to catch the sun on the back porch of his small rented Noe Valley house. He spoons tea—loose orange pekoe—from a tin.

"This is San Francisco, honey. No queen can afford to miss the rays when they're out." With that, he leans back, shades over eyes, a very attractive, cleanly muscled thirty-two-year-old with the hard features of a latter-day Tyrone Power. We have met to talk about ideas, especially about the inherent contradictions in the merging of power, equity, and fairness, contradictions that have brought Queer Nation into existence and also seem capable of ripping it apart.

We speak about the war against Iraq, which has just ended. Distinguishing itself from most other gay groups, Queer Nation had gone to the front lines of disruptive antiwar civil disobedience. In the beginning, Jonathan was out in the streets with the Queer Nation contingents, shouting, picketing, blocking the doorways to the Federal Building. But when the second SCUD missile plowed into the outskirts of Tel Aviv, he left the protests. Upset about the assault on Iraq, convinced that it had been unnecessary, he suddenly found himself worried about the fate of

Israel. And because Saddam Hussein had declared his determination to incinerate Israel, because death had hit Tel Aviv, he, a queer Jew living safely in San Francisco's gay cocoon, could no longer stand against those who were, at least for the short term, the guarantors of Israel's survival. So without fanfare, without impassioned debate, Jonathan Katz—an intellectual finishing a Ph.D. dissertation in philosophy and art history, an activist with a bullhorn—quietly disappeared from the antiwar demonstrations.

The war, even the defense of Israel, was not, in his mind, about morality any more than the picketing of Martinelli's had been about fairness. His commitment to both the defense of Israel and to Queer Nation's assault on a restaurant's apparently homophobic policies, he tells me, are about territorial *realpolitik,* and both derive from a fundamental sense of contingency in the world, of being an outsider who exists only at the sufferance of greater powers that can snatch away that existence at any moment. That is the story of the Jews, the story of two millennia's oppression that only a handful of Gentiles ever seem to comprehend fully: that farms, houses, bank accounts, and jobs can be liquidated in an instant, that homeland is, at its simplest, a home that the mortgagee cannot reclaim at his whim. For Jonathan Katz, a leftist radical who abhors Israeli policies, Israel is that home. "Seeing *Night and Fog* and other Holocaust films," he tells me, "spoke to me more directly about what Jewish power is about, which is that it always stands at the indulgence of real power. It's temporary, and it can always be very quickly removed, quickly obviated. So keep your passport. And make sure Israel lives, because you need a place to go."

Being a Jew and being queer seem interwoven in Jonathan's mind. If the heritage of pogrom and Holocaust helped shape his childhood consciousness, he developed too an anxiety about the perilousness of homosexuality. His earliest memories of homosexual contact are about being found out, with no place to go. "I'd been having boy sex since I was six years old, and my mother caught me with my friend Ed in the garage," he says. For young Jews born to the Holocaust generation, Israel presented itself as a refuge; but to the child who would also be homosexual, there was no place fully free from opprobrium, epithets, and, all too often, murderous baseball bats.

The idea of Queer Nation has drawn deeply on the territorial model that Israel embodies—both cover a territory that cannot be conventionally geographical. The idea of queer separatism holds as little appeal to queer militants as Jewish separatism does to most American Jews. For activists like Jonathan Katz, the territory of the queer nation is claimed through the recognition of cultural uniqueness. He returns to Zionism and to the questions of fairness: "There has always been a dialectic with Zionism in Israel. Does Israel operate according to a higher ethical standard than its surrounding neighbors? To what benefit? If not, then is Israel properly the idealistic vision that Zionism originally spoke about? I'm not a right-winger, I'm very much a Peace Now–nik and believe very much in the Palestinian state. But I think that it's fair to say that I would side with an Israel that cared more about its survival than about its ethics."

And so the marches on the malls, the whistles and vomit tactics to demand the firing of a waiter, become clearer: "I see this as pragmatic politics. If we are unfair to people, my attitude is, basically, I'm not going to promote that. I'm not going to say we should go out and promote something unfair, but if it happens, I'm certainly not going to mourn it.

"If some waiter loses his job unfairly, jeez, I'm sorry. Queers get bashed on the head every day. I think a large social good can be accomplished, and I therefore concentrate on that larger social good, and I pay less attention to individual casualties."

This queer-rage argument is not a part of the moral call for civil rights. It is not about right action or seeking human harmony through spiritual transcendence, and it is not predicated on the notion that individual human goodness will eliminate bigotry and replace it with universal brotherhood. More than anything else, queer rage rises from the belief that respect is inseparable from fear. "As the product of a Holocaust mentality," Jonathan says, "I think [human beings] are essentially evil, and what keeps them in

line is essentially fear." The pragmatic, in-your-face queer politics
he and his confreres have pursued presumes that personal freedom
and collective welfare will emerge not from high-minded example
but from tough, unpredictable survival strategy. "That very act of
uncaring, on my part," he goes on, "rather than being detrimental
to the movement, is, in fact, key to achieving authority and power
within the American political scheme. We need to be understood
as a threatening and perhaps unpredictable social force. I don't
want us to be predictable and I don't want us to be always fair. I
do want us to be threatening, because for me, change is about
power, and I want to project that image of power."

Power. Threat. Force. Counterforce. These were the instincts
and emotions underlying 1990's "I HATE STRAIGHTS" manifesto, which seemed almost to call for terror strikes on heterosexual couples daring to roll their baby strollers into gay
neighborhoods. Still, the rhetoric of the flier and the actions of
Queer Nation were essentially a strategy of psychological warfare:
language and limited civil disobedience as weapons for provoking
disequilibrium in the majority culture. But some activists, either
out of frustration or perhaps in tribute to the revolutionary *ban-
dolero* politics of the Black Panthers, have also looked to the Israeli
model and at least talked about going a step farther, about taking
up arms.

Late in the summer of 1990, in New York, where death and
decay seemed like daily companions on the street, where the hospitals were in collapse, where AIDS desperation seemed endless,
and where gay-bashings had, according to the police, doubled in
twelve months, some people began talking about guns. The most
outspoken and prominent among them was Larry Kramer, the
playwright and founder of ACT UP. "I keep wishing that some
group of men and women more courageous than I would start a
terrorist group," he told a reporter for *Outweek* magazine. For
years, Kramer had inflated the language of rhetorical overkill,
denouncing the federal government's leading AIDS researchers as
genocidal murderers for their apparent lethargy in prosecuting the
laboratory war against AIDS. Kramer's anger, directed both at

gay hedonists' denial and straights' indifference to the epidemic, seemed to many of his old friends to be self-indulgent despair. (Most of his real friends, he would retort, were dead, and it was indifference to their deaths, like indifference to gay-bashing, that had led him to his state of rage.) His call for terrorism, repeated frequently that summer, drew direct parallels to the Zionist founders of Israel, particularly the Irgun guerrillas who blew up Jerusalem's King David Hotel in 1946. Only direct and dramatic action, he seemed to be saying, could refocus the attention of the nation and of gay people in particular on the dual decimations of AIDS and street violence.

If Kramer had become the Brünnhilde of queer rage, others with softer voices were also taking the idea of counterviolence seriously. "Tempers and patience are now worn to the breaking point. . . . No other community would have endured this violence without responding in kind," warned Matt Foreman, the director of the New York City Gay and Lesbian Anti-Violence Project. Foreman said that he was strongly opposed to armed self-defense but feared that firearms would take a place along with hyperbolic rhetoric and civil disobedience in the arsenal of queer responses to attack.

And once again, an anonymous samizdat appeared, this one in the pages of *Outweek*.

> As lesbians and gay men, dykes and fags, bulldaggers and queens—as queers—we are not safe anywhere in this world. We have nothing—not one square foot—that cannot be taken away by the jagged edge of a broken bottle. Our most cherished pleasures are stolen from us. . . .
>
> I have my fear of being ambushed by teenage boys who get off on bashing queers, and I hate my response to that fear: There are moments when I hide my identity as a gay man—walk faster, arms swinging, look tough like a "real" man—while inside I feel the shame, humiliation and self-loathing of a traitor. . . .
>
> We have no idea of who we might be if we were free of

the threat of physical violence, let alone if our love for each other were supported in the world. In the midst of all this hatred, violence, killing and the neglect of our community, we have always refused to use force ourselves. We have been above it. In our daily battle with homophobia, we seem to have only two choices: One is to swallow all the insults, stay in the closet, avoid our desire and let our true selves shrivel slowly away until very little is left. Or we can respond to every cutting and fag comment with a hearty "fuck you," start swinging when someone grabs us on the street, kiss our lovers whenever we damn well please and face getting hurt or killed. We are forced to choose between a sudden, violent death at the hands of our haters and the insidious, lifelong murder of our souls. Quick or slow? We cannot live with these options, they create a rage that is too large to be contained. It is no wonder that we turn to thoughts of guns.

Most people—even gay men and lesbians bursting with rage—do not move from thinking of guns to buying them. Some have, however, turned to target practice. A prominent gay AIDS activist who knows guns and served in the Army's Special Forces unit spoke of walking past a gun-permit office and seeing a long line of applicants, nearly half of whom he thought to be gay men.

Robert Hilferty earned considerable notoriety when he told an *Outweek* reporter that he was thinking about taking up target practice and wanted to "be a menace to homophobic society . . . to be an anti-anti-gay terrorist." Later, during a long conversation with me in his cavelike East Village New York apartment, Hilferty acknowledges that he made the statement half as a giggle, half as a provocation. No, he hasn't yet begun target practice. No, he wouldn't really buy a gun—probably not, anyway.

Hilferty is a Princeton-educated writer, a filmmaker, a precocious fellow who in his mid-twenties was a personal assistant to director Robert Altman. In 1988, he was one of the ACT UP demonstrators who scored national TV time by shutting down the Food and Drug Administration during protests against delays in the release of AIDS-fighting drugs. The next year, he was a participant/documentarist among a group of ACT UP protesters who disrupted Easter Mass at New York's St. Patrick's Cathedral as John Cardinal O'Connor officiated. His documentary about the disruption, *Stop the Church,* was attacked as anti-Catholic propaganda when it aired on the Public Broadcasting System.

There is a wary self-consciousness about Hilferty, as though he's looking at himself through the lens of his own camera while he talks. His anger is real—at his "wasted" college years before he came out; at the response to AIDS from the government, the medical establishment, and the Catholic Church; at the vicious gay-bashings of recent years—but a sense of calculated self-presentation always underlies the release of that anger.

Shortly before our conversation, on an August evening in 1990, Hilferty and a friend were walking home to the East Village when six black and Latino kids attacked them. Wearing brass knuckles, the kids pummeled Hilferty's friend in the head. Neither man was seriously injured, but the assault left Hilferty convinced that the police are either unable to or uninterested in protecting lesbians and gay men. "I won't be surprised the day a gay man takes out a gun and shoots someone who's threatening his life," he says, his voice plain and flat. "I think it's a viable self-defense option for many gay people. We've been talking about it. Let's start doing it!" Moving from observation to incitement, mindful of the microphone, how much of what he's saying does he believe? How much is preparation for buying a gun? How much is rehearsal for his next film? Then, his words retreat to the at-hand problem of gay-bashing: "What do you do if someone has a bat and broken bottles?"

For today's gays—and maybe for homosexuals in all eras who have explicitly identified themselves—style and presentation are ever present. Not, of course, that gays have a corner on style. The romance of the student radicals of the 1960s was a white *hommage* to Malcolm X and his declaration that political power grows out of the barrel of a gun. The Black Panther Party for Self-Defense stole Malcolm's line, discarded his dour Muslim black suit, conservative tie, and white shirt, and replaced them with a television-perfect image: cordons of movie-star-beautiful black men, wearing leather, berets, and bandoliers, shoulders back, jaws out, the personification of black-man-as-seductive-mean-mother-fucker. That image, and the picture of Huey Newton seated on a wicker throne holding a spear and a carbine, sent shivers up the spines of many white people. Of course, there was more than just image here: The Panthers bought real guns, entered into real shoot-outs with the police (and, tragically, with one another), and took the violence they knew from ghetto life onto the nightly news.

Black violence was and is real, endemic, ordinary—an almost natural part of daily life. Ivy League–educated queer activists—until they are attacked—know violence only as theater. Gay anger over violence arises from its unnaturalness, from its crude, absurd intrusion into lives that have otherwise never experienced it. For men, antigay violence punches at the core of manliness. *Real men fight back. Only sissies and queers don't fight.* Fighting is the ultimate gesture in the theater of butch: A few minutes into almost any gay leather porn flick, one encounters the macho dudes who "beat" their boys into submission, slapping them hard across the jaw and the ass, yanking a mouth to a mock-macho crotch, as the yanked-on one moans, "Yeah, Daddy, yeah!" For the most part, however, this is all theater, like so much of the role-playing and mannerisms of gay behavior, invented in counterpoint to the rejected gender roles heterosexual society presents. Face real brass knuckles on real mean streets where most police would rather look the other way, and the line between real response and theatricalized response can become very fuzzy: To buy a gun and take target practice? Or to mount in the papers and on television guerrilla theater of buying guns and entering the firing range? Or simply to film a pornographic send-up of the bashers and the bashed where the sissy victims play out their erotic fantasies on their butch assailants who then, finally, submit in screams of ecstasy.

When Larry Kramer calls for a new gay Irgun, when Robert Hilferty, preppy and clean-cut even in his black T-shirt, black boots, and black leather, declares his dream of terrorism, they are speaking in voices of real rage, real anguish. But those voices are also tinged with camp, irony—even as is heard when my black journalist friend Brenda reaches into her treasury of jive anger and "does the dozens" on confused white liberals, even as was seen in the diabolical flourish of the uniformed Panthers preying on white anxiety. Even among those who say no to the call to arms, there comes a tingly charge when gay men turn to talk of guns. "I deeply love the rhetoric," says the former Green Beret who opposes gay men's carrying weapons. "People who want to pick on us should know that some of us are dangerous. We're going to hurt you one day. Fuck with us and we'll feed you your face."

In less than two years after its birth, Queer Nation all but degenerated into Queer Civil War. The two key founding groups, in New York and San Francisco, collapsed, largely over rancorous internecine disagreements concerning the concept of "safe space." Tantalizing in its spontaneity, its embrace of both men and women, its celebration of all queer sexual outsiders, its passionate commitment to ribald wit, the movement finally foundered on its naïve understanding of difference. There were deep differences in the dreams, experiences, and styles of university-educated white men, Filipino youths living with their parents, and ambitious black women who were the first in their families to go to college. What many of the Queer Nationals wanted was a kind of "safe space" where they could both discover the language of their own personal fulfillment and find unquestioning loyalty from their queer comrades, where they could be as eccentric as they wished and at the same time win total acceptance from the wider world in which they lived. As a social movement, Queer Nation was exhilarating. As a political organization, it produced squabbling and recrimination.

In San Francisco, the QN crisis came to a head over the matter of the police. Although the SFPD had long waged an aggressive recruiting campaign to bring lesbians and gay men onto the force, particularly for patrols in the Castro, community resentment had run high since 1989, when city cops beat several demonstrators at a gay rally. Then, late in 1991, two off-duty lesbian officers came to a Queer Nation meeting to participate *as queer citizens.*

Standard procedure at QN meetings—which were conducted strictly by consensus; a single objection could block any group decision—was to ask all law-enforcement officers to identify themselves. When the women did, a vehement debate followed. How could police be admitted to a meeting at which people were likely to discuss pending actions of civil disobedience? On the other hand, how could Queer Nation, which was committed to the embrace of all queer people, exclude queer sisters? To resolve the issue, an *ad hoc* group was formed, and the battle proceeded. Two weeks later, at a general QN meeting, a vote was called on a motion to exclude from the organization all law-enforcement officers. But debate was far from finished, and many people were upset because they had not had a chance to speak. One of the officers' defenders stood and blocked the vote. Instant chaos erupted. The man who had blocked the vote was denounced for having exercised his inherently aggressive male style, condemned as an abject exemplar of white male privilege. His attackers were castigated as shrill and exclusionary. But beyond ending the debate over the police officers' presence, the eruption let loose all the rage beneath the authorized QN rage—all the pent-up angers of race and class and ethnicity and sex that bubble beneath the crust of contemporary American life.

Within weeks, all that was left of Queer Nation was one of those marvels of American communications technology, a telephonic bulletin board: On the Queer Line, each of the QN affinity groups, insulated from embittered cross talk, could "post" its projects and events. Queer Nation had becoming an answering machine.

Similar battles between men and women, among blacks, whites, and Latinos, among gays, bisexuals, and transsexuals, shredded Queer Nation meetings in New York and hobbled the organization's growth in Los Angeles. Even in its wreckage-strewn wake, however, the idea of queer sensibility has persisted—in the recognition that sexual dissidence involves more than white boys in tank tops; that bigotry and violence are not to be meekly tolerated at the hands of thugs, politicians, or employers; that the public display of affection will not be restricted to straight couples kissing each other good-bye at the morning commuter stop.

three

Celebutantes

◆

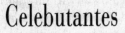

Fabricating

the

Fabulous

Man

10:15 P.M. Saturday night, March 13, 1991, the Coral Sands Motel, Hollywood. Just as General Norman Schwarzkopf is rolling his tank blitz across the sands of Arabia toward the mother of all battles, the gnomish Ggreg Taylor, his head shaved and covered with a black motorcycle cap, totters on blue-mirror platform shoes alongside the motel's courtyard pool.

Ggreg (who always signs his name with a triple G) has hired San Francisco's funky hippie bus, the Green Tortoise, which for nearly two decades has crisscrossed the nation, a rolling museum of the counterculture outfitted with diner tables and, in the back, foam mattresses. Renaming it the Lavender Tortoise, Ggreg and thirty-six "fags, dykes, and drag queens" have set off into that heart of blinding cultural darkness, southern California. Included in the tour are two nights at the Coral Sands, a slightly tacky gay hostelry, a promenade along Hollywood's boulevard of the stars, a quick pop into Frederick's of Hollywood, a solidarity appearance at the Queer Nation chapter in L.A. followed by a twirl through the underground funk-punk dance clubs, and, finally, a day on the rides with Mickey, Donald, Cinderella, and friends at Disneyland. The trip will be, as the rock-music critic Don Baird is to write, "a respite from the battles facing this community's various political activist groups, the occasional dreariness that sets in on our usually vibrant club scene, the sorrow of the constant loss of many loved ones, or the slings and arrows of life during wartime."

Or, more simply, a party.

If Jonathan Katz fancies himself the radical theorist and Robert Hilferty the cinéaste terrorist, Ggreg Taylor and his band of kindred spirits are the court jesters of the queer movement, recapturing the playful irony that marked the beginnings of gay liberation in the late sixties. On this evening, Ggreg has gathered his troupe at poolside and is running though his routine as drag adviser and tour coordinator. Many of the motel rooms have their doors ajar, for the place is also something of a sexual minimart, where "straight-acting" husbands, businessmen, and other tourists come for fun with men. Some leave the lights on; others, awaiting strangers, prefer the dark. As Ggreg runs down the items on his clipboard, war reports blare out from CNN.

"Be positive, proactive," Ggreg instructs. He is talking strategy for the next day's queer excursion into Disneyland.

"It's the happiest place on earth," shouts Tyler Bob, a member of a San Francisco performance group called the Popstitutes, quoting Disneyland's longtime self-promotion.

"Exactly." Ggreg grins wide, a dizzier version of Our Miss Brooks. Like Miss Brooks, however, he has rules to impart to his charges. "I want to be queer, I want to be militant, but we're gonna have to cover it going in. Once I'm inside, I plan on zipping up my jacket and looking like I'm in a space outfit.

"Now one thing: We're going to push the limits of heterosexism. You can do what the straight couples can do there. Straight couples can't deep-tongue kiss there. No-o-o-o! They *can* hold hands. They can pet. You can't make out in the park—it's a *family* atmosphere. So I encourage everybody to have your hands around each other. Hold hands!"

A warning comes from someone near the end of the pool: If they try to stick Queer Nation's PROMOTE HOMOSEXUALITY stickers around Disneyland, they could all be bounced out.

"Don't sticker inside the park!" Thoroughly in charge, Ggreg turns to a thinning-haired Radical Faerie. "Buzzy?"

"Is there any evidence that we can *wear* those stickers?" Buzzy asks.

"Freedom of speech, Buzzy," Ggreg answers in his best Eve Arden manner. "Now, the ones that say LABIA [a lesbian affinity group within Queer Nation], that's where you're pushing it. When you start talking about pudenda—"

"Dicks!" someone in the crowd adds.

"Inside the park, I want to be educational, not confrontational. It's not that I want us to be good queers, but I think that we're groovy and we're hip, and I'm out to use drag outreach to fight queer invisibility and educate these *tired* people from Des Moines who've never seen a phenomenon like *us*. We are everywhere, and we have come to you."

Ggreg has been through this litany before, individually with each person who paid $170 to join the trip, promoted as "Obscure Tour No. 1," and collectively aboard the bus as it rattled through the California produce valleys toward L.A. He has also advised all his would-be Mouseketeers that a few days before the tour began, he received a call from an Anaheim police detective who had been well briefed on the nature of the expedition. (Cooperative security agreements between Disney's guards and the Anaheim police are well known; it usually takes no more than a few minutes for the unkempt, the unruly, and the disruptive to be scooped up and expelled from the park.) Admonitions complete, Ggreg announces that he's going to find his party clothes and hit Hollywood's underground queer clubs. Most of the rest head for their own makeup kits. A few search out sexual adventures in the darkened rooms of the Coral Sands's other, slightly older clients.

Ggreg Deborah Taylor knows that he is a concoction. Even

his name is a self-promotional device, legally recorded on his driver's license. "I'm a product. I tell everybody I'm a product," he says. "I'm amazed everybody doesn't know that about themselves."

He will tell you how he began consciously inventing himself late in his teens, when he escaped Spokane, his hometown, where his father was a professional drag car racer. Ggreg ran off to Seattle, waited tables awhile, and then realized how much money he could make as a nineteen-year-old hustler. It took him only a few months to land a sugar daddy.

His name, the bad-boy autobiography, the shaved head, the mélange of butch leather paraphernalia and retro-drag styles of the late fifties: These are the surfaces of a carefully calculated, media-savvy outrageousness, the queer product (the queer *as* product) that Ggreg spends nearly all his waking—mostly nighttime—hours inventing and reinventing.

The calculated Ggreg Taylor self-invention process truly took off in the summer of 1989. The previous two years he describes as his bimbo phase, during which he persuaded his benefactor to buy him a one-way ticket to San Francisco and soon took up with a thirty-year-old high school teacher. The San Francisco Ggreg encountered barely resembled the mournful city of only a few years earlier. Gay men had seemed shell-shocked as the AIDS deaths mounted. For a while it seemed possible that every gay man in the city was doomed, that the whole sexy, exuberant fairyland, the gay Mecca, would perish. But gay men did not disappear from San Francisco. Many continued to migrate there, correctly believing that they would find more tolerance and better health care there than anywhere else in the country. (And, of course, discos still boomed the nights away.) Still, it wasn't until 1988 that a youthful zest returned to the city, part of it born of the first wave of militant AIDS activism, more of it brought in by a generation of young gay men, guiltless about their sexuality and emotionally removed from the toll AIDS was exacting on older gays. With them came "boy clubs," parties at which hundreds of fresh-faced youths in T-shirts danced and caroused. Older men weren't overtly blocked from the boy parties; rather, the organizers simply printed hundreds of small invitation cards that their street flacks would hand out only to pretty boys.

It was at about this time that Ggreg Taylor found the third G in his first name and returned to his semi-abandoned journal. The title of the opening entry is remarkably candid about what would be required to turn the young man into marketable product:

06.27.89 (Tuesday)

* Intellect * Ego * Image * Acceptance * Attitude *
Environment * Limitations * Events * Involvement

Journals are surely the province of confessional self-assessment, but Ggreg Taylor's (which he eagerly offered for inclusion in this book) is almost embarrassing in its tone of cold strategy, in its revelations about a young man convincing himself that the persona—the product—he is ready to create is the right one, that it will be effective even if it is not altogether sincere. (For the sake of privacy, the names here have been rendered as initials.)

Day After the Gay Day Parade

Life's been pretty amazing lately. I feel I have progressed immensely in the last two years since I moved here. I finally have met the kind of people I have been looking for since I felt the need for a new type of acceptance. Apparently I have become an adult. Somewhere in there something happened. I am proud of who I am, accepting of who I have been, and excited about who I will be.

I still have to conquer many downfalls before I will be where I want to be, but at least I am conscious of them. . . . I feel the people with whom I am involved as well as myself are movers and shakers of the future, not to be limited to the gay community. . . . G. is amazing. . . . His wit is cunning and oh-so-hip. I find myself amazed that he includes me in his circle of friends and considers me to be one of the "fabulous people," a category in which he sees himself.

A few lines further, Ggreg boasts, "I cannot help but be the way I am. I have always been somewhat of a subversive." A nearly obsessive soliloquy on subversion permeates the diary. Who is a subversive? he asks. How does subversion take place? What is it that he is subverting? Most important, what is the difference between subversion and personal marketing? In a society where nearly all political life seems to be refracted through the television screen, or at least assessed through the number of minutes won on television, how is the cultural rebel to market himself in real life?

Late in July, after a few nights of sticking gay propaganda labels on doors, windows, and mailboxes, Ggreg fancies himself a gay "guerrilla graffiti artiste," and he returns to deliberations on the construction of his identity.

07.24.89 (Monday)
. . . *Style the world Ggreg,* I say. I was talking with D.G., the cutest of the Stud's doormen. He's so dreamy. Too bad he just wants me for my conversation. Anyway we were having a most amusing dialogue about all sorts of wacky topics, but the one of most recurrence was Ggreg Taylor. It was quite amusing how hatefully egocentric I was being, however I just hope he didn't take me too seriously in my stuporous egocentrism. But the best part of the conversation was when a woman approached me to banter about my ensemble for the evening, Auschwitz-A-Go-Go disco drag with fun fur fringed vest, during which she declared me to be the "coolest person" of the night. . . .

Days later, at an "anarchist picnic" in Dolores Park, Ggreg is out again, wearing rhinestone glasses, fake-fur vest, and blue-mirrored platforms. There are a few hippies, whom he finds dreadfully tiresome. They remind him of "the type of nerd who plays Dungeons and Dragons for the rest of their life. It annoys me that people stop progressing, and get stuck in a time with which they are most comfortable, whether or not it still exists. It is said that one hates most what they fear; perhaps I am fearing the day when I will be stagnant. Naw. I just think they're tired. Give it a rest, boys."

At last, Ggreg begins to feel himself to be surrounded by an entourage, but he is uncertain about its membership. Some of his circle can provide valuable contacts. Others seem to project style and glamour sufficient to join the supporting cast of his emerging theater of the outrageous. A few he envies, as young stand-up comics envy Joan Rivers and Jay Leno. And a handful are plain liabilities.

ON D.: I actually carried on a more than civil interesting conversation for about an hour. I was surprised, because I take his snottiness to me to be indicative that his position with me is one of tolerance. . . . I don't recall what we talked about. . . .

ON F.: F. is such a flake. It's been fun watching him blend in with his surroundings and take on the look of the crowd he wants to accept him. Now he's punk . . . sporting the standard shaved head, dog chain, leather jacket and with god only knows what pinned to it (a cockring, I presume). Why clone yourself to fit in? Why lose your identity to gain acceptance?

ON R.: R. is also trying to be cool, however he just doesn't have anything near what it takes in him other than appreciation. It takes personal innovation, guts, lack of inhibition, and good style to be super groovy in my eyes. And he just has appreciation. Poor R. I don't quite understand how he sees himself in the nightclub and food chain. . . .

ON C.: C. is great. I hope to be a good influence on him.

I hope he gets focused on something at which he excels and does some real damage to this wayward society. He is a sweetheart. He's another one who I would like to corrupt and style.

ON A.: A. was peddling X [ecstasy, a dance-your-ass-off, mildly hallucinogenic drug], however unsuccessfully. Apparently S. is beating him out of the marketplace, consistently getting to those who would buy from him before he can get to them. I did a little bit of sales inquisitions for him, but didn't come up with any leads. Poor little A. It probably costs him as much to be hanging out to sell the X as he will make in profit.

Then comes the most "outrageous" of events: "B. . . . brought little Agnes to the Stud last night."

(Little Agnes is a beloved heroine of San Francisco arcana, an infant of Yerba Linda, the first Spanish settlement in the area, who died and was buried in the cemetery of the original Mission Dolores.)

It was the 136th anniversary of her death after living ten months, four days. Apparently L., the Ps, and G. had broken into the Mission Dolores for a soiree, and B. had absconded with little Agnes's tombstone. I had heard about this around a week or so ago. Well last night being the 136th anniversary of her death called for a night on the town for her to show her a good time. B. had wrapped her in his ermine coat with some roses and brought her down to the Stud for an evening of fun. He propped her up on a stack of beer boxes near the doorway, wrapped in black lace, ribbon, and silk floral bows with a candle in front of her. B. tells me that L. wanted to sell the tombstone to make enough cash to get back [home] which made B. decide that L. was not a good person. . . . Later in the evening she [Agnes's tombstone] was gone from her place at the door. I assumed that B. had whisked her back home, but discovered him dancing with her on the dance floor. He asked that I wish her a happy anniversary, so I kissed her cold, hard face.

A few days later, Ggreg turns away from caustic assessments of his associates and returns to self-appraisal.

08.07.89 (Monday)

Elevating myself to celebutante status is going quite well. I find it to be very similar to my calculated garnering of my journalism award in high school. The first step is merely to make myself very visible, while meeting the people who can help me make more of it. I want to meet and enjoin [sic] the Ps, G.P. and Co., D. and Co., who are the personalities who have spoken so very loudly in the past. But I also need the assistance of artists and publicists on my way. . . .

Honestly I want to have notoriety, but I'd much rather have social impact, and with a creative brain and drive like I have I think anything's possible. By managing the people around me I think I will be able to use their energies to create a strong social force. We're all just clamoring for something to enjoin [sic] us in expression and rebellion. I feel like I have to hurry because I will have lost this enthusiasm by the time I'm 26.

I've decided to check out ACT UP this Thursday, going to a meeting at the MCC [the gay Metropolitan Community Church] to see what they are all about. I don't mind being an additional body in the count to make the crowd look bigger, whether or not I do anything else. Plus I think this is a powerful group which would be good to infiltrate as far as self-promotion goes, and which might also teach me some good societal guerrilla tactics. But I like a lot of what they do and how they do it . . . so what the hey. It's fun to be rebellious; why not be officially rebellious?

The search for social privilege through style, the drive to become a *celebutante,* is hardly unique. Perle Mesta's and Pamela Harriman's Washington dinner parties for the political cognoscenti were fabricated of the same impulse, even if those hostesses began their trek farther up the ladder of respectability. To invent oneself as a social actor who must be watched, followed, and assessed is an old and honorable American tradition, noted by Tocqueville in the 1830s, brought to scandalous proportions in that decade at the soirées of the down-home outsider president, Andrew Jackson, and his unofficial first lady, Peggy Eaton, and rendered with conspicuous indulgence through the second and third decades of this century. If we Americans have always been the definitive *arrivistes,* a people that could never reliably count on inherited class status to grant a secure social niche, this newest crop of self-proclaiming queers is a people that seems to have no background at all on which to establish its standing. Even the reigns of Hollywood's *faux* nobility are predicated on two of America's most cherished values: the conspicuous display of wealth and the adulation of respectable middle-class entertainment seekers. For a twenty-four-year-old prematurely balding queer from Spokane to pursue some equivalently lofty place in the world requires, at the very least, outrageous chutzpah.

Throughout the summer of 1989, Ggreg and a handful of his choicest friends immerse themselves in a public art/poster campaign against Senator Jesse Helms's anti-"perversion" diatribes against the National Endowment for the Arts. They band together as "Boys with Arms Akimbo"; their logo is a picture of a small child wearing a shirt, tie, and short pants. They produce a series of silk screens labeled SAFE and UNSAFE. One SAFE work depicts a man licking the head of another man's erect penis; the copy reads, "Always pull out before cumming or wear a rubber when you're getting a blow job." Another SAFE poster shows a condom-sheathed penis entering a rectum, and reads, "Always wear a rubber and use only *water-based* lube for fucking." One of the UNSAFE pieces combines a head shot of Senator Helms and the following copy: "North Carolina Republican JESSE HELMS is the chief philistine, misogynist, homophobe, and AIDS bigot in the United States Senate. He has lead the right-wing legislative attack on freedom of expression, on the National Endowment for the Arts, on reproductive rights, on protecting lesbians and gay men from hate crimes, and on health care and human rights for people with AIDS. Helms' largest corporate political donor is Philip Morris Companies, Inc., manufacturer of Marlboro Cigarettes. BOY-COTT MARLBORO!" Other UNSAFE posters portray George Bush, Health and Human Services Secretary Louis Sullivan, and the Reverend Lou Sheldon, whose fundamentalist Christian Traditional Values Coalition is virulently antigay.

08.11.89 (Friday)

Our favorite pederast and I were talking over dinner last night about Boy with Arms Akimbo. His thoughts on its function were different than my initial thoughts, in that he and G. had spoken of it being much more radical, reactionary and destructive. His description was of "using bombs" to get our point across. I don't know what to think of this. I am exceptionally openminded, however, I don't know if actual terrorism is a good means of social reform. I wonder how much positive social change has been brought out by groups like the Weathermen. . . .

He added that our second action, our next project, should be really big. I do not know whether I agree with this or not. I think we need to get practiced at rabble-rousing first, before taking on a project which can be potentially disastrous. Of course that's just me. I also assume that most of these projects will have to come under my direction, just because I will take it on and do it. Nothing would get done unless someone with some drive pushes it forward. I have to be the one. I'd rather come up with ideas and procedures than manage a mob of cute boys with short attention spans.

08.14.89 (Monday)
We did it. Boys with Arms Akimbo struck successfully last night at the Federal Building. I am amazed that it turned out after all the problems which occurred early on, and that we were not scared away from our actions.

[We] spent the entire day from 11 A.M. on preparing for the action . . . went to make photocopies of additional artwork to put on the building . . . added a Man Ray and von Gloden. . . . After getting the glue at the Sears on Geary we went to my house to start putting together the posters. . . .

We hopped in the cars around 11:45 [P.M.] or so and drove down to the Federal Building to raise hell. Rounding the block we spied a guard walking into the building on the side which we were to attack. After circling the block once we heard sirens, and all of a sudden there were cop cars appearing all over the place . . . guys running around, flashing lights under cars, looking for someone obviously. . . . We went back to our house to wait an hour or so until whatever was happening was over. . . .

Once at my house we decided to hit the wall across the street . . . with our big lesbian bondage picture. . . . We hopped out of our car and start plastering it to the wall, but it was difficult, being our first attempt. . . . I heard G or someone yell, "Cops!" and all I could do was panic and run. I ran behind the Harvey Milk Library and down a dark street, and hid under the car.

Sure enough the cops caught me and questioned me. They were actually pretty cool about it. I handled myself extremely well, if I don't say so myself. . . . They handcuffed me and decided that they were going to run me in for resisting arrest, sticking me in the backseat of their patrol car. . . . We discussed the situation, and they agreed that if I would remove the poster they would not cite or ticket me, but would rather give me a verbal warning. They released me, and I walked across the street to the awaiting van with the poster, my symbol of my success. I called home from a pay phone across the street to inform all there that everything was just fine, and that I'd be home in a jiffy so that we could go on with the action at the Federal building as planned.

08.21.89 (Monday)

. . . The action went off amazingly well. I was elated that we received coverage all week. First we were covered in the Examiner the next day, then the Weekly and the [gay weekly] Sentinel ran stories without pictures. Sunday an article appeared in the book review section.

08.22.89 (Tuesday)

Too much pressure on these days. I have now gained the respect of many of my peers, but the expectations of others are hard to live up to. . . . I am careful now where my name gets used in advertising. I would not let P.A. use it on a flier for his outlaw party because I would be lost among a million other names in the middle of the flier where his name would fly on top with the Club Kids from New York appearing bigger than the celebs from here. I no longer need to be validated by appearing on every possible medium. . . . I'm over doing everything for free. . . .

On an entirely different train of thought, Lypsinka was excellent . . . ferocious. She presented the ultimate diva in a blender performance. The other professional drag queens were threatened by her performance, calling it the same old Broadway shit, etc., however I think drag queens will always put down those who threaten them. Others are angry with me because I am bringing in talent from afar rather than using locals. To this I say if you want to get up on stage and I don't hire you for one of my events, throw your own party. . . .

I am having a hard time keeping all the wild tangents of my life together.

Somewhere between the handcuffs, the tongue-on-cock poster, and the front page is the emerging product: Style-the-World-Ggreg.

From the earliest days of gay liberation, activists—even the underground Mattachine Society "homophiles" of the 1950s—have declaimed on how homosexual people must invent their own lives, fabricate their own families, stylize anew the rituals of mateship. These are the acts of counterconstruction, rebellions in which style is integral to action and performance.

Style and the ongoing inventions of gay identity have always been inseparable. While heterosexual mockery of homosexual men as nelly sissy queens does exploit stereotypes of actual behavioral styles, far more important is the way in which queer people, those denigrated outsiders, have used style—style of speech, of mannerism, of clothing—to assert control over their lives and to stake out a territory for their own existence. And queer people are not alone in the oppositional use of style. Since the civil rights movement of the 1950s and 1960s, white Americans have gradually grown accustomed to the ways in which black Americans use—and have always used—style as a tool of cultural rebellion and as a technique for establishing their own social space. Field calls and gospel songs fashioned during slavery days became invisible tools of black communication and resistance to white authority. Much later, during the Harlem renaissance, when performers flaunted a special, newly fashioned sense of body style, whites were variously intrigued, envious, or frightened (contemporary jive and rap have much the same effect). Black Americans have always been deft at constructing a universe in which the whites were, at most, voyeurs.

Gay men during the glorious flaunting years of the 1970s

were enjoying their own version of the Harlem renaissance in New York's West Village and San Francisco's Castro district—albeit a rebirth framed solidly within a middle-class, largely suburban, and essentially white perspective. Every night was prom night, and fashion meant finding the Levi's, Lacostes, and leather that would best display all the meat that ex–sissy boys had pumped up all over their bones. No longer salivating in solitary locker-room guilt over the halfback's perfect and apparently untouchable buns, the remade sissy-faggot found out how to make his own buns, pecs, lats, and abs. The very body whose forbidden desires and responses had for so many years been the source of shame itself provided the raw material of psychic transformation. With a few hours a week in the gym, every gay man could become the couturier of his own flesh, stitching and tucking himself into movie-star beauty. That first generation of liberated gay men stole away the Jack La Lannes from their suburban mothers and gave themselves what conventional straight men denied themselves but imposed upon their women: the *style* of self-sculpted desire fashioned, and continually refashioned, for the amusement and delectation of the lover. Of course, beyond the domain of dandy wealth, Edwardian foppery, and the artistic salon, that concentration on style had always been the preserve of women. (Perhaps the most obvious example of the persistent femininity of style is the invention in the late sixties and early seventies of newspaper "Style" sections, elegant remakes of the traditional women's pages that continued largely to be written and edited by women.) Aside from a touch of cologne, or the periodic shift from single- to double-breasted suits, most American men before the Calvin Klein era eschewed and even reviled body awareness and decoration. The essence of maleness, as most boys learned it, was its immutable lack of susceptibility to the capriciousness of style: Style was feminine exactly because it was flighty, uncertain, always on the edge of change. Hemlines were always going up and down, in and out; trousers were, eternally, cuffed or uncuffed. "Real" men went to gyms for buddy bonding (via basketball, tennis, or racquetball) or to develop physical health or strength, not to apply an exotic array of toning devices whose only real purpose was to better define this or that pretty muscle. Young gays, meanwhile, turned their trick of self-reinvention by merging gym life with the hairdresser's salon, forging a stylized new image that found its apotheosis in those first Calvin Klein underwear ads wherein an Olympian young man languished in the sun against white stone and azure sky. Theirs was a style of presentation that evoked the musk of the jockstrap *and* a highly self-conscious, cologned elegance. In the two great cities of the national dream, the New York of unlimited ambition and the San Francisco of unlimited self-reinvention, American consumerist prosperity invented the gay man, a completely new stylized product.

Style, however, is always a one-night stand. Generations age quickly in consumer America, and style as an emblem all too quickly turns stale and becomes the stuff of parody. More painful still, when prosperity turns to recession, the plumage of one generation can become the symbol of resentment and renewed rebellion for the next.

Unlike the vast majority of seventies "clones," with their mustaches, muscles, and lumberjack shirts, Ggreg Taylor and his queer entourage came of age in a time of deep economic anxiety, plagued by an epidemic that knew no end. Raised in the working class or, at best, in a middle class that had lost the confidence of its social and economic security, they arrived in a city, San Francisco, that had all but obliterated the last traces of its working-class institutions. Industrial workers had been gone for decades. Hotel and restaurant service workers, if they still lived in the city, were mostly new immigrants—or gay. The unions that had once provided succor struggled for their own survival. For boys growing into homosexual manhood and entering San Francisco during the Reagan era of the 1980s, when the dream of a universal middle class was disintegrating, the gay model embodied in Castro domestic life seemed not only unappealing but also economically unavailable. And in New York, the fast-track scenes of West Village discos and Fire Island summer shares crashed into triple epidemics of AIDS, crack-dealing youth gangs, and relentless fiscal limitations for every class of people: The cold humidity of hopelessness chilled the city's streets.

The prospect facing most twenty-year-old Americans—gay or straight—in the mid-1980s was hardly one of limitless possibilities. If anything, the view was one of low-wage survival when housing costs were up, education unaffordable, and union protection a joke. Like English punkers of the 1970s, queer punkers arrived in San Francisco, one of the world's consummate cities of middle-class grace, and took the fashion of anti-elegance as their armor of rebellion: the tattered, worn-out look of the fifties—ideally, the actual garments of the fifties, retrieved from thrift shops and welfare chests. The clothes were not only cheap. They also reflected and highlighted the tattered fraudulence of the national middle-class ideology that the clones had replicated in the now disease-wracked Castro. In New York, young gay and AIDS activists did much the same thing as they avoided the West Village for the funk and low rent of Alphabet City. Black was their color, diesel and ozone their perfume. Outsiders to the straight middle class, nauseated by the nation's reassertion of conservative sexual mores, these young men—and women—fused fashion and politics into a new style of rebellion that celebrated and promoted the queerness of being Queer.

Unlike Gay is Good—the implicit message of the Castro clones who showed themselves to be butcher than the butchest straight boys—Queer snatches the body back from the conventional image makers. Where Calvin Klein models took every Hollywood stereotype of the matinee idol and pushed it to the edge of pornographic display, Queer stylists take the secret of the macho model and turn it public: Even if he looks like Steve Reeves, he probably gets fucked at least as often as the silly queen. Being queer, they say, is about refusing to be imprisoned by heterosexual conventions about what is male and female, about how a male or female should look, about how to sculpt, display, and dress a body. A queer body is a body whose plasticity, use, and presentation are controlled by its inhabitant—not responding exaggeratedly to the cultural and commercial styles of some moral, respectable majority. If the "gay body" was a body of compensation (for everything it had been denied in adolescence), the "queer body" is the body of subversion (of all the roles and behaviors it wants to sabotage).

For talented guerrilla artists and rebel impresarios like Ggreg Taylor, however, there is a perplexity: a contest between the search for a self-affirming world of difference and the yen for the media eye. The validation of the media wrenches the stylized life away from rebellion; it sands off the ironic edge of its critique and then lacquers it for the all-consuming camera as another titillating "life-style" suitable for post-breakfast and pre-bedtime amusement. Without the posters of an UNSAFE Jesse Helms and a SAFE cock, without the tips to the TV assignment desks, the irony languishes in the salons of aesthetic queerdom; it is elegant and not entirely invisible but nonetheless innocuous, an intellectual entertainment on the scale of Weimar Berlin's boîtes. As a Queer Product, Ggreg Taylor seems to understand that he is as much an invention of the commercial image packagers in the gay and straight media as he is of the subversive mind and freak queer body he believes nature gave him.

Impresario Ggreg, leading his dyke and faggot troupe to Disneyland, is not only the insurgent fashion boy flirting with and laughing at Pluto and Cinderella and Alice in Wonderland. Product Ggreg is, as he tells Alice, always at the edge of becoming another Disneyland animal.

Resplendent in his white quilted leisure suit and blue mirror platforms—an up-to-date parody of the now-thrift-shop-available seventies—Ggreg walks up to Alice. The shameless Orange County sun bounces off her soft golden tresses, illuminates her pleated, puff-shouldered blouse. Beside her stands Cinderella, whose golden hair is arranged in a tight bun, not a single strand dangling loose.

"Are you from Wonderland?" Alice asks Ggreg. As she asks the question, Alice smoothes wrinkles in the mock linen gloves covering the hands of her other companion, a large, black-nosed, six-foot mouse. The mouse wears a yellow Dutch-girl cap.

"N-o-o-h," Ggreg answers with a verbal dip. "I'm from San Francisco. Can't you tell?"

"Well, we simply must talk later," Alice answers, floating off across the asphalt with Cinderella and the mouse.

"Sometimes it's hard to tell who's really queer," Ggreg observes, adjusting his leather biker's cap.

four

Spirit and Transgression

◆

**Looking for
Ecstasy in the
Penetrated
Man**

There is a windmill at the foot of a sand dune a few hundred yards from the ocean's edge in San Francisco. It was constructed at the end of the nineteenth century to tap large underground aquifers and supply irrigation water to Golden Gate Park, one of the grandest and most beautiful urban playgrounds in America. The windmill no longer serves the park, though presumably it could if California's periodic droughts require it. Now it is mostly a landmark separating two very contemporary playgrounds: an open field used mostly by Asian and Filipino soccer players and, amid the shrubs, brush, and live oaks, an outdoor orgy ground.

Dr. W., a gay physician who cares for many patients, was the first to rhapsodize to me about the windmill. We had been watching an Italian television documentary I had helped produce on San Francisco's response to AIDS. The conversation drifted to the matter of gay men's appropriation of public park space as sites for sexual encounters. Dr. W. was surprisingly militant on the subject. In most public parks, he argued, gay men cannot show even casual physical affection; so why shouldn't they take over places like the windmill grounds? There was anger in his voice, and then softness as he described the pathways beneath the windmill: the blotches of sunlight falling through the tunneling archways of juniper and oak; the wind-twisted limbs polished to a satin finish by the tens of thousands of hands that have gripped them in varying poses of ecstasy and anticipation.

"You must go," he urged me. "It's one of the most beautiful walks you'll ever have."

Just behind the windmill, east and away from the ocean, is a knoll covered with a grove of trees and bushes. There are some trails through it, but it doesn't have that shiny ground wear cruising parks usually show. A group of young men appears at the center. They're noisy, talking, shouting and rustling the branches; they can't be gay men, I think. I'm alone. A little worried. I could get beat up. Why are they here? They must know why a man is walking alone on these trails, stopping occasionally to lean against a tree and wait.

I continue along the periphery, stepping out into an open meadow, then cross back, up the east side of the knoll. Glimpses of blue jean flash through the leaves and branches. A stick—fourteen or so inches long—is hurled up toward a treetop. Then another. And at last I see it: a great green parrot, his tail feathers sleek, clean, extended. He is perched high above the men. On the fourth toss, the stick flies within a few feet of his perch and the parrot casts off, his wings spreading wide against the afternoon sky. He circles, then dips to the right, sailing in a slightly downward arc to the northeast. The men leave. They are not looking for sex, or for me.

The cruising men are to the west of the windmill, near a gully stretching out on either side of a long dirt roadway. Beyond is the ocean and the Great Highway. To the east is a meadow, but the trail itself is shrouded by bushes and low trees. These men are older—in their forties and fifties—than the ones who crawl through the steep trails above the Land's End cliffs a half mile away. Their facial expressions, the uncertainty of their movements, betray loneliness. A few are Latinos. Two are black, and another two are Asian. The rest are white.

By four-fifteen I'm growing bored. The sun has been warm enough, the wind civil enough, for San Francisco at the beach. I think of going to A Different Light bookstore to collect the latest gay magazines. Must keep up. But unfulfilled expectation propels me toward one more promenade up the dirt road, then back through the labyrinthine trail. And this time, patience is rewarded.

Florida—six two (my height), red-and-white Florida State letter jacket with a diver's logo—passes by on an inner path just against the chain-link fence separating the highway from the grove. He looks to be about thirty. His eyes are on me. The only man who has shown any interest all afternoon, except for another balding, gray fellow who shamelessly wears his red cap backward, ACT UP style. I follow Florida a few steps. He looks back. This is no mistake. I stop, thumbs hooked in front pockets. He stops. I retreat into an alcove of live oak and bay. He follows. No speech. No pause. Zipper down. Flesh out. Nice. Soft. Full. Growing firm.

He has a round, meaty face and wide, open features; his eyes are brown, his hair short, black, and parted to the left. His mien is boyish but hungry. He opens his mouth, lips thick and extended. His tongue flows out, lapping down toward his cleft chin. We lick. He has the sour taste of old beer.

Only when the stub of a broken twig jabs into the back of Florida's head do I risk breaking the cast of anonymity.

"Your name?" I ask, raising my eyes.

"David."

No more.

Nothing to block, clutter, intervene, qualify, distract, or explain. As though to ensure that no civil discourse pollutes the exchange, he pulls at my belt, looses the buttons on my jeans and yanks them down.

David is the first name I ever matched with desire. I was

eleven. In peach-harvesting season, late July. Someone from town had brought a hand-cranked ice cream machine, the kind that makes two quarts in a tin suspended inside a metal-strapped wooden bucket filled with ice and rock salt. You had to crank it for hours and hours until, as the old cookbooks put it, the arm rebelled. Those southern cooks knew about the power of the flesh to give itself or to rebel against the giving.

We still grew peaches then, and the fuzz of each peach as you picked it left an itch that crawled up the skin of your arms to greet the mean little sweat bees that lodge their stingers in tender elbow crooks and armpits. On the stone steps beside the kitchen door, baskets of peaches rested, awaiting the paring knife that would slice their flesh away from pit and skin for dumping into the ice cream tin with raw, lumpy cream, left three days to rise in a crock before skimming. We little boys cranked the ice cream maker until, yes, the arm rebelled. That was when David—the town boy known as the Demon—appeared with his parents. He was fourteen or fifteen, with a bristling black brush cut and a green plaid shirt unbuttoned, hanging loose over his summer-brown torso. As he swung his hands to the rough wooden beam over the shed door in a languorous stretch, his shirt parted farther, and I saw the hard, round, crinkly nipples, black as currants.

Eating the tongue of this David in this park, his shirt discarded along with the Florida jacket on an oak limb, that one word, his name, lets loose new fantasy making. A gallery of past Davids pass before the mind's eye—David the dancer from Morgantown, David the seminarian in Berkeley, David from Senegal who sat down next to me at the Paris Cinématheque, David the film critic who died in the epidemic, biblical David and his sweet friendship with Jonathan. All these Davids of mind and memory press in on the present tissues of the David before me. They will not leave us free of our pasts.

We do not stop. Our appetite grows more urgent, lost in hopeless determination to resist memory's order, futile in the desire for a desire that imagines no past, no future, no knowing that the mind can mediate.

We climax, then hold on to each other in the ritual of embarrassed loss.

David reaches for his letter jacket.

"So you're a diver?" I say.

No. He shakes his head. "My lover. He died a year ago."

"You live here?"

"New York."

He is only visiting his brother with whom he grew up here, with whom he has just had lunch. In forty-eight hours, he will be back on the Upper West Side, in an apartment with an unlisted phone number. And then to work, in a suit, the letter jacket of the dead diver hanging in a closet.

A half hour later, I stand at the pay phone inside the Cafe Flore, mission control for queer style, on Market Street, near Castro. Warm, dappled sunlight has given way to the chill gauze of fog that always leaves visitors shivering. On the ledge beneath the phone is a small stack of cards.

Big Ironworx
The Biggest Sex Club
for Men & Boys in the
Universe

Private Party—Deep Underground
Invitation *only*
Saturday, June 1st

Drinking & Fucking
from 11 P.M. 'til dawn

Iron info line: 773-XXXX

I call. A recording:

"Big Ironworx. The biggest fuck party in the universe, from eleven P.M. 'til dawn, Saturday, June first.

"Go to the corner of Third and Townsend in front of Burger

Island. Look for the mailman and ask for your mail. He'll give it to you. Follow the directions on the map to the biggest fuck party of your life. So come on down to Third and Townsend and we'll fuck 'til we drop at Ironworx. See you there."

The voice is a young baritone, studied tough, like the insolent attitude of the new studs featured in the Falcon porno line. They moan but never sweat. Almost raunchy, but not really, the recording gives you the sort of voice you'd expect to hear in a Method acting class. And the "mailman" who'll "give it to you"? Droll? Must every generation discover the old clichés anew? (Turns out that the mailman at Third and Townsend—black jeans, T-shirt, baseball cap turned backward—seems more like a college freshman home on midterm break who's picked up his old job mowing lawns and as a bonus got a couple of extra hours' work handing out orgy maps: "Go back down to the other block, look for the orange traffic cone, and use the double doors.") These are the new sex boys, making the new sex parties. Ironworx would be a scene for the new, younger hot-and-hunkies, new young men looking for their own wild times.

Sex for its own sake—raw, naked, wanton sex—made a comeback sometime around 1988 in the gay wards of New York and Los Angeles and San Francisco. For a while, five years or so, the pall of AIDS had hung so heavy that sex talk seemed filtered through nostalgia. Therapists spoke about how many of their gay clients used up their fifty-minute sessions talking about sexual dysfunction. Newspapers and magazines, hetero and homo, devoted thousands of column inches to reports about how gays had "grown up," matured beyond the sexual "self-indulgence" through which they had "acted out" during the bacchanalian seventies. Then, to the surprise of the sage observers, along came Queer and a new sexual fierceness.

By the spring of 1991, New York, L.A., and San Francisco had seen the proliferation of the revived sexual underground. Gay male "invitation" clubs reappeared, a half dozen at least in each city. They weren't bathhouses with cubicles, cots, and doors, but open rooms in the warehouses of depleted industrial zones, where in the small hours of the morning, young men lined up with their buddies to probe, caress, and gnaw at one another's flesh in dimly lit tangles of animal abandon.

It was at the dawn of the sex resurrection that I came back to San Francisco to produce the radio report on how AIDS had affected the country's most famous gay community. I recorded a long conversation with Armistead Maupin, probably the most successful gay writer ever published. Armistead had written a series of novels, most of which had originally been syndicated in the city's two daily papers, the *Chronicle* and the *Examiner;* collectively known as the *Tales of the City* books, they have sold more than a million copies worldwide. A North Carolina gentleman transplanted to San Francisco, Maupin is a witty raconteur, the sort of man who makes straight women lament about straight men's underdeveloped sense of grace and charm.

"Sex," Maupin tells me, "is the reason this liberation movement came about." Instead of his normally puckish manner, he has in his voice a trace of the same controlled anger that I heard in Dr. W.'s talk about orgy parks. Maupin's ire seems directed not so much at censorious, uncomprehending heterosexuals but at certain gays who, during the eighties, seemed set on desexing gay life, recasting gay people as just another community of polite American consumers for whom sex acts are merely incidental, private behaviors. Maupin is a big man, and his exasperation pushes itself out through a body just on the trim side of portly. The long, soft vowels of a Carolina childhood tighten and relax, tighten and relax again, as he slides between recollection and polemic. His straight sandy hair tumbles repeatedly down over his forehead.

The parks and the bathhouses have been places of freedom and fraternity in Maupin's life, places where the cares and duties of the day dissolved, where barriers of class and education and profession might temporarily evaporate. "I learned," he says with a chuckle, "that you could tell the difference between a nice guy and a bastard in the dark." In the baths, he found remarkable qualities of communication with men whose names he never knew, men with whom he did not even have sex, with whom he embraced and then moved on, all of which left him with a nearly religious feeling. "I felt very close to God," he says. Then, perhaps mindful that our conversation is being recorded for radio broadcast, he breaks the mood and adds, "My friends say that's because I was always on my knees."

When my report aired on the radio, Maupin's wisecrack left many people uncomfortable. A few recoiled at the graphic image of the writer on his knees in a bathhouse, but even more flinched at the religious allusion. How could anyone suppose that falling into a darkened, anonymous orgy room could be elevated into a religious experience? At best, they said, Maupin had lowered himself to sophomoric blasphemy. And yet, as anyone could hear, there wasn't the slightest hint of sacrilege in his tone. His words seemed like a genuinely spiritual confession to which his droll passing remark had been offered only as comic relief.

A few months later, I find myself conversing with another man, a once devout Catholic who had entered adulthood as a Christian Brothers novice. Bruce Boone is as thin, intense, and brooding in his manner as Armistead Maupin is full, voluble, and amusing in his. The son of wealthy parents, he is, today, perennially poor. We meet at a Chinese noodle house where the smell of rancid grease encourages anything but thoughts of ecstatic sex.

"The first time you suck dick," he begins, "it really is like Holy Communion. Mystical. Know what I mean?" Boone holds a Ph.D. from Berkeley. He is a specialist in contemporary French literature, a translator, a short-story writer in the modernist vein, a teacher without a seminar room. His head—gray hair at the temples, skull bones close to the surface—tends to tip forward on an overlong neck. His eyes peer out through thick round horn-rimmed glasses.

He expects me to be shocked.

I explain that I wasn't raised religious but that equating cock-sucking with communion seems like a cliché.

"No, you didn't listen carefully," he answers. "I said Holy

Communion. It's different." We pick at the slippery noodles from thick plates painted with red dragons. "This isn't shocking the way people think—it's about dissolving the self." He reminds me that Holy Communion is not about fellowship, as Protestants might conceive of it; for those deeply driven by the spiritual quest, Holy Communion is literally to eat the flesh of God, and so to be one with God. To eat God is to be liberated from the alienated division of the self, to lose the self. In Boone's quest, to eat cock was in some profound measure to find the unity that divided the dictates of his spirit from the drives of his flesh, and so to eat cock became a Holy Communion.

Bruce Boone was the first man who spoke to me about the links between his Catholicism and his sexuality. At first, his discourse seemed as exotic as the psychosexual analyses of Krafft-Ebing or anthropological accounts of sexual symbols in New Guinea. But as I explored the subject over the next two years with homosexual and heterosexual men and women, the association between sex and God came to seem extraordinarily common. What I had taken to be nothing more than arcane and probably questionable footnotes to the lives of the saints was as familiar as incense to people raised as Catholics who were struggling with the enigmas of their sexual drives. No story I encountered was more germane than that of the sixteenth-century saint Teresa of Avila, who recorded in her journal how God had entered her with a long golden spear, at its tip "a point of fire" penetrating to her entrails with a pain so sweet that "one can never hope to lose it." The temptation to read St. Teresa's revelations as a barely disguised metaphor for orgasm is strong, but Boone, the careful metaphysician, demurs. Why not instead see the orgasm as a metaphor for spiritual penetration?

On another occasion, we discuss San Francisco's gamy South of Market district, which for a half dozen years in the 1970s housed the world's largest collection of leather bars and S&M clubs.

"There were lots of people, naked, milling around, some suspended in leather slings," Boone says. He pauses to be sure I'm listening attentively. "As you walked on, each room was more scandalous than the last—all these figures moving in the dark. When you realized, after your eyes adjusted to the darkness, what the shapes were doing, it seemed even more scandalous to me."

The manner of his description seems more archaeological than prurient, though at times he lets out a titter. He isn't embarrassed, just bemused at his own mental picture of himself surrounded by raunch.

"In the last room there was this table and a guy was strapped down on it and he was sucking one guy at the end of the table and his butt was being whacked hard by two or three older guys at the other end, older guys who were really mean-looking."

Boone pauses for a long moment.

"It was all in murky shadows like a grainy film, and the shocking part was the sound of this guy being whacked. WHACKED! HARD! and LOUD! So you knew it really hurt.

"Here was one person deliberately inflicting pain on another—and the guy getting it was *wanting* this pain. It was shocking because it was beneath the surface of these ordinary, sweet, liberal social democrats. . . . Something was happening there . . . they were doing something . . . that couldn't be realized by the daylight world . . . something monstrous. And contagious . . . so wasn't I a monster too?"

"Monster" is one of the words that brings Boone to a giggle. "Monster" is what the anthropologists might call liminal, or betwixt-and-between, creatures. Charles Manson and Dr. Mengele and John Wayne Gacy are called monsters: They performed hideous, monstrous acts upon other human beings. Yet there are other monsters too, the fantasy monsters that hide in children's closets, and the plastic and wooden creatures that live in toy boxes or beneath the pillow. Bruce Boone finds the monsters in the whacking warehouse both real and fantastical. They transmogrify, dissolve back and forth into one another. They inhabit civil men who help arthritic ladies across the street. They sit with dying friends in the hospital wards. They make contributions to the homeless. And at night, they beat their brothers to the point of raising blackened welts on their backsides. They harbor psychic monsters who travel between the mind and the flesh, reflecting the vibrant instability of the spirit.

There are stories, true stories, from the West Side docks of Manhattan, from the trails of Griffith Park in Los Angeles, from the warehouse catacombs along Folsom Street in San Francisco, of men whose journeys into sadomasochism led to suffocation, mutilation, dismemberment. Before the AIDS epidemic, these were dark tales at the periphery of the great gay adventure, the stuff of gossip and crime-blotter summaries printed in the back pages of the daily paper. The arrival of AIDS changed all that. Mystified by a disease that seemed only to touch gay men, researchers began in earnest to explore the behavioral particulars of homosexual desire. They were regaled with tales of the kinkiest and most bizarre uses of the body, of violence and torture and abuse. They were stunned by matter-of-fact accounts of men whose nipples were attached to chains and stretched, whose testicles were twisted in leather thongs, whose mouths were gorged on the penis of one unknown man while another would plunge his fist and forearm so deeply into their bowels that he could feel on his fingers the contractions of the heart.

Usually, when the researchers would repeat such stories, they would maintain a cool, professional detachment. Only in the glance of the eye, the slightly raised brow, would they offer any normative comment; yet the comment, however politely passed, was always present: The homosexuals have gone too far. Though the scientists were too considerate, too worldly, to charge homosexuality outright as a violation of nature, they offered a variant: If you press the body beyond its limits *as an organism,* you will violate the rules of self-preservation. It was within that *"bionormative"* context that "safe sex"—as a slogan, as an approved list of behaviors—was born.

At first, safe sex seemed simple, like following a cookbook. 1. Do not exchange bodily fluids. 2. Reduce the number of sexual partners. 3. Avoid anal intercourse (or, at least, use a condom). 4. Do not engage in fisting (anal penetration by the fist and, sometimes by the forearm as well) or rimming (oral-anal contact). If gay men were simply to adjust their sex lives to conform to these simple rules, they could easily protect themselves from HIV infection. Nearly everyone bought the program—at least for a while. Some, however, found the rules bizarre.

Consider Rule 2: Reduce the number of sexual partners. Why? Because epidemiologists found high correlations between the number of sexual contacts men had and infection with HIV. As a matter of probability, a man who has sex with 1,000 different people has 999 more chances of engaging with an infected partner than a man who has sex with only one partner. However, if the monogamous man's partner is already infected, then probability analysis provides little protection. Moreover, in following Rule 2, gay men often feel they've been given subliminal permission—if not outright encouragement—to forget Rule 1. (Indeed, by 1990, researchers had discovered through behavioral studies that unattached gay men were significantly less likely to expose themselves to HIV through risky sex than were men in serial monogamous relationships.) Apparently, then, the reduction in number of sexual mates has nothing to do with the prevention of viral transmission. So what is going on?

Michael Callen, the singer, songwriter, and AIDS activist, tells of entering a government office building and seeing two "young, presumably straight" men giggling over a photocopy. He asked to see it. In traffic-sign silhouette, it showed two men, one bent over at the ass, another standing close behind him as though fucking him. A prohibition circle and line had been superimposed over them. The cartoon was, in visual form, Rule 3: Avoid anal intercourse. But if condoms are effective, Callen asked, why avoid anal sex?

Stranger still is the rule against fisting. By 1984, it was clear that AIDS was the result of some microbe—HIV, and possibly other agents as well—that could be transmitted via the blood or semen. Yet what, it was asked, could possibly be transmitted from the fist to the rectum so long as the fist was clean or, at least, gloved in rubber? Researchers answered that inappropriate objects inserted into the rectum could cause abrasions or fissures through which HIV could later gain entry. But by the same logic, a mishap during *any* anal sex could also result in cuts and abrasions that, if the area was later exposed to blood or semen, could lead to HIV infection. Nonetheless, these scientists asserted, such practices are dangerous, dangerous because the rectum was not designed by nature to be penetrated by objects (unless, apparently, those objects were put there by a licensed doctor).

Dr. Joseph Sonnabend, a longtime and controversial researcher on the epidemic, believes the confusion about anal penetration is the result of heterosexual anxiety over the use of the rectum as a site of sexual pleasure: "The rectum is a sexual organ, and it deserves the respect that a penis gets and a vagina gets. Anal intercourse is a central sexual activity, and it should be supported, it should be celebrated." Instead of having instructed people to repress anal sexual desire, Sonnabend argues, AIDS advisers and public-health officers ought to have taught them how to explore that desire within hygienic, HIV-prophylactic constraints. Yet to have done so would have legitimated, openly and publicly, an act that still constitutes a criminal felony in nearly half of all American states and in most nations worldwide. Little wonder, then, that when health officers invented the rules of "safe sex," they conflated commonsense advice about viral protection with a blanket protection of the body against *any* "unsanctioned" penetration.

There are few rituals more heavily guarded and codified than the penetration of the body. In nearly all cultures, the opening of the flesh has rested within the domain of the sacred, whether in the name of surgery, ritual scarification, outright sacrifice, or the blessing of union. In the case of procreative sex—the most ordinary and often the most abusive of penetrations—the rules and even the techniques of physical union are commonly understood, even if, as during rape or sodomy, they are widely violated. As Michel Foucault and other scholars of sexual history have shown, the rules of sexual behavior are everywhere reflective of broader cultural relations of power, right, and privilege. It hardly requires the learning of Freud or the bent of radical feminism to see that phallic penetration of women by men is inextricably linked to social positions of power and subordination. Nor should linking power and penetration relegate one to the exotic fringe that denounces and abhors heterosexual penetrative sex. The point is simply that the act of *being penetrated* requires some release of power over the self. The penetration of the self—not merely the body, but the gestalt of body, mind, spirit, and memory—is, by almost any definition, an entry into the most private and sacred zones of individual identity. Marriage, the most prevalent social ritual governing living people, provides sanction both for penetration of the body and for mutual entry of each self into the other. It confirms intimate and public power relations through which individuals and societies protect and secure their future. If the reinvention of marriage rituals reflects contemporary struggles about the terms of the power equation—*if the prohibitions and privileges within marriage are shifting*—society still retains a critical interest in arbitrating the rules through which we give ourselves over to direct physical and broader symbolic interpenetration. Even for radical feminists, who attack marriage as an instrument that men use to reduce the personhood of women to a status as disposable property, there remains a redemptive societal objective: The terms and methods by which we enter one another's lives and bodies should reflect common values of equity, mutuality, and personal autonomy. Acts that transgress those values constitute a new set of taboos: Men may not force sex upon their wives. They may not enslave them in the house and forbid them to work elsewhere. They may not deny them political franchise. Though particular taboos may change as the struggle for social reconstruction advances, still some system of taboo persists. And yet it is against even that "liberated" system of taboo that Bruce Boone pursues the monstrous animal of desire, a desire that while it may be shaped by reformulated and redemptive taboos is in fact still committed to acts of transgression and self-obliteration.

As he finishes describing his night in the S&M whacking room, Boone wants to be sure that I understand the full import of what he is saying. "This isn't the seventies message of 'Gay Is Good,'" he admonishes.

"Gay is bad. Straight is bad. Sex is bad. It's animal, out of control. Scary. Scary like Stephen King, not cute scary like Steven Spielberg."

In Boone's world, there may be Safe Sex, but there is really no safe sex. Whether it is the first touch of the tip of the tongue to the tip of the cock, the rending of the sphincter, or the ritual pain of the S&M parlor, sex is inherently a sacred journey through ecstatic pain. Boone is a student of the late French writer Georges Bataille. In his best-known work, *Erotism: Sensuality and Death,* and in a small volume of art history, *The Tears of Eros,* Bataille posits the unity of the erotic and the sacred, how at that white-hot tip of sexuality burns an essential transgression of all civil rules. Most of the time, we respect established taboos, abiding by the routines of the social contract that protect us from chaos. We come to common agreements among ourselves and describe them as history, law, medicine, economy, religion. Only in the transgressive moment do we solitary humans relinquish the social identities that individuate us and distinguish us from the wild, polymorphous animal force of Eros that unifies all being.

The bohemian response to civic taboo is to deny the rules of convention, to declare oneself free of taboo's boundaries. But Bataille goes further. To deny taboo, he would say—to claim to have erased it from how we build our lives, choose our mates, seek sex—is simply to live within a different safety zone of complacency. Only by acknowledging and searching out that framework of taboo, and then by entering *into* its violation, by feeling its fire, is there the possibility of shattering the self and gaining rebirth—not some distant rebirth into an eventual eternity, but a continuous rebirth that comes of touching the eternal in the present.

Here lies the problem for those who see in gay liberation a movement of liberal social progressivism, heralding a multisexual, multicultural, multierotic system of desire, a "safe space" for the celebration of diversity. For Bataille, eroticism can only be "good" insofar as it dares to penetrate and touch the "bad" that dwells within the sacredness of the self. Inside that self remain all the demons of pain, fear, bigotry, and abuse that constitute the world as we live it. As Hannah Arendt has argued, we individually and collectively harbor the same motives and capacities for evil as the architects and engineers of the Holocaust. The Mengeles, the Gacys, and the Mansons of this world are not another species. In the call for an inclusive "safe space" wherein we celebrate the charm of diversity, we too easily blind ourselves to our own elements of darkness and thereby risk another totalitarian program, a program that recapitulates the binary system of order vs. chaos, pain vs. pleasure, good vs. evil, us vs. them. As we embark upon a new project of social redemption, claiming to insulate or to free ourselves from the abuses and inequities of the world, are we not instead simply insulating ourselves from the terror of losing control over our own demons? And if we are successful, will we not suppress the essence of desire that Freud called the *jouissance* of exploded limits?

In the spring of 1988, an obscure journal called *October* devoted an entire issue to the manner in which AIDS had confronted American cultural life. The issue was published at the depths of the epidemic, just before the new queer resurgence, when many feared that the whole gay enterprise of the previous twenty years would be snuffed out by the virus. One of the journal's most disturbing essays was entitled "Is the Rectum a Grave?" Its author, Leo Bersani, a neo-Freudian literary critic at the University of California at Berkeley, saw in (the heterosexual) Georges Bataille's deliberations on the ecstatic and in Freud's early essays on desire the possibility for a radical opening. Per Freud, Bersani reminds us, normal male development progresses from an anal phase characterized by a polymorphous sensation of desire involving all orifices of the body to a hierarchical ordering of desire, centered on the penis, in the post-Oedipal phase. During the transition, boys (and girls) develop identification with their own gender and focus desire on the opposite sex. Along the way, both sexes also replicate male and female social roles exemplified by their parents—roles that in most households take in the mastery of men and the subordination of women. Boys learn early and continually not only that they hold power over their own bodies, but that they hold the sanctioned power of penetration of the "other" body, the female's, which is anatomically incapable of penetrating the male's. In his essay, Bersani turns the mastery-subordination question upside down. The organization of male desire around phallic power, around the power to dominate and penetrate, covers up the existence of a counterdesire within men, "the perhaps equally strong appeal of powerlessness . . . the loss of control." Homosexual desire among men presents a threat to conventional arrangements of power and identity in society, Bersani asserts, because it acknowledges the will to shatter the authority and integrity of the male self. By equalizing the potential for penetration, sodomy steals authority over the most sacred of acts. By celebrating his own penetration, the male offers himself as both an actual and a symbolic sacrifice and places his social identity at risk.

Sex is good, Bersani argues, *only* to the extent that it "demeans" the social, rational individual who carves up, categorizes, and orders daily life. In being "demeaned" by penetration, the male imperils the fundamental arrangements of power through which we have trained ourselves to know one another.

Bersani goes further, drawing parallels between antihomosexual campaigns and misogynist nineteenth- and twentieth-century accounts of prostitutes as wanton, polluted creatures possessed by unquenchable desire. Such tales were often offered as a means of protecting people from venereal diseases; but public health wasn't the only reason for circulating these stories. Criminological theory throughout the nineteenth century argued that women—who unlike men are capable of ongoing and repeated orgasm—are in essence more animalistic than men—and are therefore, when criminally inclined, less redeemable, less correctable, than men. "Normal" phallic, penetrative sex is limited by the duration of the male erection and is spent at orgasm. It is limited in time and physical, bodily territory. Ecstatic, continuous sexuality that does not end at a single orgasm rejects the authority and control of the penetrator male. And that is just what happens when the hairy, muscled male spreads his buttocks and releases himself to penetration by another. He has ostensibly relinquished control over the course of his own pleasure to the man who is entering him. But because his pleasure is not directed toward a spending orgasm, he is in his "powerless" submission capable of outlasting, and forgetting, his top man, who, upon orgasm, can be replaced and replaced again. Like the "wanton whores" who so upset the blue-blooded reformers of the nineteenth century, the penetrated man is, in theory, insatiable, and as such is an enemy to maleness itself. Such a man only intensifies the fear of expendability, of cosmic contingency, in phallic man. The "disordered" male's desire to be penetrated threatens to dislodge the phallic man, at least symbolically, from his position of authority.

The image of the insatiable man obsessed AIDS researchers, most of them straight men, in the early days of the epidemic. And it is the image they repeated over and over to the public: the men who had sex with ten, twenty, thirty men a night, hundreds a year, thousands per decade. It hardly mattered that few men enjoyed or wanted to enjoy these delights. The promiscuous specter seemed monstrous to the researchers and to the public at large. Public-health officials, able only to consider viral and bacterial transmission, could come up with only a single response: Close the sphincter. If they had cared to explore the terrain of desire in actual practice, if they had spoken to female prostitutes and male hustlers who had long been protecting themselves against venereal disease, they would have learned that disease can be controlled. But instead, public-health strategy derived, Bersani argues, from horror of penetration—and, even more, from a horror of seemingly uncontrolled *promiscuous* penetration.

"Gay men's 'obsession' with sex, far from being denied," Bersani concludes,

> should be celebrated—not because of its communal virtues, not because of its subversive potential for parodies of machismo, not because it offers a model of genuine pluralism to a society that at once celebrates and punishes pluralism, but rather because it never stops re-presenting the internalized phallic male as an infinitely loved object of desire. Male ho-

mosexuality advertises the risk of the sexual itself as the risk of
self-dismissal, of *losing sight* of the self, and in so doing it
proposes and dangerously represents *jouissance* as a mode of
ascesis.

Bersani relies on Freud and Georges Bataille as he tries to work
through modern America's anxiety over straight sex, homosex,
and disease. For him, the general phobic discomfort seems to be a
subconscious realization that the sodomized rectum harbors more
than a viral infection, that instead it presents a subversive grave for
the machismo of the phallic male. But there exist as well other,
more common metaphors that offer a parallel insight into conventional society's fears and anxieties.

Until I began to allude to my own adventures in the parks,
liberal-minded straight friends would occasionally slip into the use
of animal metaphors when discussing gay sex, asking how homosexuals could permit themselves to behave "just like dogs." They
said that they found within themselves no aversion to men loving
and mating with one another (they understood, they said, how we
all share bisexual impulses), but they could not understand how
these elegant, polite, witty men—their friends and decorators,
favored playwrights and pianists—could so "debase" themselves
as to behave like wanton animals in rut. As long as we gay men
maintained an orderly sexual life, as coded and restricted as the
finest town councilman's (or, at least, as long as we conducted our
lives in public as properly as the councilman conducted his), we
were comprehensible. But when, through the window of AIDS,
the number of our assignations became commonly known, then
we, like the fallen women of the nineteenth century, came to
appear as beasts in the jungle of Eros.

It was, in fact, during a conversation with just such a liberal,
straight male colleague at the Fourth International Conference on
AIDS in Stockholm that I first heard the image of the jungle. A
paper had been presented by a Dutch social scientist who argued
that "safe sex" had nothing to do with promiscuity—that the
whole campaign against having multiple sexual partners was

purely about sexual fear and prudery. It was easy enough for my friend, an experienced science reporter, to understand that condoms could prevent disease transmission, but, he insisted, there were other issues besides HIV.

"People aren't animals," he told me, "and several thousand years of civilization have surely taught us something about curbing our desires. We've learned not to live like beasts in the jungle."

But aren't we jungle animals? And what is this image of the jungle? For as many centuries as Europeans have wandered about the Western Hemisphere, the lure of the forest and the jungle, that fecund, dangerous territory of darkness, has preoccupied the magisterial mind. Nathaniel Hawthorne's Young Goodman Brown placed his very soul in peril when he wandered out of his orderly, covenanted New England community into the twisted shadows of the night forest. Priests and conquistadores fell before the sensual corruptions of tropical America's flora. The jungle—perhaps more so the *idea* of the jungle—is a place where order and civilization fall before the irresistible forces of savagery, desire, and unrestrained wildness. A Capuchin missionary, working in the Amazon earlier this century, expressed his terror of the wild:

> The jungle is a degeneration of the human spirit in a swoon of improbable but real circumstances. The rational civilized man loses self-respect and respect for his home. He throws his heritage into the mire from where who knows when it will be retrieved. One's heart becomes morbid, filling with the sentiment of savagery, insensible to the pure and great things of humanity. Even cultivated spirits, finely formed and well-educated, have succumbed.

Few stories demonstrate the potency of jungle degradation as eloquently as that of the turn-of-the-century writer and diplomat Roger Casement. Casement was an eminently civilized and highly educated British consul whose reports on savage European massacres of natives in the Congo and on South American Putumayo rubber plantations, recounted in relentless, lawyerlike detail to

Parliament, scandalized Britain. He once explained that it was his own identity as an Irishman in the maw of British imperial thuggery that tied him to the African and South American victims. But his identification ran deeper than anticolonialist ideology. "I realized," he wrote, "that I was looking at this tragedy with the eyes of another race of people once hunted themselves, whose hearts were based on affection as the root principle of contact with their fellow men, and whose estimate of life was not something to be appraised at its market price." Eventually, Casement ran afoul of his own radical sentiments and was implicated in gunrunning during the Irish uprising of 1916. Despite his prominence, he was tried for treason, found guilty, and sentenced to be hanged.

A campaign arose among writers and intellectuals to save Casement. But the clemency campaign was easily sabotaged when British authorities circulated passages from Casement's personal diaries wherein he had recounted in exquisite—to his enemies, lurid—detail his homosexual fantasies and liaisons. Citing the diaries, Home Office lawyer Sir Ernley Blackwell advised the prime minister's cabinet that Casement had been "addicted to the grossest sodomitical practices" and had finally "completed the full cycle of sexual degeneracy and from a pervert has become an invert—a woman, or a pathic, who derives his satisfaction from attracting and inducing [men] to use him." Worse, Blackwell wrote, Casement's descriptions of the number of men who had taken him seemed so "incredible" as to be an unbelievable "hallucination." To ordered, imperial, mercantile English minds, even to the most progressive inhabitants of that society, Casement had succumbed to the uncontrollable, degenerate desires of the jungles in which he had spent so much time. He had gone savage, had been overtaken by a wildness that could subvert the orderly progress of civil authority. (It was not only in England, of course, that men were preoccupied with the contest between civil order and nature's chaos. Throughout Latin America, the emerging governing and commercial classes, who often accumulated their wealth as brokers for European investment, were at least as anxious to secure the future through containment of the unruliness that their tropical jungles represented. In Brazil, the leaders of the new republic took their search for order beyond law and commerce to the design of public parks, for which they imported the trees, flowers, and shrubs of French, German, and English gardens, eliminating native plants as crude, irredeemable weeds; it was hardly by accident that this immense Amazonian nation, forever reciting a soliloquy about the powers and dangers of its mixed-bloods, chose "Order and Progress" as its watchword, then stitched it to the Brazilian flag.)

Casement was hanged.

Now, fast forward sixty years and hop an ocean and a continent to discover the observing eye of a 1979 CBS television documentary crew as it portrayed the "notorious" Buena Vista sex park in San Francisco. Finely wrought Victorian houses, emblematic of the city's reputation for civility, ring the hilly park. There are benches by the sidewalks and elegantly sculpted entrances to winding stairways. From the plaza at the top, visitors can look north to the Golden Gate Bridge or east along the bay to downtown and on to Berkeley. The view is charming—or might be, in the documentarists' view, were there not hundreds of men stashed behind, beneath, and between high bushes, buggering and fellating each other with raw, animal abandon.

CBS called its documentary *Gay Power, Gay Politics*. It was one of the first close-up examinations on network television of the gay campaign to win full participation in American political life, and with good reason it focused on San Francisco, the city in which gay people first became a potent political force. *Gay Power, Gay Politics* aired two years before the first signs of the AIDS epidemic. While much has changed since then, both in gay male behavior and in public attitudes toward it, the documentary remains emblematic of most television and press coverage of gay sexuality.

CBS hung its report on the mayoral election in which incumbent candidate Dianne Feinstein vied with challenger Quentin

Kopp to attract an estimated one hundred thousand gay voters. In his introduction, Harry Reasoner, the very image of the staid, sober, authoritative male, set the tone:

> For someone of my generation, it sounds a bit preposterous. Political power for homosexuals? But those predictions are already coming true. In this report, we'll see how the gays of San Francisco are using the political process to further their own special interest, just like every other new minority group before them. Gay power, gay politics, that's what this report is about. It's not a story about life-styles or the average gay experience. What we'll see is the birth of a political movement and the troubling questions it raises for the eighties, not only for San Francisco, but for other cities throughout the country.

In a "tease tape" shown immediately before the Reasoner introduction, gay activist Cleve Jones talks with CBS reporter-producer George Crile. "So, what's the message today?" Crile asks. "The message is 'Look out, here we come!' " Jones answers. Even the most dull-witted of viewers can hardly miss the point: Something strange, something heretofore unthinkable, something "troubling," is happening here, and it'll be in your town soon as well.

The gays are pressing *their own special interest,* Reasoner says, *like every other new minority group*. The "troubling" question lurking throughout the report, however, is just what that interest is. In the producers' presentation, it seems to be wanton, uncontrolled sex. Reporter Crile declares that there is a "consequence to the homosexual life-style here," and cites what he calls a "Kinsey" report: "The average gay man here has had sexual encounters with at least five hundred different men; twenty-eight percent with more than a thousand." He then sets out to document the city of desire with repeated images of boy cruising on Castro Street, grainy footage of men meeting in Buena Vista Park, the city's annual Halloween drag ball, and a visit to an S&M shop and an S&M "torture chamber." At the park and at the Halloween party, the camera focuses on how "innocent" children become frightened or are, in the view of their parents, threatened by these homosexual escapades. When reporter Crile goes to the S&M shop, though, he himself becomes the shocked innocent. Street cruising is "just the tip of the iceberg," he explains. "When you take the next step, you find yourself in places with no counterpart in the straight world."

He asks the S&M shopkeeper: "What kind of people will use this sort of thing? The . . . is it the lunatic fringe of the community?"

"It's . . . no, it's everybody. It's bankers, lawyers, doctors. We sell to all types of clientele," the shopkeeper responds.

Later, after angry complaints about the show to the (subsequently defunct) National News Council, CBS was forced to acknowledge that more than 90 percent of the S&M shop's clientele were heterosexual. Even so, the network's defense was telling. "For one thing," a CBS spokesman declared, "to the extent that heterosexual S and M exists, it is not institutionalized but in fact is an 'underground' activity. While it is true that its practitioners buy or rent equipment from such establishments as depicted, there is no other public manifestation of their activity. Not so in the case of homosexual S and M, which is institutionalized to the extent that so-called S and M or 'leather' bars are an institution in the gay community. They are public establishments which serve as a gathering place for homosexual sadomasochists, and to one degree or another, some sadomasochism takes place in a number of them. A second significant difference is that while homosexual leaders are quick to defend homosexual S and M, we have observed no one among heterosexuals who would defend heterosexual S and M, at least not publicly."

Gay Power, Gay Politics implicitly portrayed gays, at least gay men, as a threatening force of degraded animal wildness. Bad enough they had taken over the small, formerly Irish working-class neighborhood called Eureka Valley and renamed it the Castro. Worse, they were threatening to extend their decadence into the parks of decent orderly people, they openly discussed the range and nature of their sexuality, and they dared, in violation of accepted social codes, to introduce the matter of sexuality into *public* discourse.

Years later, a friend of mine, left-wing and heterosexual, who owned a house at the top of the ridge separating the Castro from the yuppie neighborhood called Noe Valley, acknowledged to me his apprehension of the gay frontier. "They" were on the verge of swarming up and over his still-heterosexual hillside, he told me.

"So you'd have been rich," I said to him. "Any people eager to buy into a new neighborhood always push the property values up."

"That's not the point," he answered. "They were taking over. They would have driven us out. And I'll tell you one thing. If AIDS hadn't happened, they would have taken Twenty-fourth Street and the rest of Noe Valley. The only reason they didn't is because they started getting sick."

Filmed just a year before the first purple lesions of Kaposi's sarcoma appeared on the legs of gay men, the CBS documentary tapped the heterosexual panic inspired by the open street lust in the Castro, the parks, and the leather district south of Market Street. No one could any longer be condemned and hanged as a sodomite, as Roger Casement was when his diaries were circulated in the London of 1916, yet the tableaux of unrestrained desire, the dark, shadowy images of loins in jungle heat, seemed nearly as hallucinogenically wild in 1979 as they had to the British six decades earlier.

For many gay people intent upon winning a respectable place in the traditional civil rights coalition through which outsiders—blacks, Asians, Latinos—secure social respectability, the CBS documentary was a libel against an entire community. By focusing on the tawdry shenanigans of a few, they felt, the network condemned decent people whose only distinction was that they loved others of their own gender. Moreover, these gays were *themselves* mortified by the raw sexuality that kept the parks full and the bathhouses booming. "I don't know of anyone who is responsible who feels that the Buena Vista situation should be condoned or encouraged," Burleigh Sutton, a subject of the documentary, told the National News Council. "It's a matter of embarrassment to most of the people I know. It's a small percentage of the gay population that's involved in that scene, and we don't even condone that." Gay journalist Randy Shilts was one of harshest critics of the sexual demimonde. Early in his 1987 book, *And the Band Played On,* he describes a fist-fucking scene in a bathhouse, and then enters into the mind of a young Wisconsin émigré who seems sickened by the act:

> Where was the affection? he wondered. Where was the interaction of mind and body that creates a meaningful sexual experience? It was as if these people, who had been made so separate from society by virtue of their sexuality, were now making their sexuality utterly separate from themselves. Their bodies were tools through which they could experience physical sensation. The complete focus on the physical aspect of sex meant constantly devising new, more extreme sexual acts because the experience relied on heightened sensory rather than emotional stimulation.

Somehow, the to-do surrounding *Gay Power, Gay Politics* seems layered with disingenuousness. As a credentialed, respectable, middle-class professional—an ordinary person who reports, writes, and speaks through the airwaves about conventional social issues of family, economy, health, and politics *and* who pursues the limits of lust in parks and sex clubs—I continue to wonder whether CBS was really incorrect in its characterization of gay men. Without question, its producers subordinated, even distorted, the gay petition for basic human and political rights. They ignored issues of concern to lesbians, many of whom had never participated in public sex rites and, at the time, were deeply critical of the Castro body worship. And they failed to address fully the complex question of sex in private and public spaces. The total effect was that of a strident alarm, a warning that the hidden agenda of the campaign for gay power was the legitimization of sex in the streets.

Nonetheless, the sexual revolution upon which the gay social movement built itself has indeed probed the limits of wildness. For all the talented dancers of *A Chorus Line, Cats,* and myriad other Broadway shows, for all the courageous and eloquent AIDS activists, for all the dedicated civil rights lawyers and public officials, for all the doctors, designers, and urban planners, there remain the people who frequent the windmill and Land's End in San Francisco, Griffith's Park in Los Angeles, the Black Forest in Washington, the Ramble in Manhattan's Central Park, the Fens in Boston, and the Woods, with their hanging plastic shopping bags of condoms, on Fire Island. Indeed, respectable community leaders and park habitués are very often the same people. Everywhere, within a few steps of the civil rights agenda of social acceptance, there still murmurs the wild man of jungle lust who appeared in the Casement diaries. If at the level of civic politics there are homosexual people who do not want to be known solely through what sex they have or where and with how many they have it, it is nonetheless absurd to claim that sex is merely ancillary to the gay male agenda. The problem for civil, nominally straight, society, for CBS, its producers, and, probably, most of its viewers is the implicit threat of disorder contained in all that desire gone wild. To them, what is wrong with us homosexual people is that we are always available (potentially); what threatens them is their anxiety that *all* men harbor a desire to be penetrated and to surrender to the universal impulse toward wildness, an impulse that if allowed to go unchecked would proliferate into a thousand jungles of desire.

One April morning in Washington, D.C., just as the rhododendron were blooming, a journalist friend of mine altered his usual route to work to stop at a foreign-newspaper shop on Connecticut Avenue. It was a little after 9:00 A.M. As he thumbed through the French and Italian newspapers, he noticed the profile of a man, wearing soft shorts and a runner's tank top, listening to a headset radio, who was about to leave the shop. The man returned the journalist's glance, then lingered for a moment on the street outside.

The journalist, catching up, introduced himself.

"I hope you won't be offended," he stammered, feeling flushed, "but I think you have the most beautiful body of anyone I've ever met."

The man (his name was Derek, and he was black; my journalist friend is white) answered plainly, "It's just genetics. It's nothing I have any control over." He then began walking down Connecticut, the journalist strolling beside him. Generally, the journalist got to his desk by ten, though on this day he faced no deadlines. Derek, he learned, was an accountant at a large firm, supervising payroll for several dozen employees. He'd decided to take the morning off, he told the journalist. He'd already put in too many ten- and twelve-hour workdays that week.

Derek did not formally invite the journalist up to his apartment. The journalist said he never suggested it. They went there automatically, as though they'd been arranging such trysts for years.

A few hours later, after multiple orgasms, they finished their sex. The accountant had a lover of several years, he told the journalist. The lover was a white man who lived in another apartment in his building and who occasionally accompanied the accountant to family gatherings, otherwise all-black events in an upper-middle-class neighborhood. Since that morning, he and the journalist have had periodic sex dates.

Usually, when I recount the story to heterosexuals, they have one of three responses. 1: "Why are gay men so obsessed with sex?" 2 (from straight men): "You guys don't even have to try to get it." Finally, however, comes 3: "Aren't you afraid of what could happen, going home with a stranger from the street?"

During the summer of 1991, newspaper readers and television viewers throughout the country were drawn into the ghastly story of a new sex-crazed multiple murderer. Jeffrey Dahmer, thirty-one years old, a chocolate-factory worker, attractive, fair skinned, with the sort of plain, open face you might find on an astronaut, told Milwaukee police how he murdered, sawed open, dismembered, boiled, and ate upwards of seventeen people in as many years. His victims were men, often black or brown, whom he brought to his apartment for sex. A few were decapitated; Dahmer boiled their heads in a stewpot until the flesh fell away, and later stored the skulls on a shelf. Tracy Edwards, the one intended victim who got away, fled Dahmer's apartment in handcuffs. He later told a reporter his story. He had been invited home by Dahmer to drink beer and, apparently, was drawn to the killer.

"He tried to make me, but I talked to him and [got] him to trust me. . . . I was a prisoner about four hours, but to me it seemed like ten minutes."

Usually, we perceive time moving slowly when we are in unpleasant circumstances.

Edwards continues: "The guy just changed from Mr. Right to Mr. It. It was like I was confronting Satan himself."

Mr. Right?

Although the reporter writes that Edwards ended the interview in tears and then "went upstairs where his girlfriend was waiting"—a girlfriend who also knew the woman identified as "Dahmer's girlfriend"—there seems to be little doubt that some sort of sexual liaison had been under way with this Mr. Right.

In this allegory, the moral is clear: Even nice neighborhoods in broad daylight, even the shopping mall, all sleek glass, plastic, and granite, may contain monstrous creatures who from one moment to the next can transmogrify from Mr. Right to Satan. The evil forest into which Young Goodman Brown ventured, the jungle in which Roger Casement debased himself into animal man, exist in the disguise of ordinariness all around us. Casement's accounts of the Putumayo massacres, European fantasies of tribal cannibalism, the dismemberment confessions of Jeffrey Dahmer—all are testimonies and reminders of the monsters that live close by in our collective closets. As symbols and images, they are the same monsters that the ex-Catholic novice Bruce Boone visited in the S&M chambers in San Francisco's warehouse district, however much those monsters are part-timers whose rituals are consensual, with both the drama *and* limits of theater. And just as surely, they are the monster images cast up between reporter and viewer when CBS's George Crile asked of the S&M shopkeeper, "What kind of people will use this sort of thing? Is it the lunatic fringe of the community?" What is most terrifying about Jeffrey Dahmer, what was most "troubling" to CBS, what the British found most unforgivable about Roger Casement, is the external normalcy and respectability of those who acknowledge, examine, and touch the monstrousness within themselves. "Bankers, lawyers, doctors," the shopkeeper told CBS; they are the people who buy the toys through which they invent a theater of transgressive desire and enter into the symbolically exploded self. For Jeffrey Dahmer, the membrane between theater and action dissolved. We see in him the link between death and Eros: a convicted sex offender, a confessed necrophiliac. For the CBS producers, the membrane between act and symbol seems not to have dissolved; it is merely invisible. The implied threat to "community standards" and civil decency is that doctors and lawyers, people who not only look as appealing as Jeffrey Dahmer but are also power holders in the establishment, are on the same Satanic journey as the Milwaukee cannibal took.

Sorting through these accounts of murder, lunacy, cannibalism, and desire, I come back to the inquiries of an Australian anthropologist and psychiatrist, Michael Taussig, who has spent two decades examining how Europeans projected "wildness" onto the natives of the Amazon. Taussig, like Roger Casement before him, was fascinated by the recurring inquisitions and massacres that Christian Europeans visited upon the South American tribes in the era after the European Inquisition, when the Catholic Church was struggling to purge Europe and the New World of Satanic Forces. Time and again, the colonizers invested the Indians with special demonic powers that rose up out of the jungle and gave the Indians supernaturally destructive abilities. In the orderly European eye, the natives—however enslaved, tortured, and repressed by colonial power—still retained a dark and threatening strength.

Taussig renders the conquest of South America as a "chamber of mirrors" in which sorcery, desire, rebellion, and sedition threaten the colonizers at every turn. More worrisome, the visage of native disorder threatens to unleash the ancient, suppressed "wild man" of pre-Christian European myth, made manifest in the Visigothic barbarians whose lingering specter in the Middle Ages "implied everything that eluded Christian norms and the established framework of Christian society, referring to what was uncanny, unruly, raw, unpredictable, foreign, uncultivated." Less dramatic, though no less threatening, is the prospect of atavistic man harbored within the loins of apparent grace, an image so beguiling and so disturbing in accounts of casual homosexuality. That the players can be as ordinary as accountants and reporters on a busy block of Connecticut Avenue, as commonplace as bankers and lawyers in San Francisco, only reminds us how little removed the totemic wild man is from the orderly corps of briefcase carriers who claim to run the world.

Self-serving gay propaganda might easily claim that men who get fucked are the anointed liberators of a world in chains—a notion so far from sense or reality that it hardly deserves note. Leo Bersani acknowledges that there is nothing inherently liberating in the classless nakedness of bathhouse and park orgies—or, as Armistead Maupin put it, one of the things bathhouses teach is how to identify a bastard in the dark. The pursuit and recovery of the sacred and the ecstatic in contemporary life is a journey separate from the path to equity, democracy, and justice. It promises only a quality of knowing unavailable to the Rousseauistic mind of social contracts. The impulse toward the ecstatic speaks of neither good nor evil, neither protection nor redemption. It speaks only to remind us that the permanent human condition is exposure, and it reveals that the new activist demand for sexual "safe space" is little more than a silly oxymoron. On the one hand, "safe space" denies the darkness and violence humans face in nature, and on the other it concocts a language of banal, "redemptive" sexual management that would suppress the inherently transgressive nature of desire. Fearful of facing the terror squarely, we invent a new "radical" mythos, complete with its own system of privilege and taboo. We actively contrive to inoculate ourselves from one another, struggling to deny that in the messiness of human affairs the only genuinely safe space exists in an urn of ashes. We forget the simplest, plainest truth: To be alive is to be at risk. *Nowhere* can sex be altogether safe, because sex is, for most of us, our primary, residual, atavistic connection to the realm of animal existence.

five

From
Front Lines
to Home Front

◆

first met Jim Corti in Miami, on a hot, sticky night in May 1989. We were both seated in the restaurant of the Howard Johnson motel on the north edge of the city, a sad establishment that had seen too many tropical summers since its last paint job. We were at separate tables, exchanging looks from time to time. I was alone. The man I guessed to be Corti sat with three other men. He and I had not yet been introduced and were not sure how to recognize each other. I had come to witness and record an "underground" treatment of four HIV-positive gay men, two of them with full-blown AIDS, who had volunteered to be injected with a promising but possibly deadly Chinese drug. Corti, I had been told, was a famous, or at least notorious, crusader. A doctor, one person told me. A nurse, said another. A nurse and a smuggler, by his own account.

Corti and a small alliance of gay men had been pressing the

limits of the Food and Drug Administration's tolerance since 1985, when they began importing unauthorized drugs for friends and acquaintances dying of AIDS. To obtain a drug called ribavirin, they had gone to Mexico City and Tijuana wearing color-coded pins on their collars to identify themselves to their pharmaceutical contacts. They had negotiated discount deals for dextran sulfate from Japan. But nothing in four years' efforts had spread as much hope and excitement as this new drug, derived from the root of a stubby Chinese cucumber and popularly known as "Compound Q." Its imminent arrival in the United States was sending shock waves of eager anticipation through AIDS-decimated gay ghettos of New York, Los Angeles, and San Francisco; even the most sober-minded and skeptical men were ready to anoint it as a mystical elixir from the East that would save all their gay brothers whom Western science had failed. One friend of mine, the head of a prominent AIDS service organization, told me that thanks to Compound Q, AIDS would be a moot issue within a year. That was April 1989. My friend's inside knowledge helped me make the contacts that led to the shabby Howard Johnson that for one weekend would become a makeshift AIDS clinic under the direction of nurse Corti.

This HoJo is stashed between a freeway interchange and a golf course. Outside, next to the parking lot, sleepy-eyed Cuban security guards lounged on bent folding chairs, tossing cigarette butts under the bougainvillea. The elevator reeked of too much spilled beer. Mold seemed everywhere on the march.

Three rooms had been reserved by and registered (under a phony name) to a man who directed that the motel's maid service stay away for the entire weekend. In many cities, such requests might alarm the management. In Miami, through which half the nation's cocaine is imported and where most of the covert operations against Central America have been mounted for the last quarter century, hoteliers take such nonstandard bookings and requests in their stride. Miami is still America's Casablanca.

At 8:00 P.M., from the motel lobby, I called the name I'd been given. I was invited to a room upstairs, where I met Corti and his coconspirator, Paul Ellis, a young, doe-eyed man who sometimes used the name Paul Sergios. Thanks to an old-fashioned air conditioner inserted in the wall, their room was clammy cold. Ellis was laying out an array of syringes, swabs, thermometers, and IV bottles that had been obtained from a friendly local doctor.

"This is totally illegal; essentially holding an experiment which is not FDA approved," he exclaimed. He seemed to thrive on the film-noir ambience of the operation. He also made regular complaints about how horny he had been since his arrival in Miami, a condition he illustrated by periodically groping beneath the elastic band of his red short-shorts. Over the next two days, he would emphasize several times that he had undertaken great risks, not only to save lives but to revise the way this nation views medicine. "This is a revolution against the FDA, and I'm happy to be a part of that," he would proclaim.

Yet if Ellis was the orchestrator of the operation, nurse Corti, a bear of a man, 230 pounds, six foot two inches tall, was still the boss. He moved about the room in a black-and-white kimono and sandals, displaying the calm but intense bedside manner of the avuncular doctor. On the bathroom-sink ledge that served as his lab table, he opened up a box of ampoules containing the miracle drug, formally known as trichosanthin. He had two sets of ampoules, one containing a weak solution that he would use to test his patients for allergic response, the other, undiluted, for full-strength infusion.

All four volunteers passed the allergy test and by ten o'clock were ready to undergo the treatment. The two who had full-blown AIDS, Bob and Nick, knew that this was a last-ditch gamble. Both had essentially no immune system left and could contract a fatal disease at any time. Both knew that trichosanthin, which in test-tube experiments had seemed to kill the AIDS virus, was itself potentially lethal and had never been formally administered to AIDS patients. Both understood that many drugs that work in the laboratory have little or no effect in the body.

Nick, a trim, tall man with deep, inky eyes, went first. He dropped his pants down about his knees. Brownish-purple spots, the lesions that are the mark of Kaposi's sarcoma, disfigured his back and legs. Forty-seven years old, he had moved to Fort Lauderdale to live with his elderly mother, who herself was frail. They were in a ghoulish race to see who would leave life first. Nick gripped hard onto the shoulder of a friend who'd accompanied him here, then squinted and sucked in a sharp breath as Corti plunged an inch-and-a-quarter-long hypodermic needle into his left buttock.

"Okay, honey," Corti said, giving a friendly slap to the other buttock. "You're a done deal."

For the next two days, there was little to do but wait as Ellis, Corti, and two volunteer nurses monitored the four men, noted vital signs, and prayed that none would lapse into shock or, worse, into the coma that an earlier volunteer had suffered.

During the waiting hours, Corti told of his exploits in Mexico, Japan, Switzerland, and Paris, of the charms of the boys of Bangkok, and of a lover whose death in 1987 had turned Corti into a radical. And he told me of his just-completed trip to obtain the shipment of Compound Q.

That tale begins in Shanghai, on Monday, May 1.

Along with a translator he found in Hong Kong, Corti has made his way to the most chaotic and freewheeling of Chinese cities in the middle of May Day celebrations. And this is not just any May Day. The entire nation is in upheaval. Tiananmen Square in Peking is still occupied by thousands of students, and revolution seems imminent throughout the country. Corti has brought an enormous roll of cash—several thousand dollars—and a couple of VCRs that he's been told could be useful gifts to lubricate the transaction. He has come to Shanghai because that is the location of the laboratory named on a box of trichosanthin ampoules that Paul Ellis had obtained by mail through a Miami doctor's office. When Corti and his translator present themselves to officials at the laboratory, they are told that they will have to deal directly with the pharmaceutical factory, an hour and a half outside the city.

A day later, at midmorning, five men—four slight, middle-aged, chain-smoking Chinese plus the relatively enormous

Corti—stuff themselves into a Fiat taxi. The dingy three-story brick building Corti sees as he pries himself out of the mud-spattered Fiat ninety minutes later hardly seems the right sort of place in which to discover cutting-edge science. The polite discussion that follows inside across weak tea served at a conference table covered with a stained oilcloth seems no more promising.

"Five hundred ampoules," Corti says to the factory officials. "We've got to have five hundred." He repeats what he told the officials at the Shanghai Research Institute earlier: The trichosanthin he means to buy will not be used for abortions, as it once was in China. He represents patients who are dying because the U.S. government's AIDS research is moving too slowly. Only they will get the drug. No one will make a profit on the deal, and the patients will not have to pay.

His Chinese hosts nod politely, attentively.

"But it is simply not possible," the head of the factory explains. She shuffles through a stack of letters received from around the world since April, when reports appeared in the scientific press suggesting that trichosanthin had, in laboratory tests, killed human immune cells infected with HIV.

"You see, there are so many requests," she says, shaking her head. Still, she proposes that Corti come to lunch in the village. She is interested in his mission and in AIDS.

Lunch is bland: greasy noodles and duck feet. Corti continues to press his cause. Near the meal's end, as the party sits with stripped duck bones piled about their bowls, a new response comes from the factory head: "It will be very difficult."

Very difficult, he understands immediately, is not *impossible.* As the visitors, crammed once again into the Fiat, splash through mud puddles on the road back to Shanghai, Corti's translator explains what he must do. That evening, when the factory head and the local Communist party clerk visit him at his room in the Shanghai Hilton, Corti must present them with gifts—the VCRs and a couple of TVs he'd picked up earlier—and pay them one hundred dollars for each of the trichosanthin ampoules.

The officials arrive at 7:00 P.M. It is clear that they have never been in one of these wide-windowed hotel rooms with such a commanding view of the city; no sooner do they enter than they press their noses against the glass. Below, in the streets, students and workers are pressing their ill-fated campaign against Party privilege and corruption.

Gratefully, the two accept Corti's bribes. But, they say, it has not been possible to bring the trichosanthin to Shanghai, and because the supply is limited, they will be able to provide only one hundred ampoules. To get them, Corti must return to the factory the next day. Momentarily stymied, he considers backing out of the deal. But he has no choice. Politely, he agrees, and proceeds to count out ten thousand dollars in U.S. cash for the one hundred ampoules—which in China would be worth, at most, a few cents apiece.

The next day brings another long drive to the country and another invitation to lunch. This time, the main dish is soup: Floating in the center of the tureen is a headless turtle. The Chinese watch, mirthfully, as Corti plunges his chopsticks inside the shell to pull out the strange, stringy flesh.

After lunch, the factory officials hand over one hundred ampoules—just enough to launch what will be the first underground AIDS research trial ever conducted.

By the time Corti finished his yarn about the Chinese connection, it was nearly midnight. Time to check on his patient volunteers and get blood-pressure readings and other vital signs before they fell asleep. Fortunately, none had had a bad reaction—nor would they throughout the weekend, aside from slight fevers and extremely sore buttock muscles at the site of the injections.

At checkout time, midday Sunday, the revolutionary Mr. Ellis packed up his needles, swabs, and unused IV bottles. Nick, Bob, and the other two volunteers drove off into the steamy, 90-degree sun, hoping desperately that as pioneers on the frontiers of research, they had stopped the killer within them. Corti, however, had one more task, one that provoked friction between him and Ellis. Half the reason Corti had agreed to run the operation this weekend was to make a connection with another underground courier, a contact of Ellis's, a wealthy young real estate operator named Dean. Dean was infected with HIV and had spent thousands of dollars trying every drug he could get his hands on. Ellis had promised Corti that Dean would deliver a supply of a new drug, called ddI, that Dean had obtained from Canadian suppliers. A chemical cousin of the AIDS-fighting drug AZT, ddI seemed to offer hope to those for whom AZT has ceased to be effective. (Two years later, it would become the second AIDS antiviral to win approval from the FDA.) Home in Los Angeles, Corti had an old friend who could no longer use AZT and desperately wanted to try this new remedy. But Ellis had stalled all weekend, first delaying phone calls and then telling Corti that there was no answer at Dean's. Finally, a half hour before Corti was to leave, Dean appeared in a flashy red Camaro, his wife beside him. Too bad, he told Corti, but somehow the FDA had found out about his connection, and customs agents had seized his latest shipment of the drug, more than a pound of it. Corti's friend would have to look elsewhere.

That weekend in Miami proved to be only a rehearsal for the most remarkable and, in many eyes, scandalous operation of the AIDS drug underground. By the end of May, Corti and other activists launched an unauthorized treatment study of Compound Q involving doctors, nurses, and more than forty patients in New York, Los Angeles, and San Francisco. Some of the experimental treatments took place in doctor's offices, some in motel "clinics," and some in the elegant condos and houses of rich gay men. What was scandalous about the experiment was that no medical agency had yet endorsed Compound Q's efficacy or safety; an authorized study of the drug at San Francisco General Hospital had only just begun. To encourage sick, even dying, patients to take a drug that is known to be lethal at high dosage violates the most basic tenet of medicine, namely, that doctors must first *do no harm.*

Norm Watkins was one of those who obtained Compound Q through the San Francisco arm of the underground study. When I first met him, he had already been given one infusion of the drug.

He looked good. Short, muscular, and trim, he had the bronzed skin of a southern Californian surfer. In fact, he was far from healthy: His "tan" was the result of one of the dozen or so other drugs he was taking. He barely had sufficient strength to get up from the couch in his living room and walk to the refrigerator for a glass of water. One of his prescriptions was suppressing his red blood cells, and he was losing his sight from cytomegalovirus retinitis, one of many AIDS-related opportunistic infections.

"I'm pretty lucky," Watkins told me on the afternoon before his second Compound Q treatment. "I'm one of the first of millions who want to get on this. And even if it doesn't work, it certainly gives you hope. Psychologically, it helps."

When I met him the next morning at seven o'clock, he was winded after having walked thirty feet from his door to my car; he held a cane in one hand and gripped my arm with the other. He hoped, he said as we drove to the doctor's office, that this infusion would not leave him as weakened as the first had done a week earlier. Of course, it was only his assumption that his loss of energy was a side effect of Compound Q. His doctor didn't know; nor did anyone else. That is part of the trouble with AIDS: When the body loses its ability to fight disease, there are infinite possibilities to explain its failures, including the interaction of potent drugs.

By nine-thirty, Watkins was hooked up to an IV bottle that was slowly dripping Compound Q into his body. By lunchtime, the infusion was complete. His energy had returned a bit, but he felt so dizzy that his walk had become a shuffle, and his stoic reserve had disappeared. "I'm really kind of scared," he told his boyfriend, who had come by to drive him home. By the next week, Norm Watkins was too frail to take the third and final infusion in the experimental series. He died before the year was out.

Throughout the study, there were a handful of reporters who had been permitted to witness these treatments, on the understanding that we would not reveal them until the experiment was complete and that we would all break the story simultaneously.

That agreement fell apart when NBC's science correspondent, Robert Bazell, reported the first death.

Robert Parr, a San Francisco real estate broker and former British Royal Air Force fighter pilot, had fallen into a coma two days after his first Compound Q treatment. For three days, he lay motionless, hooked up to life-support equipment; then he began to stir. Two days after that, he could speak in a hoarse whisper. But then, on the next day, a Saturday, Parr apparently vomited in his sleep, sucked the stomach floods into his lungs, and suffocated. On the Monday evening news, Robert Bazell reported Parr's death. Leading AIDS specialists denounced the experiment as wildly irresponsible and the participating doctors as medical "cowboys" flouting the rules of research, desperate zealots who were all too ready to sacrifice ethics to ego. The FDA announced it would investigate. The trial's organizers promised they would take on no more patients. Notably, the patients, who had undergone the greatest risk (and who *had* been given serious warning of the drug's dangers), continued to praise the study. All fifty-one stood fast and continued the treatment for two more weeks until the project was complete.

Two years after the underground study ended, Compound Q had shown only limited value. Some who continued using it (but who had been generally healthy at the time they began) said that their health had improved. Those who were sickest when they first took it got little benefit; most of them died. The sanctioned studies that followed offered no more hope. In fact, none of the anti-AIDS drugs that activists have smuggled into the AIDS underground have delivered any measurable clinical benefit. Yet, as desperate as gay men are to find the AIDS breakthrough, the clinical effectiveness of potential cures is not the most important measure of the activists' impact. More telling is the effect AIDS activism has had in challenging fundamental presumptions and procedures in American medical research and, by consequence, radically altering the relationship of health and homosexuality.

Jim Corti, the smuggler nurse, is blunt when he talks about his smuggling operations: For gay men, "there was no other way." He is firmly convinced that neither the government nor the medical establishment would have done anything about AIDS were it not for the desperate moves he and his comrades made. Not until five years into the epidemic, when hundreds of thousands of Americans—not to mention millions of others, most of them Africans—had been infected, did the federal government begin to address AIDS as a national threat. Even so, the Centers for Disease Control have long been prevented from promulgating the sort of prevention measures most public-health specialists recommend. Without question, the most effective AIDS prevention programs—whether in Germany, Australia, Zambia, or San Francisco—are those that tell people plainly and graphically how to have sex and use drugs safely. The problem, however, goes beyond American politicians' squeamishness about funding sexually explicit public education. At root is the historic place of homosexual people in the health-care complex.

Born into a society whose medical establishment told them that because they were homosexual they were diseased, then let loose into the orgy of the bathhouse era, when gonorrhea was a minor inconvenience dispatched with a shot of penicillin, gay men who came of age in the days before AIDS have had good reason to see themselves as outsiders to the medical codes that most people live by. In the sixties and seventies, the last thing that most gay men were willing to discuss with their doctors was the sexual habits that exposed them both to communicable microbes and to denunciation as psychological and moral degenerates.

The gulf between health and homosexuality first became clear to me at an Army induction center outside Detroit in 1969. I had registered with my Kentucky draft board as a conscientious objector and then had my case transferred to Michigan, where I was an undergraduate. While the Selective Service System was making up its mind about my fate, it ordered me nonetheless to appear for the standard physical exam. Most of the other young men at the center had come for immediate induction and eventual shipment to Vietnam. Hundreds of them, clad in nothing but their Jockey shorts, were inching along a cold cement floor to a series of examining stations. Outside the armory windows, the sky was a dirty industrial gray. Half a world away raged a war in which many of these boys would soon perish.

At that time, very few nineteen-year-olds were ready to embrace homosexuality publicly. Given the war, however, "pleading homo" had become one of the outs that desperate college students used to avoid service. I never learned whether the thin, slightly stooped boy directly in front of me really was gay. I do know that the doctor with the round, red face who sat behind a long table spared nothing in releasing his venom on the boy.

"Your body is God's temple. How dare you defile it with perversion!" the doctor spat out loud enough for everyone to hear. Most of us got only ten or fifteen seconds at his station before we were passed on, but this boy had to stand, shivering, humiliated, for ten minutes as the doctor ranted on about "vile sickness."

Probably, the boy in the armory escaped induction into the Army. If he was not gay, the melodramatic little episode may have quickly disappeared from his mind; it might have been risky to have a "homo" sheet in your draft file, but it wasn't as risky as fighting with the infantry in Hué or on Hamburger Hill. If his confession of homosexuality was only a draft-dodging ruse, then he had not really "defiled the temple." But suppose, on the other hand, he *was* gay, or had, at least, thought he might be. (I, at that time, had slept with one man and believed I was passing through an "experimental phase.") Even if he was not religious, even if he did not consider it a perversion to pursue the pleasure in his own flesh as his own flesh wanted it, still, he could have been left with little doubt about the viewpoint of official medicine. He was a diseased human being.

One might suppose, of course, that the sort of civilian doctors who hired out to run Army physicals were exceptionally unenlightened. In fact, in 1969 the vast majority of doctors regarded homosexuality as a disease, and an incurable one. Consider, for example, how Dr. David Reuben treated homosexuality in his 1969 mega–best-seller, *Everything You Always Wanted to Know About Sex but Were Afraid to Ask:* "The homosexual must constantly search for the one man, the one penis, that will satisfy him. Tragically, there is no possibility of satisfaction because the formula is wrong. One penis plus one penis equals nothing. There is no substitute for heterosexuality—penis and vagina." To be homosexual was to be unhealthy, outside the pale of medical normalcy.

By the time of the great gay sex explosion in the mid-seventies, it was no surprise that gay men with plenty of money, health insurance, and prestige still sought out public VD clinics—or private gay doctors running what amounted to commercial VD mills—rather than mention the annoying side effects of their sex lives to their regular (and, presumably, straight) doctors. To most Americans—even, I suspect, to most family physicians—a case of the clap was deeply shameful: Quite apart from homosexuality, it was the mark of having consorted with the wrong kind of people. Gay men, many of whom had the oozing pus repeatedly—four, five, six times in as many years—were even more loath to go to their own doctors for VD. And so, as other areas of gay life were estranged from the "normal" world, homosex was cut off from the conventional territory of medicine and good health.

By the time the first purple lesions appeared announcing AIDS, or GRID (Gay Related Immune Deficiency), as it was then known, the sex frenzy had hit its height. VD clinics were running at peak capacity. Even though openly gay men were graduating from medical and nursing schools in greater numbers than ever before, there were not nearly enough of them to serve the rapidly expanding gay enclaves in New York, L.A., and San Francisco, much less the second-wave communities in Miami, Houston, Atlanta, Chicago, and New Orleans. Doctors and gay men remained, at best, suspicious of one another. When a handful of men organized the Gay Men's Health Crisis in New York in 1981, they did so because they saw too many of their friends dying and too few doctors and public-health officials paying any attention. There was, in fact, little that any members of the medical establishment could say that would carry much credibility; they seemed always to have been preaching against gay sex. Warnings that sex could give you cancer—in the form of KS lesions—sounded like just another barrage of homophobic prudery. Even the activists who founded GMHC were denounced. One gay New York writer accused activist Larry Kramer of self-hating melodrama over Kramer's attempts to draw attention to the mounting number of KS cases. "I think the concealed meaning of Kramer's emotionalism," Robert Chesley wrote to the *New York Native,* "is the triumph of guilt: that gay men *deserve* to die for their promiscuity. . . . Read anything by Kramer closely. I think you'll find that the subtext is always: the wages of gay sin is death. . . . I am not downplaying the seriousness of Kaposi's sarcoma. But something else is happening here, which is also serious: gay homophobia and anti-eroticism." To which Kramer responded that it was "stupid to rail against the very presentation of these warnings."

Far earlier than most, Larry Kramer understood the enormity of what AIDS would do to the gay world, that the disappearance of his own closest friends presaged "the death of whatever community there is here in New York." But the division of Chesley and Kramer over Eros and disease, the tension between sex and medicine, ran through gay neighborhoods all over the country, and it shaped both the progress of the epidemic and of gay men's eventual activist response to it. In San Francisco, a rancorous battle centered on the closing of the city's bathhouses in 1984. Prominent gay activists damned the bathhouse operators as profiteering murderers, and they themselves were in turn denounced as self-hating quislings for assisting the health department. An editorial in the *Sentinel* warned that all gays would soon be taken to concentration camps.

From the rage, paranoia, and confusion around the epidemic emerged a social and psychological upheaval in the historical dynamic linking homosexuality and health care. The conception of "the homosexual" was an invention of nineteenth-century scientism, when modern medicine devoted itself to the exhaustive labeling of human differences. Not until 1973 did the American Psychiatric Association (urged on by gay liberationists) remove homosexuality from its catalog of pathologies. Yet by the middle of the 1980s, activist homosexuals had propelled themselves into the vanguard of the American public-health system and were challenging nearly everything about the way health care in this country is organized and medical treatment delivered. Never before had those suffering from a disease hired their own buses to haul themselves hundreds of miles to Washington, D.C., to storm the government bureaucracy that regulated the drugs they could obtain. Never before had any group organized an international pharmaceutical distribution system to import its own drugs. Never before had the ill been members of the councils that designed the policies governing how doctors and hospitals and health insurers should treat them. What's more, as the AIDS lobby gained power over the vision and practice of health care, they managed to introduce Eros into it, making hot sex central to a campaign for good health.

Any residual doubt about the place of sex—hot, sweaty, raunchy sex—in the AIDS-prevention campaign disappeared at the fifth global conference on AIDS in Montreal. For five days the discos were packed with gay doctors, nurses, activists, and researchers shamelessly cruising one another. A nearby bathhouse was doing land-office business. A JO (jack-off) club posted promotional fliers in the conference exhibit hall. And in the middle of the hall a monitor was showing a "safe sex" video sponsored by a West German health agency. The video was played and replayed all day long for two days, and there seemed never to be fewer than twenty-five or thirty viewers—men, women, straight, gay—gathered about the screen in a fidgety semicircle. Two men who except for their blondness might have been Michelangelo's models were demonstrating a wide array of "safe" erotic possibilities, including an exquisite tongue bath one man gave the other, laying a wet track from ankle to crotch and consummating with a nonorgasmic, voracious blowjob sans condom. (That the German hunks weren't wearing condoms, and that the German health ministry's safe-sex guidelines seemed to condone unprotected oral sex, fueled a still-ongoing debate in AIDS circles over the wisdom of the latexless blowjob. Reflecting what may be broad differences in American cultural attitudes toward individual freedom and propriety in all guises, New Yorkers tend to call the act unsafe and Californians tend to gobble one another up with little thought to condoms. Then again, it may simply be that Californians will do anything for a blond.)

Most of my straight friends have told me that they cannot fathom how an AIDS conference can also be a sex carnival. My standard, flip response has frequently been "But what else could it be?" The lust of men for other men has not evaporated just because funerals and memorial services have become nearly as ordinary as an evening at the theater. To a considerable degree, those gay men who have committed themselves to trench duty in the battle against AIDS have done so exactly because they would not and, perhaps, could not relinquish passion to death. Simple survival as whole human beings forced them to face AIDS squarely and to determine how much they would permit it to control them.

The idea that we have the capacity to limit the effects of a terminal disease seems strange at first. Suggesting that those who succumb are to be blamed for their failure of faith, it carries the fragrance of trendy New Age spiritualism, a route many have followed, eschewing standard medicine for curative visualization, and seeking the redemptive light of self-ordained and self-enriching priests and priestesses. Hunger for redemption has been an integral part of the American landscape since Jonathan Edwards launched the "Great Awakening" early in the eighteenth century; there is nothing like a global pandemic to renew the impulse. The militance of the gay response to AIDS, however, has been something else. Though it contains deeply spiritual elements, it draws more heavily on the language and behavior of resistance. To that extent, parallels with the Holocaust become inescapable.

One of the first men I spoke to when I began this inquiry in 1988 was Yoel Kahn, a young rabbi in San Francisco. Kahn is not only a minister to his congregation but an acknowledged Talmudic scholar, and is probably the best known gay rabbi in the United States, if not the world. His temple, Sha ar Zahav in the Castro, is made up almost exclusively of gay men and lesbians, and since he arrived he has been surrounded by dying and death. As a Gentile, I had been uncomfortable speaking of AIDS as a holocaust. All too many groups have bid to label their sufferings as new equivalents to the Holocaust, and in doing so they have risked diluting the meaning of that consciously genocidal project. The young rabbi, however, saved me the awkward question.

"AIDS is like the Holocaust," he told me, "in that we have to go on living as though it were not happening, just as Jews in the camps could bear their existence only by living *as though* they were not facing death in the gas chambers and the ovens." To live in the shadow of AIDS, to live in the communities where one of every two gay men has been infected and seems sure to die, is to live a life of resistance, he told me. That life of resistance is at once spiritual, militantly political, and irrepressibly intimate in its sense of collective nurturing. AIDS has permeated the media with tales of suffering and sacrifice, of heroic and tireless hospital teams like those on San Francisco General's famed Ward 5-B. The rabbi was claiming more: Nurturing is not only to care for the fallen, but to go on living as an act of positive resistance, not in denial of disease but *in spite* of it, knowing elsewhere in your mind that you will surely succumb to it. As Kahn spoke, I recalled a line of Sartre's that I had read many years before, about his own life in the French Resistance. He was never so free, he said, as when the Gestapo was on every corner. Though there was continuous terror and mourning all about them, those in the Resistance understood that it was the texture of their lives, the vitality of their spirits, that was most at risk. To cooperate or to become resigned would have been to give away more than life; it would have been to give away the reason for living.

The link between the idea of resistance and the gay response to AIDS became even clearer to me two years later, when I was interviewing Herbert Daniel, the best known of Brazil's AIDS activists. As a young man, Daniel had been a commandant in a guerrilla group fighting the Brazilian military dictatorship; later, he fled to France, where he began to write novels. During his insurrectionary years he fell in love with another man, a fellow guerrilla, with whom he has shared his life since. Daniel told me of how in 1989 he consulted a doctor about a persistent lung infection. The doctor looked through Daniel's lab results and told him flatly that he had AIDS and would not survive long. The doctor stayed with Daniel for all of thirty seconds and then left him for the next patient, having performed an instant intellectual triage in which Daniel saw himself written off, discarded as both terminal and homosexual. He calls it a "death before death," a social death in advance of biological death. AIDS-era resistance is the assertion that we have *not* disappeared, and that we continue to pursue the fullness of our physical, political, spiritual, and emotional existences, acknowledging that the alteration of any one of these is not the elimination of it.

Inevitably, the passage through a time of resistance distinguishes a generation as a set of people who have in some special way danced with history. They may be the families of those who perished in the camps, the snipers who assassinated the Gestapo, or the civil rights marchers who defeated Bull Connor in Birmingham. A collective transformation seems to result both in the relations among the resisters and in the way they are perceived by others. Since the first AIDS cases were reported in 1981, 160,000 Americans have died from AIDS. More than 9,500 men have died in San Francisco, and nearly 30,000 in New York. In Rabbi Kahn's congregation, 50 have died. Death and dying have become so generalized, so routine, that many gay men rarely pass a week without speaking to someone who has visited a friend in the hospital or gone to a service. At the gym, a man opens the door to the steam room. Through the mist, he looks healthy. His stride is sturdy, his shoulders high and strong. When he sits down on the tile bench, I see dozens of KS lesions. A day later, I go with a group of friends to the movies. "How's Bill?" Dan asks. "Physically, he's great, feels okay," Lee answers with a shrug and a laugh, "but he's completely bananas, nuts." The answer is not meant to be callous. Six months earlier, Bill would have been with us, making the same comment about someone else. In the interim,

Bill had a stroke, and even before that he was losing concentration. Had he been struck down in a crosswalk by a speeding truck, the emotional impact of his destruction would probably have been much harder on us, his friends. But his death has been coming on steadily, inexorably. His gym-pumped body has been subsiding beneath his clothes. His color has dulled. His mind has slowed. The process has advanced as it would with a revered grandparent, but Bill is not a grandparent, not an elder; he is one of us. The tenuousness, the fragility, of his life hangs palpably among us, disarming us, stripping us, of our carefully constructed layers of self-protection.

Those of us who survive this epidemic will never altogether escape the odor of untimely death. We will probably never enjoy sex fully free of the anxiety that we may be embarking on a journey that will end with a remark from some old friend that we have finally gone bananas. To a degree, this is the dirge of the Romantic poets, of Keats or Shelley or Millay: every pain our pain, every struggle our struggle, every death our death. At a more pedestrian level, gay men in the 1980s became premature septuagenarians, learning to prepare for death twenty, thirty, forty years before our proper time. We have already experienced what my father did as he approached seventy, and accumulated black-bordered obituary notices sent by his college association. We have become a people for whom death is as familiar as brunch.

Among the elderly, obituary notices are one of the signals modern society sends to familiarize us with our proximate disappearance. Departing the prime years of personal power and individuality, we begin to dissolve into our final collective experience, eased along by funerals, retirement dinners, nursing homes, and Social Security checks. If we are lucky, the process lasts a decade, sometimes two. For gay men in the age of AIDS, the process of disappearing lasts perhaps a year, rarely longer. Those of us who survive the deaths of our old friends, followed by the deaths of our replacement friends, frequently grow chary of getting close to others yet again, fearful that we will graduate into premature octogenarians, lone survivors of a disappeared generation.

*   *   *

Reed Grier was thirty when he first began to confront death among those closest to him. It was early in the epidemic, 1983, and Leo, a doctor, fell first, to cryptococcal meningitis, a fungal infection of the brain and spinal-cord linings. Reed and Leo were part of an extended network of lovers and sexual playmates, the sort of arrangement that writer Edmund White once labeled the "banyan tree" model of gay family life. Five San Francisco men were at the core: Reed, Leo, David (Reed's original lover), Don (David's final lover), and Stephen (David's earlier lover, who owned the duplex Reed and David shared, and who lived in the apartment below them). They were all white, all professionals with advanced degrees: a health-policy analyst, a doctor, two urban planners, and a psychologist. Both Reed and David had had affairs and, occasionally, joint trysts with Leo. It was Leo's passing that removed death as an abstraction for the entire group.

By 1983, Reed had finished a master's degree in planning at Berkeley, returned from fieldwork in Micronesia, and, as he told it, transformed his relationship with David, one of the two urban planners in the quintet, into "brother love." They kept house together, ate most meals together, shared finances, but slept in separate rooms. Reed even introduced David to Don, the other urban planner and a rugged outdoorsman, who became David's lover and took a small room in their house.

"In effect, what we had was a ménage à trois," Reed tells me. "It was an emotional ménage à trois. David and I were married. We shared a household together. We were family. I took care of him and he took care of me. I was his confidant in ways that Don never was. I knew his spirituality, inside and out. I knew all his fears and all his shadows, and he knew mine. He was there as a financial support and buffer for me. He really took care of me . . . to such an extent that he made provisions for me in his will.

"David was one of these people where every one of his ex-lovers turned into family, turned into this sort of brother-sister-friend who never left his life. David and I had previously been involved with Leo. Leo was our doctor.

"First, David had to have an emergency appendectomy. He collapsed in the doctor's office . . . a full-blown ruptured appendix. It was a four- or five-hour procedure, a type of surgery people don't survive well, that involves removing the entire intestinal system from the cavity and brushing it off centimeter by centimeter, flushing out the cavity so there's no more gut in there. Then they don't stitch you closed. They put in about five suture bars for spacing, to kind of bring it together, and put two drain holes in with tubes, and then they send you home. You take baths several times a day in a salty, sterile solution to draw the stuff out, and eventually you close from the inside out. That was the beginning of the caregiving." From that point on, Reed became David's chief nurse and lifeline.

At first, a visiting professional nurse came to take David's vital signs, and the nursing service provided a social worker for counseling. "He's going to die," the social worker told Reed one day. Reed dismissed her and the service, insisting that David was only in postsurgical recovery. Though he knew that David was HIV-positive, Reed couldn't yet acknowledge that the virus was killing his companion.

From time to time, David seemed to regain his health. Several months after his surgery, David had recovered enough strength to accompany his sister and Don to Yosemite National Park. As a young man, David had been an endurance runner, for three years a top contender on the rugged Dipsea Trail across Mount Tamalpais in Marin County. But without AZT, without aerosolized pentamadine, without Bactrim, without foscarnet or ddI or ddC or any of a score of emerging drugs that people with AIDS would later use to buy extra months of life, David was unable to prevail over his illness. His trek to Yosemite Park turned out to be his last journey.

The final siege came in the spring of 1986. Reed had been in downtown San Francisco at a conference on aging, discussing parallels between AIDS care and geriatric care. At four o'clock in the afternoon, he called his answering machine and heard an urgent message from Don: David had collapsed and been rushed to

Pacific Presbyterian Hospital. Diagnosis: pneumocystis carinii pneumonia, PCP.

Reed says, "I remember just turning white, freaking out, running into the hotel bar to the people I was talking with. 'There's an emergency,' I said, grabbing my briefcase and *running* out the door to the BART, to the hospital, as fast as I could get there. He was already in ICU."

Don and his sister Shelly were at the hospital when Reed arrived. The doctor was explaining that David's lungs were so blocked with pneumocystis that they appeared white on the X ray.

"What do you want us to do?" the doctor asked David. "Do you want to fight one more time? Do you want to go for it again? Or do you want to give up now?"

"I want to go one more time," David answered. "Let's try one more time." David survived the hospital, but he never remembered being there. The last weeks after David's hospitalization were the most troubling times for Reed.

"I don't know whether it was brain damage from oxygen deprivation in the treatment. I don't know whether it was HIV getting into his brain and causing dementia. I don't know whether it was the cryptococcal meningitis reaching his brain. I don't know whether it was MAI [a form of tuberculosis] also getting into his brain. But he never recovered mentally from that hospitalization."

Once Reed brought him home, David required continuous care. A nurse came three to four times a week, and Reed cut his work hours in half. David's insurance and disability benefits covered household bills.

"We had to spoon-feed him. Tapioca. Applesauce. We had to toilet him . . . pick him up and put him on it. His digestive system failed. We had to give him medication a half hour before he ate to start the process, then give him an antidiarrheal after the meal to stop the whole process."

Meanwhile, David's mind had gone away.

"Oh, gee, it's really lovely," he would say, looking out the window at blooming flowers. "This must be Switzerland." Sometimes, he thought he was in Australia.

The more David lost his mind to dementia, the more Reed lost himself in nursing David. Feeding. Wiping. Changing. Counting pills. Fixing doses. Only rarely did David speak. The David who had been Reed's soul mate, confidant, and sustainer became the object of his care.

"I was in such denial about his dying, I couldn't face it or see it coming," Reed admitted to me. The drugs may have eased David's suffering, but they became essential to Reed. He found himself forcing the medication into David, on schedule, around the clock.

"I'd wake him up, lay all the pills out, give him a little sip of water, actually put it on his tongue. It got to the point where he was tonguing them. They'd go to the side of his mouth. They wouldn't go down. I was almost sticking my finger down his throat to push them down.

"Then one night, I screwed up. I'd put the midnight dose off to two A.M., and he was actually refusing. He said, 'NO!' Like, 'No, I don't want to,' or 'No, not anymore!'

"It was the first coherent thing he'd said in weeks. And I thought, *I'm pissed. You've got to do this! You've got to stay alive!* And it's like, he won't. Don is saying, 'Let's just let well enough alone,' and I'm insisting, *'We'll at least get this series down. We've got to get this one down!'* And I say, 'I've got to tell the doctor about this.' I go to bed furious. Angry! I'm angry!

"I call the doctor in the morning. And he says, 'Stop all meds! He has told you it's over. Stop all meds!' " From then on, there was nothing to do but maintain David's morphine-based pain relief.

A few nights later, around midnight, Reed heard groans coming from the bedroom Don and David shared. He went in. David's next morphine dose was not scheduled for another two hours. David's breaths were rapid, shallow, short; then he'd gasp deeply; then rapid, shallow, short; then another deep gasp: It was the Chain-Stokes breathing that immediately precedes death. Reed gave David a half dose of morphine, checked his oxygen flow, and went back to bed. At 2:00 A.M., Don came to wake Reed.

"David's died," he said. "I just woke up. He's gone."

The two men cleaned their dead lover, wiping a string of saliva from his mouth, and dressed him in an old pair of jeans and a T-shirt. They wrapped an Ace bandage around his jaw to hold his mouth shut. Then they placed coins on his eyelids.

Reed stops the story for an instant and points to his cat, once David's, curled up next to him on the sofa. "While all this is happening, she just flipped. Raced around the house for an hour or so. Don and I were methodically doing our things, taking care of the body, had some of David's favorite music playing. I had lit incense all over the house, opened the doors and windows, and we really, we . . . felt . . . something." He looks down at the cat. "She felt something. Later in the morning, I went downstairs to tell Stephen, who was also sick, not as sick, but slipping slowly, surely. I came down, and Dan, his boyfriend, said, 'We know. David died last night, didn't he? We could feel it.' "

When Reed told me this story, five years had passed since David's death. His voice broke often as he forced his way through it. Midway in the telling a watch alarm went off: the AZT alarm. He stopped to swallow the tablet, one of the many powerful and expensive drugs that had kept him relatively healthy. Drugs had not, however, saved the rest of his family. Stephen died six months after David. Don died last, three months before my conversation with Reed. Two years after David's death, Reed entered into a relationship with a man named Ron. Their first year together, Reed said, was blissful, but early into the second year, Ron fell ill; he died within a few months.

There have been thirty-eight deaths in Reed's life, he tells me. His remaining close friends are heterosexual. Recounting the demise of his gay family, Reed slips back and forth between self-consciously academic analysis—sociological theories about family and community, jargon-filled reflections on dependency and codependency—and still-unresolved grief. He says that he "watched his boundaries" more closely during Ron's dying, left the most painful nursing details to others but stood by to offer emotional succor. And he was there, too, as a caregiver for Don, who in advance of his own end had made out an elaborate chart of friends and colleagues he wished to handle his affairs.

All of the dying has had a double impact on Reed. He seems wary, even fearful, of getting close to other gay men, as a friend *or* potential lover. He is not optimistic about how much time he himself has left. At the time of our conversation, Reed has been taking AZT for two years, about the duration of the drug's protective value. In his remaining time, he tells me, he cannot risk becoming the caretaker for another dying mate. The lesson of the last five years has been plain: Those he loves will leave him; he will survive only to be buried himself. Although he knows intellectually that not every man he might meet will get sick, he says nonetheless, "I'm afraid of connecting with people." Even his gay friendship network is dying. Several years ago, he and nine others organized a weekly support group of HIV-positives. Now the group has only five members. "When Micah dies, there will be only four of us, two in a couple, and that's a nonstable group. We either dissolve it or reform it into another thing where we don't do support or invite others in. I don't know when, but we know it's coming." These are the presentiments as well of the very old who have outlasted all their friends and mates, of people whose loss is nearly inexpressible because there is no one left alive with whom they share memory. It is loss that goes beyond personal grieving. It is the loss of a world disappeared.

As the last survivor, Reed inherited many of the personal artifacts of his extended family. Jewelry. Photos. Furniture. Journals. Some of them he has stored; some of them populate his small, rather woody apartment on Bernal Hill. They often become props in his recollections. He picks up a small figurine. "That was Leo's. And the bookcase behind you—that was Leo's too."

There is another dimension to relentless and premature gay death. It concerns the sense of fate among gay men, and it is not restricted to those who are sick and dying. In those gay communities hardest hit by AIDS, counselors and therapists have reported an undercurrent of self-destructive behavior among uninfected men. Frequently, survivors say that their dead lovers were not sexual adventurers but were almost prudish, that they had one unlucky experience and contracted the virus. "It should have been me. I was the one whoring around," they say, finding both guilt and injustice in their own survival. They watch their gay family disappear, and face profound dilemmas of separation and self-worth.

Psychologist Walt Odets has written with terrible poignance of survivors who during or after their lovers' dying consciously sought to infect themselves with HIV. One of Odets's patients was "so conflicted about finding his former lover, John, repulsive and dangerous [that he] wished to introject John by lying in John's bed and by taking John's semen into his body." Gradually, the patient began to "grow into" some of the aspects of his ex-lover's life, taking up the sick man's hobbies and political activities; eventually, he began to represent himself as HIV-infected, blurring the discrepancy between his fate and his late lover's and reducing his own sense of guilt. Odets saw his patient's behavior as a response to the unfathomable nature of fate. Though he had been found to be HIV-negative, the patient could not believe that the tests were accurate. He was certain that he would get AIDS anyway. "The sense of fate," Odets concluded, "may simply fulfill the wish not to survive, but it also often includes the feeling that one will not be *allowed* to survive because of his unworthiness. Thus, one's belief that he *will not* survive can be a passive form of *not wanting* to survive. The feeling rests on largely unconscious, childlike and primitive, magical thought processes, sometimes associated with conscious or unconscious beliefs in an omnipotent being—God or parent—who sees to it that people get what they deserve. Such magical thinking provides a compelling vehicle for the passivity which those who are feeling depressed and helpless so often experience."

Modern, white, middle-class, urban America is not a place where fate is given much quarter. Our national ideology teaches us virtually from infancy that we are the individual masters of our own destiny. As we mature, established medicine and pop psychology—even "legitimate" psychoanalysis—tell us that we are the authors of our own predicaments. (I have a friend who spent four years in psychoanalysis and was billed for the session she had had to cancel because she'd been in an automobile accident. Why did she expose herself to such an accident? her analyst asked at their next meeting, suggesting that accidents are never accidental.)

Gay men, however, especially those who have experienced the caregiving, have found themselves in that crucible where fate and identity are forced to face each other. Few gay men who came of age in the 1970s or before escaped the enticing torment of sexual self-acknowledgment. That first intimation of aberrant desire sometime in early adolescence—whether embraced or repressed—is the beginning of a mysterious confrontation with fate. That desire may lead us to contest convention, that it seems to have nothing to do with rational choice, ensures in us a measure of respect for a mystery that is beyond our control. Unlike the 90 percent of humans who apparently take their desires and biological responses to be universal and therefore find no cause to examine their own sexual orientation, the homosexual person experiences fate as a constant companion that almost inescapably provokes a profound examination of identity. Yet, just as that first intimation of fate as desire is almost always private and individual, the later acknowledgment of untimely death is collective and requires a public response.

For Reed Grier and uncountable others, AIDS has become the agency of collective transformation. Gay men have not "matured into" or recoiled from sex, as many observers began to report after many of the country's bathhouses closed in the mid-1980s. They have learned to integrate sex and communal caring. "Sex and desire are still a major portion of what makes us a community," Reed told me, "but it's not the only thread anymore. Something else happened. You no longer necessarily look at another gay man as a sexual object, but as a brother, as someone who's in this together with you, someone who has gone through this thing with you, someone who is facing the same issues of mortality, who is there to be cared for, cherished, nurtured, someone to be intimate with. Those are my brothers out there. There is a qualitative shift in the nature of the relationships between men in this city in the age group who've gone through this."

Gay men—and lesbians—have established many institutions to defend and provide for those stricken with AIDS: food distribution, home nursing, legal aid, shelter, medical clinics, even pet-care services. Not to mention the organizations that smuggle drugs, stage street demonstrations, and lobby politicians. The electricity of that network struck me profoundly when I returned to San Francisco in the spring of 1988; I began to see the gay response to AIDS as a form of creative cultural resistance. The city's gay community, which had once been best characterized as a post-adolescent meat rack in the perennial pursuit of ecstasy, had grown into a complex, angry, exuberant, and politically forceful community of human beings struggling to make sense of the elemental forces of death and survival.

The signs of transformation that Reed Grier described had taken on a subtler and more intimate color, at once fraternal, spiritual, and sexual. One such change is the emergence of new kinds of recreational sex clubs. Next to bars, bathhouses were the most prominent gay commercial institutions of the 1970s. Without their advertising dollars, few of the fledgling gay newspapers would have survived. Most of the bathhouses have closed, but in their place have emerged venues for men to get together sexually. Like the baths, they are hunting grounds for recreational orgasm. Unlike the baths, where men walked around clad only in a towel, sex-club patrons are generally fully dressed. The cold, objectified tyranny of the naked body that so dominated the bathhouses has been diminished, and the responses between hunter and hunted have become more complex. Men of varying ages (though mostly young) arrive in groups, talk, and spend social time with each other, then wander off into quieter halls or corners. If the most common experience among men in the youth-obsessed baths was cold, public rejection, the more common gesture in the clubs is the affectionate caress that may or may not go further. The style of competitive prowess seems to have been supplanted by an ethic of shared adventure.

For Reed, the appearance of the clubs represents "a qualitative shift in how you relate sexually and personally." He doesn't hang out at them much himself, he said, because he has lost some of the drive for recreational sex. But he finds their appearance important, even reassuring. He sees in them a resurgence of the communitarian spirit and unapologetic desire that first drew him into the gay world. "Every one of these places has a different position on the continuum of desire, but the interesting thing about them as an archetype was this wonderful combination of a jack-off party where you're getting down and dirty and being sexual, a cocktail party where you're politely and very charmingly standing around and dishing things, a church social where you just hang out with a bunch of buddies—all wrapped into one. It's all going on simultaneously. Somebody you start having a cocktail-party chat with may end up fifteen minutes later holding, cuddling, and jacking you off, and then will come back and talk about the kind and price of fertilizer you're putting on your garden."

six

Reconstructing the Extended Family

◆

Sheldon, my New England doctor friend, called one evening. He was unusually melancholy, so much so that he'd taken a mild tranquilizer. He'd been suffering boy trouble. A new—and, it had seemed, promising—relationship seemed to be petering out. That, however, was only a surface irritation—certainly not enough to lead to tranquilizers. The real disturbance on Sheldon's mind had developed the previous weekend when he'd flown to Boston to visit his brother's family.

Sheldon had taken boxes of toys, including a large, inflatable penguin that, he said, propelled his five-year-old nephew into gales of glee. It was a weekend of children—child talk, child development, child screaming—all of which provides much of the reason Sheldon goes to see his family. Late afternoon on Sunday, Sheldon's sister-in-law announced that she had rented the video of *Longtime Companion,* the 1990 movie about gay men confronting

AIDS. She and Sheldon's brother had been eager to see it, she said. The kids wandered off to their own room, and the adults gathered at the set.

Ten minutes into the movie, Sheldon's brother stood up and walked out of the room. No comment. No explanation. He went elsewhere in the house to watch Sunday-afternoon sports. An hour and a half later, he came back, just after *Longtime Companion* had ended. He asked what he'd missed.

Sheldon didn't answer, leaving it for his sister to explain. He drove to the airport that evening, wondering why he continued to visit at all.

"What seems so hypocritical," Sheldon told me on the phone, "is that they expected me to be so attentive to all the taking-care-of-baby stuff that occupied every minute of the weekend, but none of them had any insight into how really rude my brother was, how he had completely discounted who I am and what's going on in my life and my friends' lives."

At first, Sheldon's complaint seemed to be little more than self-indulgent whining. Aren't all modern parents unrelievedly concentrated on the details of child rearing? Even straight married couples without kids express exasperation over how their onetime hiking–dancing–touring buddies have disappeared into the territory of burble, bottles, and kiddie-proof cabinet latches, most of them capable of only broken snatches of intelligent discourse. Sheldon, I thought, might have shown more forbearance. Or should he have? As I replayed our conversation in my mind, I realized that it was not the children who had upset him so much as the fact that once the kids were absent, his sister-in-law and, particularly, his brother had demonstrated no real interest in his life. Even worse than being overtly hostile (which would have provided at least an acknowledgment of Sheldon's existence), his brother had displayed the subtler hostility of indifference. As a homosexual man, Sheldon was presumed to be without family. To the extent that he could have family, it would be as the peculiar uncle to the standard procreative family his brother and sister-in-law were building. Whatever lovers, ex-lovers, soul mates, and devoted companions Sheldon had would disappear as he walked into his brother's house; or, if their names did emerge, they would be taken by his blood family as nothing more than passing consorts. Such people would not, apparently, merit the status of genuine family.

Derek, the Washington payroll accountant, tells a similar story with an important variation. Derek grew up in a stable dual-income family with a number of brothers and sisters. Nights and weekends, he took classes and worked part-time as a massage therapist. His lover, Gunther, was a Swiss whose family Derek had visited in Zurich. One day, more than four years after the two had become a couple, Derek's mother spoke to him about his future.

"Why don't you and your sister buy a house together?" she asked. "You've both got good jobs, you're single, it's a good investment, and your father and I could help with the down."

Derek began to consider the idea, musing about how he and his corporate-lawyer sister would get along. And then he shook himself.

"Mom, I can't buy a house with Liz. If I were going to buy a house with anybody, it'd be Gunther."

"Gunther could be gone tomorrow."

"And so could Daddy."

Gunther was not unknown to Derek's mother; Derek had brought him to family gatherings. No one in Derek's family had ever been rude to Gunther, but there was no denying that he precipitated a measure of discomfort, for Derek's family is black, and Gunther would usually be the only white person present when the group assembled.

Derek's account of his family relations certainly bears some similarity to Sheldon's. In both, the homosexual's gay family seems invisible to his blood relatives. Maybe Derek's mother and Sheldon's brother find it too painful to think of the details of daily gay mateship. Maybe they are genuinely unable to imagine what men do together. Perhaps they only comprehend gay men, who usually don't provide offspring, as sexual neuters.

At the same time, there is a profound difference between Derek's and Sheldon's family experiences. Derek lives nearby his blood family and has regular, intimate conversations with his mother and one of his sisters. He and his family are present for one another even when they annoy each other, as they regularly do. Sheldon, who grew up in a working-class Jewish family, is geographically and psychologically distant from his home ground. Like millions of other gay men, he came to a gay enclave, San Francisco, to make his own life, and to a major degree he tried to put class, ethnic culture, and family relations behind him. Not that he denies his Jewishness or his family connection, for both are important to him; but he acknowledges without hesitation that his gay identity has far more impact on his life than his Jewish heritage, and that his connection to blood family is a matter of occasional visits, not regular Sunday dinners.

Different from either Derek's or Sheldon's family situations is Reed Grier's experience as chief caregiver to two dying lovers. When Reed, a health policy planner, told other health professionals how he cared for his dying lovers, they were stunned. "Why did you put yourself through all this torment?" they would ask him. "Because we're family," he would answer. "This is what you do for family." All the members of Reed's extended family sustained their commitment to one another through crises; they were there for one another just as surely, he declares, as his blood family has *not* been there for him. "The key word," he told me in our conversations, "is support. Emotional, practical support. And why? Because we care about each other. We have meaning to each other. Not instrumental meaning, as in 'this is where I can get help,' but unqualified support because we care for and take care of each other. Because of my experience in this overly individualistic society and with a family that was dysfunctional, I tried to create my own tribe, my own sense of communal solidarity with other people."

These three men—Sheldon, who seems displaced and disconnected from any family, Derek, who seems to have negotiated a comprehensive life within both his families, and Reed, whose dysfunctional blood family sent him on a quest to construct a replacement—tell common, perhaps archetypal, gay tales. Yet these are more than gay tales. Each story also seems emblematic of the anguished search for a place of solidarity, a search that is haunting all Americans in the late twentieth century. As any number of sociological reports and blue-ribbon commissions have demonstrated, the footloose character of American life, combined with powerful economic and demographic pressures, has torn our families asunder. More and more, we are a scattered population of pairs and individuals dislocated from familiar geography, the memory of ancestors, the traditions of race and religion, the confidence of gender, and the predictability of class. As the one historically stable institution in American social life, the nuclear family has been asked to carry so much weight—the burdens of sex, intimacy, economic security, child rearing, moral instruction—that it frequently fractures under all its obligations. In earlier times, extended families distributed duties. Older children cared for and instructed their younger brothers and sisters. Adult in-laws, aunts, and uncles counseled and relieved one another (and were forgiving targets for pent-up anger). One even went to the family for financial help—and was spared the 18 percent credit-card rate. The family not only provided solace and devotion but was, equally important, fundamentally utilitarian. The American family was the reliable base from which its members went into the larger world and performed their social responsibilities. Today, the purpose, the structure, even the utility of the family eludes us. (How often do parents of teenagers complain that the family shares supper only once a week?) In the wake of family dislocation, we are, as a nation, learning (and often resisting to learn) new ways of behaving with one another, searching desperately to construct new kinds of family security even as we are dogged by nostalgia for the type of family that has all but disappeared.

One recent moral drama typifies the conflict Americans face: the Senate hearings examining whether Supreme Court nominee

Clarence Thomas had harassed his former employee Anita Hill. Though never stated as such, this unprecedented inquiry became a shadow play—at times marked by passion and eloquence, at times marred by childish, prudish sniggering—about the unrequited yearnings for the security and stability that families once provided to Americans. Beyond rhetoric and political expediency, it forced us as viewers to consider troubling problems of how men and women—regardless of their sexuality—connect with one another, with the idea of family, and with the uncertain identity of American society itself.

Two carefully drawn images dominated the scene. On the one side: a heroic, ambitious, and aggressive individual who fought his way to the top only to be, in the term used by his supporters, "torpedoed." On the other side: a woman of rectitude who, sustained by her parents and many siblings, struggled toward an ambitious career, then withdrew in disgust because of the abuse she allegedly endured from a trusted mentor and returned to her home state to be a teacher. What is so striking about these two people is not the peculiarity of their lives; rather, it is that their journeys toward national public life have stripped them of the conventional family solidarity they have so vigorously embraced in their faiths, traditions, and ideologies. Their stories are quintessentially American, and yet Americans were deeply disturbed by these stories and by the charges Hill and Thomas made about each other. Many people, including the president, spoke of their embarrassment over the "graphic sex allegations" made in the hearings. Graphic? The most graphic references were to "large breasts," "big penises," and "sex with animals." No one among the participating or witnessing men—neither the liberals nor the conservatives, not even the network journalists and anchors—was able to repeat Anita Hill's matter-of-fact charge that Clarence Thomas had propositioned, harassed, and intimidated her by boasting of his large, satisfying penis. It was as though by uttering the P-word in the Senate Caucus Room, on national television, Hill had committed a violation even greater than the harassment she said she had suffered. By bringing into the open the images and terminology of desire and abuse, she had broken an unwritten gentlemen's code that has long restricted such matters to the private club and the locker room. The offense appeared all the worse because Anita Hill seemed to be a demure, religious woman.

By the time the episode had ended, Americans everywhere decried how lurid, how tawdry, and, especially, how painful the hearings had been. Much of that revulsion, of course, came from partisans who believed that their hero—either Hill or Clarence Thomas—had been savaged. However, even impartial Americans were discomforted. The hearings seem to have touched troubles that vex all our lives—troubles not so very distant from the concerns of Sheldon and Derek and Reed, the ordinary, commonplace, and inescapable troubles that emerge when the drive for individual success, personal identity, and civic participation fractures our reliance on family security. The proceedings became a living national Rorschach test upon which we could discern signs of our own distress and dislocation in the conduct of daily life. The conflict is not new.

When Alexis de Tocqueville published his monumental study of Americans' struggle over individualism, morality, and democracy in the 1830s, he focused on the torments surrounding family life. What fascinated Tocqueville about the new American democracy was the relationship between "attachment" and morality. In their rapacious advance across the frontier, the Americans had left behind most of the attachments that their European cousins relied upon for a sense of station and identity. Kinship, religion, class, geography: All these told the European who he was and how he should behave. As they wiped out the North American continent's native inhabitants, these transplanted Europeans lived on empty ground, devoid of any monuments to psychological or moral location. Churches were makeshift affairs, and the minister was usually a circuit rider. Often residing beyond the pale of institutional law, the family alone offered refuge from the frantic, rugged individualism that became the hallmark of nineteenth-century American life. Tocqueville worried about the ability of the family to carry so much moral authority when there was so little beyond faith and neediness to sustain it. Only among the women, whom he identified as the carriers of moral strength, did he see a counterforce to the cutthroat male world of commerce and ambition. To the women he ascribed nurturing roles through which they passed on values of interdependence, Christian virtue, and civic good. No matter how much men squared their shoulders and swung the ax, it was the women who preserved and exemplified the highest of nineteenth-century virtues: sacrifice and unselfish love. Tocqueville believed that those values constituted the true foundation upon which the infant democracy survived. Take them away—shatter the family as the last point of social stability—and the moral basis for the republic would disappear. His fear for the Americans was that their hyperactive individualism, their compulsion always to take to the road and invent their identities anew, would leave them bereft of a civic base. "I have seen the freest and best educated of men in circumstances the happiest to be found in the world; yet it seemed to me that a cloud habitually hung on their brow, and they seemed serious and almost sad even in their pleasures." Americans seemed, he wrote, a people who "clutch everything and hold nothing fast."

For Anita Hill to come forward and speak of her career and her suffering, and in so doing reject self-sacrifice, was for many Americans an act of betrayal. Not only had she betrayed her former mentor (and her race, as many blacks accused her of doing), but worse, she had shirked her duty as moral touchstone. The judge told his questioners that he saw his employees—mostly women—as his family; he was their patriarch. Whatever the sins of his ambition, it followed that it was these women's duty as moral nurturers to preserve the values of personal sacrifice. When, after a decade's waiting, Anita Hill reinterpreted her civic duty, she precipitated a national crisis over the true nature of identity and its relationship to democratic responsibility, and her charges against Clarence Thomas were turned against her. When it became clear that no witness could conclusively demonstrate who was telling the truth and who was lying, the arbiters of truth could fall back only on fantasy. If Hill was not corrupt, not a certifiable liar, not a tool of sinister forces, then she must have been lost in fantasy. She must have undergone what the early Freudians called "hysteria," a false psychophysiological-perceptual experience brought on by—what else?—displacement from her natural social role. Though they never stated it as such, her attackers limned her as a woman who, in betraying her patriarch, had betrayed her nurturing identity, had betrayed the trim, schoolteacherly suit she wore to the hearings, had betrayed her parents and siblings who sat behind her in the hearing room: She was arrogant, haughty, abrasive—code words for a woman who has so departed from her nature that she is *not truly a woman*.

And that is precisely the crisis precipitated by gay people—not truly men, not truly women—who have "betrayed" the legacy of their blood families. Worse even than the sexual perversions they practice, gay people's more damning threat to traditionalists is their claim to family parity, their claim to family life as a right. As long as gay people were satisfied living as marginal individuals or urban bohemians, they were seen as distasteful but relatively harmless. But to press their unnaturalness into the heart of the family, and in so doing to challenge traditional family order and authority, was too much. Little surprise that the growing gay acceptance in mainstream social life should precipitate new and ever more virulent attacks on gay people from conservative "family values" advocates. Little wonder either that the keepers of conservative Catholic doctrine should intensify their justification for active anti-homosexual discrimination. As gay people petition for a reconstructed family of their own invention, they not only propose new terms of interpersonal solidarity, but, even more important, they argue for an altogether different notion of how gender is connected to moral duty.

Luna was born in Havana, but he was brought to Miami as a small child. Gilberto, his boyfriend, was born in Miami, in Little Havana, the enclave of Cuban refugees that vies with the real Havana as the global center of Cuban cultural life. I met them on Mother's Day, after they had prepared a joint feast of maternal tribute. In fact, of the dozen gay contacts I'd been given in Miami, all but one man (whose mother was dead) were with their parents that day. In no other place in America had I seen such close ties between gay men and their families—a closeness made all the more remarkable by the fierce conservatism of Cuban Miami.

On the front lawn of the house where Luna lives with his mother, we sit on old chairs, drinking beer. A few feet away, dozing on a couch inside the enclosed front porch, is Luna's uncle, a drawn little man who speaks no English, actually lives on the porch, and is heard frequently on local radio stations agitating for new assassination campaigns against Fidel Castro. The uncle doesn't speak with Luna about Luna's sex life. Luna, who calls himself a left-wing anarchist, doesn't speak with his uncle about Cuba. Overhead, jets roar us into periodic silence on their takeoff path from Miami International Airport.

Gilberto is reminiscing about his first male lover. "He was an older man. Cuban. And he was a top." He adds sarcastically, "God forbid that I should want a piece of butt."

Gilberto is twenty-two, sandy-haired, blue-eyed. A close-cropped goatee corners his chin. A turquoise earring dangles from his right ear. His voice is a little camp, a touch fey. He could easily pass as a Queer Nation foot soldier in New York or San Francisco or L.A.

He goes on about older gay Cubans: "Somehow, I think that they brought over that stigma that somehow you are not gay if you don't get butt-fucked. Once you get butt-fucked that makes you a queer. And you are lower in status than a top man."

Gilberto does not consider himself a top or a bottom. He has, he says, distinct sexual tastes, but his sexual positioning doesn't define his sense of masculine and feminine roles, as it does throughout much of Latin and Mediterranean culture, where no man is denigrated for homosexual activity so long as he is on top, penetrating. Such "straight" men have long kept discreet homosexual liaisons with boyish mates who behave as mistresses. The shame of being a bottom is the old-country stigma that Gilberto's first lover brought to Miami with him. I would have expected that

Gilberto's large, traditional family would have stigmatized him in their own ways—for example, deriding him for laying out a ladies' luncheon spread. But among Gilberto's family, who knew that Luna and Gilberto were lovers, there was only acceptance. Indeed, and particularly among Gilberto's elders, Luna has been taken in as a member of the family.

Toward the end of the Mother's Day afternoon, several of Gilberto's cousins arrived, tough straight, roustabout guys whom Gilberto calls Cuban rednecks, macho men who are always off, without their wives, hunting and fishing.

"Well, you got to go spearfishing with us, man," they tell him. "We got a boat." Then one of the cousins—the most redneckish, according to Gilberto—draws him in close.

"Like, you disappear! We got to stick together, 'cause, well, we never see each other anymore. Why don't you hang out with us anymore?"

Gilberto's reaction is noncommittal. "I just sort of go quiet," he tells me later. "I figure, he doesn't know how to track me, 'cause I'm gay. It's like, 'You're our cousin, and we used to do things together when we were young, and there's no reason for that not to happen now.' "

Would he like to hang on to that inherited place of butch family camaraderie? I ask. Would he go spearfishing?

"I don't know," he answers. "I really enjoyed hanging out with my cousins before. Going out and getting all muddy. Going fishing. Scaling the fish." He gets a little campy. "Getting fish guts all over my hands—the whole butch scene." He goes back to his usual inflection. "That's fun to me, and I miss doing that, 'cause I don't find too many people in the gay culture that want to go do that."

More than his Mother's Day devotion, Gilberto's equivocal attachment to his tough-guy cousins captures the complexity of his concept of family. He hopes to make a household with Luna if their relationship continues to grow. He would like them to live in a neighborhood of straight and gay Cubans, where now and then he could borrow a cup of sugar from another gay couple. Yet he is also deeply afraid of being beaten or even killed, possibly by some fanatical homophobic Cuban who might spot him and Luna holding hands on the street.

I ask about this neighborhood, Little Havana, where family seems to matter most. Could he imagine walking down Calle Ocho, the main boulevard, holding Luna's hand?

Melancholy calms his voice. "I think there'd be a violent reaction, to be honest. I like my life, and I like my head to be in one piece, and on my neck. I've read stories of gay people being bashed and killed. That really scares me. These people here are warped. You can just see it when they go to the Cuban rallies. These people really scare me, not because they know I'm gay, but just because they're really warped."

I glance at Luna's uncle up on the porch, a man who has spent his life at such rallies. He is no longer dozing. Perhaps he is formulating his next diatribe. He knows that in the front yard of his sister's house there are now three *maricons,* three faggots, chattering away, and that one of them, his own nephew, takes another, Gilberto, to bed in this house three, four nights a week. And sometimes, the morning after such a night, Luna will silently drive his uncle to the radio station from which he spreads his bitter oratory.

Many gay men say that it was because of anxieties such as Luna's that they left home and moved into safe enclaves like the Castro, West Hollywood, or Greenwich Village. Luna says that his culture, despite its potential for violence against him, is what lured him back home. At age thirty, he has lived in gay ghettos in San Francisco and New York. Coming home to Miami has been about comprehending his blood family and reinforcing his Latin identity. He says, "Having sex in Spanish makes a big difference to me—all the communication that goes with sex. We flip back and forth between different languages. If you catch me when I am just waking up, I would more likely respond in Spanish than in English, even though I have been in this country longer.

"When I count, I switch to Spanish." Counting, he reminds me, is among the earliest associations we have with language, one of the first strategies we use to order our world, one of the last things we learn to do comfortably in a new language.

Only recently has Luna come to feel the cultural resonance as a Cuban that the use of Spanish stirs in him. "I always thought that it wouldn't make a difference to me, but later on I came to realize that it does, that these are my people. Why would someone stick with their people?" he asks rhetorically, but he has no perfect answer. "The most satisfying sexual relationships I have had have been with other Cubans, even though I don't really look Cuban the way I dress or listen to the music most Cubans like. People call me a punk, and it has always put me outside of being a Cuban. Like with him . . ."

He grins at Gilberto, who says, "We just took a little vacation in central Florida, and it was really good to be able to speak in Spanish and be really sexy with each other . . . to say really hot things to each other in front of a lot of people who didn't understand."

Luna goes on. "No matter how passionate I may be feeling in English, it just doesn't come across as much as it does in Spanish. When I talk in Spanish, I think in English. But I think that I *feel* in Spanish, and think in English, and then I translate it."

No matter how much his intellect, his style, his ideology, and his pursuit of individual homosexual identity have drawn Luna away from his Cuban family, the feeling embodied in his passion for Spanish seems to be winning him back. So far, he's had to sacrifice little of his essential queerness. As for his reactionary uncle, the man is still his flesh, blood, family. "You have to draw a line. I don't educate people all the time when I hear them say really stupid things. I might say to them, 'You are really dumb,' and then move on."

Not long before our conversation, Luna and Gilberto had found cause, however delayed, for optimism. A baptism had been scheduled in Gilberto's family, and though he was expected to attend, his father had asked him not to bring Luna to the reception that was to follow at the home of Gilberto's aunt. This woman, a devout Christian, had raised Gilberto, and each time lately he had visited her, she had said that she would pray for him to find a nice girl and get married. When Gilberto was told not to bring Luna, he suppressed his anger but stopped speaking to his aunt and his father for several weeks. Eventually, Gilberto's father told him that his aunt had agreed to allow Luna to come to the baptism. Luna could even come to her house. "Only one thing," Gilberto's father added. "Anytime you guys go over, she wants you to give her some notice—so she can get her hair done."

Neither Luna nor Gilberto would claim that most gay Cuban men are able to reconcile sexual identity and family identity as easily as they have. Gilberto considers himself lucky that his father has become so supportive. (That Gilberto's older sister is a lesbian, and that their father has learned to accept her—if only after having virtually locked her inside the house—may have made things easier.) For Luna, that his mother had lived alone before he returned to Miami may have hastened her approval. Neither Luna nor Gilberto would deny that the homophobia of macho Latin culture sometimes terrifies them. (A survey of cultural attitudes conducted by the University of Texas in 1991 showed that hatred of homosexuals is one of the major prejudices articulated by Hispanic Americans.) But something more powerful than their own relationship seems to propel them into a search for family. Throughout his twenties, Luna lived in a succession of communes that included both straights and gays, Anglos and Latinos. He says that his need for fulfillment has driven him to seek out a larger living arrangement that reflects both his personal identity and his place in society. Gilberto, younger and not yet traveled in the world, feels certain that he in no way wants to lose the communal *and community* ties that his extended family and their traditions have provided him. Even when he contemplates leaving Miami, Gilberto insists that he wouldn't abandon his family altogether. "I know I'd have to come here for Christmas and New Year's," he says in a tone of absolute certainty. "I know I'd have to come here for Mother's Day, and I'd have to make a big effort to be here for my birthday."

First-generation Americans have made such promises repeatedly, but few have managed to keep them. What may alter the situation for Luna and Gilberto is the extent of the Hispanic presence in America and the steady replenishment of linguistic and cultural tradition provided by the proximity of the Caribbean countries and Mexico. Anyone who has spent time in South Florida or the American Southwest knows how completely the bonds of language and family have overcome the barriers of borders. Too often, monolingual Anglo-Americans can't comprehend the cultural insurance locked within others' languages. When Luna and Gilberto confess that sex is altogether different when they make love in Spanish, they are referring to more than hot sex talk. When they flirt with each other in street Spanish that is incomprehensible to Anglos, they are not merely playing a sassy inside joke. Like children who invent their own secret language, like immigrant parents who withhold the mother tongue from their children in order to maintain a private memory of their own pasts, Luna and Gilberto are reenacting a long-standing ritual that at once sustains them as individuals, cements them as a couple, and connects them to a cultural identity greater than themselves. Furthermore, the secretiveness of their street language and the double entendres in their camp talk intensify their sense of being "gay spies" in a straight land. All these layers of language and interpretation become a framework through which they may express the irrepressible drive to hold on to family and culture.

Since Tocqueville, the search for meaning and continuity in American family life has fascinated historians, social scientists, and culture watchers. What do we want of our families? How do we hold on to them? Why do we flee them as soon as they become established, desperately searching for renewal somewhere beyond the next mountain range? David Riesman asked those (and other) questions in his study of the urban professionals of the 1950s. Robert Bellah and his team at the University of California in Berkeley looked at the subject even more penetratingly in the 1980s in *Habits of the Heart: Individualism and Commitment in American Life*. All the people interviewed—and they were all, apparently, heterosexuals—spoke of their desire for mateship, family, community, and social justice, in the language of individual self-fulfillment. Even the social activists spoken to explained that the reason they wanted to rebuild society was to bring redress to those individuals currently treated unjustly. Bellah found that the dream of goodness, happiness, and completeness was, ultimately, everywhere expressed in terms of benefits to the solitary heart. On both the right wing and the left, the search for family was an inward process, guided almost exclusively by personal utility. Few of the people Bellah and his colleagues interviewed looked to the family as a unit through which citizens could contribute to community, society, and culture.

A few years after the Civil War ended, my father's paternal grandfather committed suicide because his hardware store went bankrupt. In those days, small community businesses were known by the style and character of their owners; almost always, the owners were evaluated by the manner in which they conducted themselves as citizens. There are, of course, deep differences in the meaning of bankruptcy then and now. A storekeeper's financial collapse in the mid-nineteenth century represented more than personal hardship; it meant the collapse of his position as a citizen. However much we might today sneer at the patriarchal implications of male elders killing themselves because their financial failure had "ruined" their families, nineteenth-century men nonetheless understood their roles and duties in grander terms than contemporary individualism supplies; it seems unlikely that any number of visits to a therapist's couch could have enabled my great-grandfather to "adjust to his personal misfortune." When his son found himself constrained to quit high school and work days while reading his books at night, he did it, I am told, not only to satisfy his ambition but to redeem the family name. Had they lived in the late twentieth century, by contrast, my forebears would have readily eluded the label of failure and found a fresh place to start over.

As much as industrialization and mass consumer marketing have broken down the family-farmer-craftsman model of idealized American social life, replacing it with the individualism of the "lonely crowd" and corporate managerialism, traces of the old arrangement persist, especially in the South. Today in Kentucky, small-town papers retain the language and sometimes the behavior of earlier times. While *individuals* are "betrothed," *families* sanction marriage. Each week during warm weather there are announcements for annual family reunions that draw back far-flung relations working in the auto, textile, and service industries of the South and Midwest. Just a generation ago, in the 1940s and 1950s, extended families were still important, to their own members and even as local political forces. Of course, they also served as vessels of noxious myth and prejudice: Children, however bright they might be, could seldom escape the stigma of being born to "poorhouse" or "food stamp" parents. Family members who were believed to carry "tainted blood"—or, more politely, to suffer from "mental nervousness"—endured quiet whispers at weddings and funerals; they were threats to family respect and prominence, points of collective vulnerability. We learned these things early and well, just as we learned that Miss Bess (seventy years a spinster, always clad in jeans and work shirt, handler of the cattle) and Uncle Walter (who never married) were "just that way." When a branch of the family became conspicuous (invariably by an upsurge in fortune), they established a collective identity and were perceived as possessing shared traits, as in "the Hindleys were always short-tempered" or "those Garrison boys have always been dreamers."

If the migration to the Sunbelt is simply the latest leg of the American journey to find individual freedom, fortune, and self-reinvention by escaping the suffocating cape of family identity, it has also led us to that lonely "land without grandmothers," as old-timers once described California. Even more unsettling is the discovery that many new arrivals in this country—the Chinese, Filipinos, Vietnamese, and Latinos—have brought their grandmothers, their aunts, their uncles, their cousins, and their second cousins with them. They have come to the land of new identity and stowed the wagons with those extended families that white individualists so eagerly fled.

One story of family meaning emerged in the autumn 1991 firestorm that destroyed more than two thousand houses in the Oakland Hills. A gay Pacific Islander who knew he was HIV-positive had dedicated himself to careful collection of antique Asian furniture in order to create an inheritance for his recently arrived extended family. The fire destroyed everything he had accumulated. Worse, he discovered that his insurance policy would reimburse him less than the purchase value of his collection. In an afternoon, everything he had built up was wiped out. The destruction would not hurt him individually, for his insurance would enable him to rebuild and refurnish his house. The tragedy was that as he felt his life coming to an end, he would now have no way to fulfill his family duty.

It was in that autumn of 1991, for the third time in ten years, that San Franciscans came together to judge the legitimacy of self-constructed families, popularly known as domestic partnerships. Once before, the city's Board of Supervisors had enacted a domestic-partnership ordinance, only to see it vetoed by the mayor. Later, voters approved the idea in a referendum. Finally, due to a repeal initiative brought by conservatives, they were asked to judge again. What is remarkable about the domestic-partnership issue is that everywhere it is debated, both sides seem to embrace the same position: American society will be a better place if human beings are encouraged to live not as individuals but as families.

The trouble, of course, comes in deciding what makes a family. Those who call themselves traditionalists find family only in the social architecture of blood ties and procreation, the last rusting links of medieval Christianity's Great Chain of Being, which bound God to King to Noble to Father to Mother to Child, all held in place by those sexless lieutenants of Christ, the priests. With the outbreak of the American and French revolutions in the eighteenth century, the connective power of both Church and

King was snapped. The nobility committed class suicide in the nineteenth century. And the fathers lost their hold during the campaigns for women's rights in the twentieth. By the time the 1990 census takers filed their reports, more than half of the marriages begun since 1970 had ended in separation or divorce, and nearly a quarter of American children lived in single-parent households. Traditional families were losing their traditions.

If the call for restoration of antique family values reflects little more than nostalgia, the campaign for domestic partnership is not much more clearly motivated. Is a domestic partnership only a symbolic recognition of two house-sharing individuals? If so, what is the societally witnessed ritual that certifies the power of the symbol? Is it only a secular contract designed to protect the property rights of the joined individuals, guaranteeing them real estate and probate privileges, granting them the right to share health insurance? If so, why shouldn't those individuals take on the responsibility of drafting legal agreements that will meet their particular needs or campaign directly for guaranteed health care? Is domestic partnership the first legal building block in the construction of new extended families not based on kinship? If so, won't it reinforce existing barriers to recognizing families more complex than than those of conventional marriage? The implications and uncertainties are legion, and gay people themselves are nowhere near consensus on how to resolve them.

During 1989 and 1990, Tom Stoddard, then executive director of Lambda Legal Defense and Education Fund, and Paula Ettelbrick, Lambda's legal director, conducted a series of public dialogues about gay marriage and domestic partnership. In October 1989, they took their movable forum to a packed gay community center in Chicago. In the debate, Ettelbrick opposes gay marriage; Stoddard supports it.

Stoddard argues that the right to marry is a classic American civil liberties matter. Any two human beings should have the right to participate in a union officially recognized by the state. And while marriage should not be held as a higher ideal of relationship, given the privileged place it *does* hold in society, people who choose to enter into it and maintain the legal responsibilities it confers should not be denied it.

Ettelbrick opposes marriage as oppressive and discriminatory, an intrusion of state authority into individual relationships. "We have in this country a system of haves and have-nots along marriage lines. Those who marry get a lot—not just health insurance, but all kinds of governmental benefits, from housing to immigration rights to family discount rates, even bereavement leave." Rather than bring gay people into the marriage system, Ettelbrick would eliminate the preferential treatment granted to married people. If gay men and lesbians were given the right to marry, she fears, a replication would occur of the discriminatory two-tier system already existing among married and unmarried straight couples; legalized gay marriage, then, would make gays who don't marry outlaws among outlaws. Consider, she suggests, gay extended families that include a number of sexual partners, or those in which long-term primary relationships include both sexual and nonsexual partners. Or consider the gay man with a lover who chooses to have a child with a lesbian who also has a lover, the four then organizing themselves into a committed parenting family. "I don't know that any of us are ready to push for more than two people getting married," Ettelbrick suggests. "If you have two women and two men who are raising that child, assuming that one of the men is the biological father and one of the women is the biological mother of the child, you still have two individuals in that family unit who do not relate legally to the child." Her concern is not restricted to child rearing. The broad nature of gay relationships—some sexual, some mentoring, some fraternal, some utilitarian—commonly involves more than two individuals. A movement to bring lesbians and gay men into the existing marriage system would almost certainly curtail ongoing experimentation with new extended families that recreate the complex emotional and practical support systems that existed in extended families of preindustrial times.

Ettelbrick's argument is intriguing. Through the freedom of exclusion, the very people who have historically been cast outside the legal and moral traditions of family are advancing useful models for a resuscitated modern family. The modern nuclear family has become a pressure cooker: The financial necessity that both parents work combined with the lack of child-rearing support from extended family members has forced couples to rely on child-care services, reducing the intimacy between parents and children. Counseling once provided by elder relatives must now be bought at prices that further deplete family resources. Wives have no time to develop friendships with other women, nor husbands with other men. Friendships developed at work are always subject to the manipulations of career ambition. Might there be something useful that nuclear heterosexuals could borrow from emerging gay households to alleviate their own stresses? Or, as Paula Ettelbrick asks: "If people were truly liberated regardless of what they were, could that help but restructure other people's lives in a broader context?"

Perhaps. Yet I remained confused about the basis upon which these regenerative families are establishing themselves. Where do they find their grounding? For whom do they exist? Is the yearning for these new-made families born of essentially private motives, for the maximization of personal happiness? Or do they provide niches of solidarity from which gay Americans can assert their sense of citizenship?

Deep into her argument, Ettelbrick made her position clear: "The norm in this society should be recognizing families in the way that they are *self-defined.*" Even in a Utopia where there was no prejudice against homosexuals, Ettelbrick would give society no authority to sanction, to reward, or even to approve one set of family relations over another. Ettelbrick's families would be created solely for the maximum happiness of their individual members. If living in a family made it easier for an individual to participate in public life, she seems to say, that might be a nice social dividend, but it would not be a fundamental objective of forming a family, and society should not be able to shape tax policies, housing programs, or educational services to reward one family arrangement over another. The families Ettelbrick foresees would find their raison d'être in the same radical individualism that Robert Bellah found everywhere he turned in writing *Habits of the Heart.*

The clearest of intentions, however, frequently have unintended consequences. In *Families We Choose,* anthropologist Kath Weston looked closely at how "kinship networks" grew out of gay sexual and friendship relations. Like Bellah, she discovered that most people place preeminent value on their right to order their own social space. Asked what she did with all that free choice, one of Weston's informants answered, "I create my own traditions." The response is painfully oxymoronic, for tradition is by definition that which is handed down, from one generation to the next, from an earlier era to a later era. To alter, reshape, adapt tradition: these are the choices we have. We are free to choose who keeps house, who rears the child, who is the primary breadwinner. Unlike habit, which is individual, tradition is a way of living that is collectively established. Unlike convention, which is a contemporary agreement on rules of behavior, tradition derives its authority from history. It's a tradition in Sicily to eat goat on Easter; it's the current convention in the Mafia to use Uzis to wipe out uncooperative judges. It's become a tradition since the time of Oscar Wilde to employ camp irony in homosexual humor; it's a convention to wear your keys on the left to advertise yourself as a sexual top man. The notion that one individual can create tradition reflects a naïve arrogance that perhaps only a self-reinvented Californian could express. A more tempered, and perhaps more social, response to Weston's question might have been to say that gay people have pushed open a social space through which individuals are searching for new kinds of family roles and relationships, and that out of the search, some as yet unknowable traditions will emerge. Among bourgeois heterosexual Americans, and especially among heterosexual American men, roles are usually separated by impermeable boundaries: brother, father, son, buddy, colleague. Gay people, however, do seem to enjoy greater fluidity in their relations as they explore a continuum ranging from lust to love to nurture to mentorship to friendship in the search for a new kind of family.

Not long ago, an old friend of mine who has been married for more than a quarter of a century, has raised and educated two children, and has maintained a prominent position in an eastern university made a remarkable confession to me. He had been suffering an especially difficult period both at home and at work. I asked if he shared his anxieties with anyone outside his immediate family. "I don't really have intimate friends," he said. And though he would be more likely to talk revealingly with female colleagues than with males, he admitted, he didn't for fear of being misinterpreted. The personal relations in his life fall into three mutually exclusive categories: colleagues, spouse, and children.

As I listened to my friend's confession of emotional insularity, I couldn't help but think of something Reed Grier had told me about the passing of his gay family. A day or two after his dearest companion, David, died, Reed "crawled into bed" with David's lover, Don. Four years later, shortly after Reed's second lover, Ron, died, Reed found himself having sex with Ron's nurse. At first, it seemed startling to me that Reed should have sought sex in the midst of mourning; it seemed a confirmation of the criticism that gay men are stuck in their sexual obsessions. Yet neither of these single acts in the midst of mourning reflected anything we usually consider obsessive. With Don, the sex seemed to be about ritual bonding, a declaration that even in the midst of an epidemic that had infected every member of these two men's family, *they* were still alive. In his relations with Ron's nurse, Reed found both comradeship and nurturing. Like many gay men who are able to blend sex with friendship, who occasionally use sex as a form of bonding not unlike an intense game of racquetball, Reed found it possible to break the boundaries that usually separate the categories of male relationship.

On balance I wonder whether by making sex ordinary, even recreational, we have learned to re-form it into a tool for building diverse forms of comradeship. By stealing sex away from the restrictive laws of marriage, by acknowledging its myriad meanings, gay men may have shown how lust contributes to the bonds of friendship. By devaluing the taboo of sex among friends, they may have begun to shine more light on the complex and various ways intimacy can be arranged in emerging gay families. This is not to deny that lust without constraint can be abusive, callous, selfish, and ignoble; the point is only that through the persistent exploration of love and lust and nurturing, gay people have helped to open up the territory of family meanings. Individual gays and lesbians may not be able to create new "traditions" of mateship and friendship in family life. But their determination to find a new sort of family may well provide vital models for the remaking of all families, straight and gay.

No matter how gay people feel about domestic partnership and gay marriage, most share a core belief: Our friends *are* our family. A great many people who came of age during the political movements of the 1960s and 1970s—the student movement, the antiwar movement, the women's movement, the gay movement—have made the same claim. For those gays who felt themselves alienated from their blood relations, comradely friendship often developed as a substitution. Yet if friendship is to offer more than escape from solitude, if it must carry the weight of family, supply the security of solidarity that Reed or Derek or Luna and Gilberto seek, how do we understand its fundamental character?

Is it possible to construct a system of abiding friendships that contain the unquestioned loyalty that Derek, Luna, and Gilberto enjoy in their multigenerational, extended families and that Reed has found only among his contemporaries? To grow up black or Latin in America is to have an exceptional cultural status forced on you by the white majority; the bonds of the family unit, even if they are frayed, offer at least a sense of collective defense. Significantly, it is in the black and Latin civil rights movements that the birth family has remained fundamental, while it is in the overwhelmingly white movements (gay included) that the family of friends has become preeminent. If friendship is to generate the genuine power of family, what must it do? When Sheldon became so angry at his brother for choosing to watch a football game instead of *Longtime Companion,* his deepest disappointment came from his brother's incomprehension that the bonds of friendship tempered through the AIDS crisis could mean as much to Sheldon as the family of his birth.

Friendship has its own dual heritage in American life. For Utopian individualists like Emerson and Thoreau, friendship was rooted in a sublime knowledge shared by two souls, but the search for inner peace, found only through solitude, forbade utilitarian motives in friendship. "I do then with my friends as I do with my books," Emerson wrote. "I would have them where I can find them, but I seldom use them." The idea of friendship seemed almost sacred, nearly an ideal of nature, a matter of spiritual presence; it came almost as an antidote to family, which was so marked by duty and the constraints of civic life. As the Puritan Americans understood it, however, friendship required not so much *self*-reliance as a covenant of *mutual* reliance among individuals otherwise alone in the wilderness. Friendship was a material covenant guaranteed by the spiritual force of God and evidenced by the possession of Christian grace. The concept, however, is not peculiarly Christian. Its roots extend back at least to Aristotelian ethics, which demanded of friendship three elements: affection, usefulness, and shared moral commitment. Most of us easily acknowledge the first: We are friends with the people we like. But most of us, like Emerson, would deny the precept that friends must be useful to one another. Yet are we not continually calculating how to spend our time most effectively—and with whom? Gay journalistic sources who were always quick to take my calls during the years that I was NPR's full-time AIDS reporter, people who were eager to have a drink and share personal stories, returned the calls less quickly and shared their time less freely when I set the microphone aside. Were they callous and self-serving? Some, surely. Yet it seems naïve to suppose that people who are no longer engaged in common enterprise will allocate scarce time in the name of mutual affection. Neither love nor liking is without context, and it is within the context of shared commitment that

Aristotle found the greatest power in friendship. We are useful to one another not only in providing practical utilities—status, income, care—but in illuminating the search for meaning and understanding.

Those gay activists who joined in international AIDS-drug smuggling operations found a place of meaning for themselves, came to understand in common purpose the limits and possibilities of their action. The intensity of friendship that emerged among those who shared affection and common objectives became a powerful, even a transforming, force. Like those French resisters who found unparalleled freedom in their daily confrontations with the Gestapo, like those activists galvanized by Vietnam, like the women who battle for equality and the right to abortion (and many who go to jail in their fight to stop abortions), those gay men who have been propelled into activism against AIDS have discovered a deeper *civic* friendship transcending private affection and reorganizing the conduct of public life. For Aristotle, as for the early Americans who so fascinated Tocqueville, it was that union of affection and usefulness driven by shared commitment to public ideals that underlay the idea of democracy. If the intensified dialogue that has emerged during the AIDS epidemic over the search for gay family and domestic partnership is to have any real meaning, it will surely have to confront these abiding American problems of individualism and commitment. Along the way, it will have to move the family of friends beyond a celebration of private happiness to an affirmation of civic participation.

seven

Parties,
Pageants,
Parades

◆

Every Easter and Labor Day, a party occurs in Palm Springs, California. It's called the Hollywood Boy Party. Hundreds—sometimes thousands—of snappy-looking young men resplendent in their International Male shorts pack themselves into Mazdas and BMWs (often rented for the occasion) and shuttle across the sands from West Hollywood to the Springs. Others fly in from New York, Houston, even Sydney. They bunk up in fancy hotels where the quarters run $150 to $400 a night. They gush and dish and guzzle till dawn, sleep for a few hours, and then totter to the poolside around midday, slathering themselves in suntan oil and eyeing the competition before the night scene gets going again.

The Boy Party began in Hollywood as a celebration of and for all the young men with good bone structure and fine skin who had come to town to seek their future in the commercial image industry. Some, like Lana Turner at the drugstore soda fountain, get spotted by older gentlemen of station and manage to find an appropriate position, either on camera or in the service sector behind it. Others become gardeners. A few reprocess themselves as muscle hunks at the Venice Beach sideshow. A fair number descend into the ranks of hustlers on Santa Monica Boulevard. Too many die of AIDS.

The Hollywood Boy Party is the L.A. stop on the growing circuit of peripatetic gay gatherings. In Washington, Beverly Hills, Dallas, Houston, Fort Lauderdale, Puerto Vallarta, and other swell places, the private Gamma Mu society has been staging invitation-only fly-in soirées for well-heeled businessmen and their buff acolytes for more than thirty years. At the opposite extreme are the nature retreats organized by the Radical Faeries, where ex–city dwellers fed up with the world of boy parties commune with the Mother Goddess and pursue the spirit of androgyny. On yet another plain is the International Mr. Drummer contest, in which men devoted to the rituals of leather, bondage, and S&M annually escape from their otherwise marginal place in the gay world and mount three days of competitions, "slave auctions" (usually these days, for the benefit of AIDS charities), and parties. Guy Baldwin, a psychiatric social worker and couples counselor, a former Mr. Drummer, and a self-described whip master, describes the weekend-long gathering as halfway between a Shriners' convention and a revival meeting of S&M spiritualists.

From the Mr. Drummer contest to the Boy Party, gay men are relentlessly searching for Mecca, even for a weekend—and their many Meccas are not necessarily mutually exclusive. When the spirit and the weather shift, many a Chicago leatherman might find himself inside a Faerie skirt in the Oregon mountains. And more than a few Queer National cyberpunks will hop a plane to Atlanta for the Hotlanta River Expo, the huge homo river party on the Chattahoochee. In a largely middle-class and mostly white male world where the images of identity can be as fluid and contradictory as a Halloween costume ball, the impulse to gather in a distant place often seems insatiable. If homogeneous, suburban America seems marked by its eagerness to shed the distinctive rituals of its forebears, American gaydom seems marked by the ritualistic pursuit of party, pageant, and parade.

Except at New Orleans's Mardi Gras, Americans tend to separate the physical, raucous celebration of parties from the sober celebration of divine or primal moments. An American party is nothing more than a distracting amusement from the duties of the day. The harvest festivals that were once centerpieces of American county fairs were doomed the minute the McCormick reaper replaced the scythe. Some might claim that New Year's Eve is the modern descendant of winter solstice resurrection celebrations, but it has become so lacking in sustaining ritual that the claim seems weak. And Easter, once the occasion for displaying the plumage of spring and celebrating the rebirth of the body, has been relegated to children's egg hunts—without even an oblique reference to pagan fertility rites.

Even though they have been marred by commercial exploitation, American Mardi Gras and the carnivals of Venice, Brazil, and the Caribbean recall for us a richer era of parties. Carnivals trace their origins to the escapades of the gods who preceded the monotheistic Judeo-Christian order. In Greek, Roman, and West African Yoruba myths, the gods brought both ecstasy and dementia to mortals whom they had chosen as mates, allies, or enemies. Festivals were offerings of appreciation for the good fortune mortals had enjoyed, or supplications for better fortune. They often required masks, which both displayed tribute and permitted a release from the tedium of daily life. Protected from divine wrath and mortal authority, slaves and peasants were free for a day or a week. They could take on the costumes of royalty, or they could paint themselves with the golden symbols of the gods; they could descend into a world of debauchery or comport themselves with princely authority. These parties were meant to amuse and distract, but they were also, as in the demented revels of Dionysus, acknowledgments of animal and spiritual powers beyond rational management. Unlike the Christmas office bash or the Labor Day barbecue, which still take their timing from the celebrations of harvest and rebirth, the party, the pageant, the parade, includes the notions of theater, of masked identity.

To dress up the Hollywood Boy Party or a Radical Faerie circle in the raiment of pagan divinity may stretch credibility. And yet there is something about them that does recall the ritual world of masks and theater. These gay gatherings, as tacky and banal as they often are, possess an aura of ritualized deliverance: They are places of collective release where masks (and what is a rented BMW convertible but a mask?) provide entry into an ephemeral realm of ecstasy.

It's 9:20 Sunday morning, Labor Day weekend, the intermission between all-night disco ecstasy and the "morning" parties (that begin around one o'clock) at which the cleverest and the cutest nosh on melon, berries, and lox, and dish over the previous evening's conquests and rejections. The air along the boardwalk is like warm honey. By noon, it will be muggy. I join the cluster of groggies waiting for the next ferry to bring the fat Sunday *Times* to the Fire Island Pines.

Fifty feet away, the walls of the Pavilion disco still pulsate. Digitalized Diana Ross is belting out "Ain't No Mountain High Enough." Shirtless men, too young or too old to know when the end is the end, are still sweating their way around the half-full floor, slipping out from time to time to squint at the new day. Two of them pass by.

"I don't know *who* that man is," the under-thirty one remarks, pumping one golden eyebrow as high as a McDonald's arch.

"Which one?" his over-thirty companion asks.

"Over there. On the stairs. Just waved and said, 'Hi, Charlie!'"

"Are you sure you don't know?" taunts the elder. "Or you just don't want to remember."

The ferry crew tosses down bundles of papers. A studiedly scruffy young man, full of Don't-touch-me-queers-I'm-straight, slips a jackknife from his pocket and cuts the nylon cords. He wants an extra fifty cents per paper—Fire Island surcharge. The *Times* is full of intimations that the world as we know it will soon unravel. Gorbachev meeting Bush in Finland. Several hundred women and children—Western hostages—to be released by Iraq. An essay on the invasion of Kuwait by Thomas Friedman, the new dean of diplomatic correspondents, pointing out that even in the Arab world, monarchs are in danger of losing their thrones.

On the way back to the sailboat on which I'm staying, I watch the harbormaster berate a young straight couple who want briefly to tie up their little rubber dinghy. "Get your ass out of here!" he barks, dismounting from his eighteen-inch bike outfitted with leather handlebar grips. His shorts are as white as the hair beneath his captain's cap. All day, he cruises around on his bike, smiling at the young meat, on the hoof or under sail.

Fire Island is the gay deliverance. For half a century, this long sliver of a sandbar has served as a summer refuge to New York bohemians. Originally, the gay district was Cherry Grove, funky and windswept, shared comfortably by men and women, colored with the affairs and foibles of the theater set, Gramercy Park painters, and Village poets (that, at least, was its mystique). By the 1970s, the hunky macho clones had taken over and moved their pretty pumped-up pecs eastward to the shifting dunes of the Pines. They danced their way into that frothy triumph of compulsive homo-consumerism chronicled by Andrew Holleran and Ethan Mordden, two of the best-known gay writers of the era. Saving every dime through three seasons, gay men (and a few lesbians) contracted shares, half shares, or quarter shares, securing a semi-private room in a plain pine-and-glass vacation house for one to four weekends a month. They left behind the city of soot and sirens and subways, straight bosses from Greenwich and young bashers from Bayonne; they awakened in a motor-free paradise where does and fawns eat out of your hand, groceries are tugged home on little red wagons, and the sweet stench of testosterone hangs heavy as fog.

Jared started summering on Fire Island in 1989, when he was

twenty-nine, just as the second wave of gay/queer activists was approaching its prime. Athletic young ACT UPers who hid their muscles under blousy black frequented New York's Chelsea Gym all winter and trooped out to the Pines for summer tans. If poppers had become declassé, ecstasy was hot. And on the disco floor, clunky Doc Martens made beefy calves look beefier.

Coming to Fire Island, Jared tells me, was bliss: "You're out there with this house full of people that you're friends with. There's nothing to do but have fun. There are hundreds of gay men in all directions, and nothing but spectacular beach." He describes the atmosphere as a merger of childhood vacation nostalgia and randy young man's lust, producing an idyllic new family. "There's something fantastic about playing adult in this little world we've created. It was the first time I ever rented a house by myself—always before, it had been my mother doing the managing. It's kind of liberating. You're playing adult because it's an expensive place to go, and it takes maneuvering to make the whole thing function. Therefore, it is a rite of passage when you're old enough to rent your own beach house for the summer. On the other hand, when you get there, you can do anything you want, so you don't have to be particularly responsible." His voice softens coquettishly. "You don't have to be a good boy."

During much of the 1980s, when gay New Yorkers were suffering the shell shock of the AIDS epidemic, the Pines underwent a fashion decline. Fear of sex and disdain for the wanton image of the island as a sex camp kept lots of young men away. Thomas, one of Jared's regular houseguests, first came to Fire Island in 1983, when he was a student at Juilliard. Now he's a Wall Street estate planner. He saw the shift. "By eighty-five, it had changed. Death. Panic. Death panic. And sex panic. The old life disappeared, and the men became tentative, scared. They saw it all collapsing on top of them."

Everyone I meet this particular Labor Day weekend, at least the men thirty or over, plays some dark riff of rage and grief mixed in strange harmony with renewed excitement. Robin, a writer and editor transplanted from Canada, seems to fear that

AIDS is only the viral side of some far greater threat to this hard-won homosexual paradise. He is angry about the rise of lesbian criticism of men in the gay movement. He is upset about a shift in attention among health officials away from white gay men and toward black and Latin women. He cites a number of popular movies concerning death and disease that seem to him like AIDS fables, except that the characters are all straight. The very existence of gays has been erased, he complains: "Even our deaths must be sanitized before they can be made into art."

Fear of loss and obliteration runs deep anywhere gay men gather—and not just because of AIDS. For centuries, homosexuals have been driven from their homes, disinherited, locked behind bars, and, even today in certain Islamic countries, executed. Oscar Wilde lost his position, his income, and his freedom for his trysts with young men, and hundreds of gay people still lose their careers in the military for acknowledging their affections. It remains nearly impossible to reach adulthood harboring homosexual desire without also harboring a sense of fate that includes the possibility of obliteration. Collective memory does not fade quickly. And yet, as any sky diver will admit, the tussle with fate is also an aphrodisiac. The possibility of loss is what enriches the theater of daily life—a universal that Oscar Wilde understood full well as he set out in search of livery boys and dockmen, and which the then powerful congressman Wilbur Mills understood when he went cavorting with a stripper known as the Argentine Firecracker in Washington's Tidal Basin.

In a homosexual island paradise like the Pines, the theater of obliteration draws on the old idea of the hunt. On the beach, in the bushes, across the dance floor, hunter and prey lose themselves to a breathless game of pursuit and rejection until the last ferry whistle blows. As important as capturing your prey is the pose of being a successful hunter—or being the sort of prey all the hunters want but rarely get. In the seventies, the Pines was wild and naughty, excessive and flamboyant: a chase into the badlands. But in that pre-AIDS era, when no one knew that half the dancers on any given disco floor would end up sick or dead by the nineties, the dance of wild abandon was, for most men, a pose, a weekend theater piece. The Pines of the 1990s has reclaimed the hunt, but this time, when Jared and Robin and Thomas head to the woods, they know that there are real bullets in the bushes.

You go to the woods just before dawn. At the western end of the boardwalk, where the ground gets muddy and the mosquitos breed, there are men waiting for you. From the branches of the pine trees hang plastic bags filled with condoms.

"It's peculiar," Jared says. His upbeat intonation, full head of tousled brown hair, and fine features all suggest the Princeton preppy he was a decade ago. "It's peculiar, because it's dark, and you don't know what's going on. There are paths through the scrub pine and there are sections that open up into sandy areas and there are certain areas where a lot of men are standing around in the dark. . . ."

I ask if he always goes to the woods to have sex.

A patrician reserve washes over Jared. He belongs to one of Newport's oldest families, from which most of the cash has dissipated but a few of the Chippendale pieces remain, some preserved in the smaller homes of heirs, others released to museums, a few occasionally auctioned off at Sotheby's as cash supplements. His hesitation in answering my question doesn't reflect embarrassment. He has simply paused to examine the proposition. Might there have been times when he went to the woods *not* to have sex?

"I guess when I go I usually have sex," he admits.

He continues. "This was an odd time. I ended up fucking somebody and he wanted me to fuck him without a rubber, which I thought was kind of interesting." "Kind of interesting," rather like ritual in Samoa. How is it that he knew what the guy wanted, I ask, since in the woods, no one talks? (Like dogs, men in group rut are deadly serious.)

"How do you know?" he retorts. "Body language. We were standing. He had his back to me and we had our trousers down, and we were, uh, kind of, uh, having"—he feigns a British accent—"*frottage* from behind, and I guess it became lubricated, and all of a sudden he was putting my dick in his ass. That was what he wanted.

"I found it inside there. Then I stopped and I put a rubber on."

Even telling his most intimate and disturbing stories, Jared seems to be about a dozen feet away from himself, peering around his own shoulder, drolly amused to discover what his body has been up to. His first summer at Fire Island, he tells me, led him to the gym, where he discovered the marvels of human plasticity. Until then, he had had a young, thin, but rather soft and unremarkable body. A year later, he'd become a head-turner, still trim but possessed of taut, rippling abs. It was during that year as well that he began to withdraw from the nominally heterosexual circles in which he had been raised, moving into an almost exclusively gay milieu. Only work, as a financial analyst for a health-care consulting firm, took him regularly into heterosexual settings.

"Quite often when I'd go to Fire Island, I'd be leaving [on Monday] to go somewhere for business. So there was always that sense of 'Now I'm dancing like a maniac without a shirt on, amidst several hundred gay men, and in thirty-six hours I'm going to be in Wichita speaking in front of a technical advisory group of the state hospital association about personnel staffing regulations.' There's this sense of 'Oh, God, am I going to make it through the day when two days later I have to get up at seven A.M. and put on my suit and get out the overhead slides?' "

As much as the old Fire Island Pines life was about transgressing the moral code of family life, reenacting the conventional beach vacation but fucking your buddy in the living room, the new Pines has found a deeper frisson, plugging a stranger and dancing with death. Men like Jared and Thomas and Robin are no longer heading out to a hideaway unknown to straights. Now most of their straight colleagues know that these men are gay and that the Fire Island Pines is the gay equivalent to the Hamptons. In New York at least, most straights probably don't care, and it might well be that Jared's health-care planners in Wichita wouldn't register much shock either. Yet to keep the mystique alive, there still needs to be a forbidden lure and a new dimension to the breach. Snuggling with a hot disco stud in full view of the mother and children building sand castles simply doesn't pack much punch anymore. The threat of impending loss, far more than the celebration of collective exuberance, is what drives the electric allure of the Island. Without it, the Pines is just another pretty gay place to mark the passage toward middle age.

Soon enough, Jared admits, that's all the Pines will be to him, and he supposes he needs to get it out of his system. "There are a lot of brainless-bimbo handsome men out there, and there's going to be some point where I'm not going to want to go out dancing every night and I'm not going to want to have the beach be one big cocktail party." Without the drugs, the sex in the woods, the virus, the threat that someone—or a brigade of someones—is ready to take it all away, it's not so clear how paradisiacal this homo paradise would be. And Jared shivers at the notion that he would still be prowling the dark trails when he's forty.

He tells another story from the previous Sunday afternoon's "morning" party. He and his friends were at a swank house with its own pool, which for the afternoon had been covered over with sheets of thick plywood. The sun was beating down hard, and the dancers were chugging along on the tail ends of last night's ecstasy and several infusions of today's screwdrivers. The plywood quivered under the weight of so much driving male dance rhythm.

At the end of the pool, on narrow platforms, two go-go boys were grinding their nearly naked loins when, suddenly, one lost all control. His body contorted. His arms flailed. The pupils of his eyes rolled into the back of his head.

"He seemed to be having an epileptic fit," Jared explains. "He was banging into the walls, around the pool, over into the bushes. And then he went off."

Alone? I ask.

"Yeah, I think so."

Bad trip?

"Yeah, bad trip."

* * *

They went as a threesome: Scott "Skinnydipper," Scott "Sky-walker," and David, who doesn't have a nickname. They didn't go as lovers; more like "girlfriends," says David, the lawyer among them. We are seated around David's kitchen table, reliving the adventures that made Gay Games 1990 a transformational experience for them and for the thousands of gays and lesbians who took part in the event. The two Scotts competed in the games, Skinnydipper as a swimmer and Skywalker as a triathlete. David, who went to watch, has lately begun to enter competitive swim meets.

Some twenty thousand people converged on Vancouver for the 1990 games to watch more than seven thousand contenders from thirty nations. Two world records, in the fifty- and one-hundred-meter butterfly-stroke events, were broken.

First organized in San Francisco by Dr. Tom Waddell, who had been on the U.S. Olympic decathlon team in 1968, the Gay Games were originally called the Gay Olympics. The U.S. Olympic Committee, which has permitted other groups to use the "Olympic" name, fought successfully all the way to the Supreme Court to block Waddell's homo partisans from calling themselves Olympians; hence, Gay Games. Though Waddell died of AIDS in 1987, the Games have continued to grow as a major international sporting event, and aside from the annual pride parades in New York and San Francisco, the Gay Games have become the largest gay event ever organized.

"The three of us reflect three wonderful sagas of romance," Skywalker announces. Although nearly a year has passed since their two weeks in Vancouver, the three seem mesmerized by the event. Each man enjoyed a fleeting affair in Vancouver, which he recalls now with almost adolescent giddiness, but beyond trysts, each fell into a near trancelike romance with the idea of being a queer athlete—a participant in a spectacle celebrating serious jocks and serious homos amid the magical romance of an entire city turned gay for a fortnight. The trio's comic-strip romances—rather like a queer version of *Apartment 3-G*—begin nearly as soon as their Air Canada flight touches down in Vancouver.

"The first person we meet on landing," Skywalker starts, "is this greeter, Jim, one of the Vancouver volunteers. Jim is obviously taken with David, and I say, 'David, go! Go strike up a conversation!'

" 'Well, what do I do?' David asks.

" 'Take a pen. Get a number.'

"He comes back a few minutes later, panting. 'Okay, I got a number. What do I do now?'

" 'Well, tomorrow, you call him up and make a coffee date or something.' "

Until arriving in Vancouver, David's only experience in the gay universe was with his boyfriend of six years. A month before the games, that relationship unraveled, and the international gay panorama in Vancouver helped the unraveling along. At the beginning, however, the manners and methods of men searching for other men—"the Olympian Cruisathon," he calls it—were new to David.

Rule number one, Skywalker instructed David: Never forget pen and paper. For the next nine days, David, the initiate in the game of gay encounters, and Jim, the frantic volunteer host to the world's largest-ever gay gathering, ran through a relay of missed assignations, crossed beeper calls, and passing hallway encounters.

Meanwhile, Skinnydipper was working hard with his teammates in the pool. This was the most serious swim meet he had ever entered, and he'd arrived seeking neither sex nor romance (at home, he was already deeply involved with another man). Then, just before opening ceremonies, Skinnydipper was noticed by a man with black hair, black eyes, a black mustache, a chiseled chin and brow, and a trim, well-proportioned body. His name was Jon, and he was a volleyball player on the team from Frankfurt (and, with his dark Turkish looks, a standout amid his fellow German athletes, all blond, blue-eyed, and completely uninteresting to Skinnydipper). Were it not, however, for his master yenta, Skywalker, Skinnydipper might have missed the Turk's salivating appetite for the redheaded six-foot swimmer from Berkeley.

Now, as they provide me with their kitchen-table recollection of these episodes, the three men slip between past and present. Sometimes it seems as though they have pushed time away and are transported back to the stadium, the pool, or the track. Skywalker is right there at Skinnydipper's ear, coaching, pressing him to relive it all, just as, earlier, he had pressed him to flirt with the eager European.

"Are you really German?" a reticent Skinnydipper asks Jon in his creaky college German.

"Well, I live in Germany," Jon responds coyly.

"A gastarbeiter?"

"Yes, I was so."

The dialogue is hopeless, but the body language, at least on Jon's part, Skinnydipper tells me, is pure Pasolini. Wet. Languid. Insatiable.

"I remember a marriage proposal in the first two minutes of conversation," Skywalker breaks in, disrupting his friend's demure narration. "This guy was ready to eat you alive on the spot. He was ready to club you and grab you by the hair and drag you to his cave!"

Opening ceremonies, patterned after the Olympics, where each nation's team marches with its flag, separated Jon and Skinnydipper, but only until each had found his way back into the stadium stands. Neither man had private quarters. Neither would ever have the chance to meet the other alone.

A sweetness comes over Skinnydipper's manner and speech, and he brushes aside the bawdy talk of David and Skywalker. "I haven't had too many nights like that before . . . where somebody is just so turned on." He sighs. "We spent hours, just sitting there under the night sky, lying in each other's laps, caressing, kissing, but that's all."

The days were full for all three Americans: The meets began at eight o'clock each morning, and the competition was tough. But it was a peculiar competition. A football team from New York that was short a man might enlist a basketball player from Cincinnati, and the Cincinnati player would bring all his hometown buddies over to cheer for New York. Instead of describing the usual rivalry among teams and nations, these three men—and many others I met—spoke of a contest that was at once private and collective. For these gay athletes, being their "personal best" meant more than besting their adversaries. They were part of a group asserting their collective exuberance as gay people, demonstrating by their presence alone that they were contenders in a greater world. Again and again, the men and women who went to Vancouver say that they were radically changed in how they understood themselves as individuals, as athletes, and as members of a movement.

"There was just this electricity to the air, from the moment you woke up until you could finally close your eyes at the end of the day," Skinnydipper goes on. "The atmosphere was charged. Everyone was living with lots of other people. It's the energy of everyone having worked for months and months for this experience. So there's all that anticipation coming to a head and meeting itself, doing the swimming events, doing these matches we'd come for, feeling the accomplishment of that. All the spectators being there. The fireworks show. The concerts. The dances. The recitals. A disco for four thousand. Being cheered just for walking down the street."

For David, the experience was an epiphany. When he caught his flight to Vancouver, he carried with him a hopeful curiosity; by the time he returned home, he had realized for the first time in his life that sport need not be the exclusive province of straight men. He saw in his friends' experience a way of joining competition with affection—something that never seemed possible in the world of straight male jockdom. He saw that the conventions governing the display of rivalry and affection could themselves be subverted. The real competition that the Scotts and many others have described is a personal, inner competition with a past that too often led them to forswear participation in the world of aggressive, putatively straight athletics. Equally, the generally *nonsexual* nature of the nonstop "Cruisathon" seemed to break down some of the usual male barriers and reinforce the possibilities of affection and interteam support. Not only could all these faggots be serious jocks; they could experience the rush of athletic performance while confounding the generic individualist sports clichés about "the thrill of victory and the agony of defeat." Lesbians who participated in the games have spoken of a parallel sense of affirmation as women, as athletes, and as queers. Until Vancouver, David had supposed that his role at a sports event could never be more than that of spectator. Within weeks of the games' conclusion, he had joined a swim group; within months, he was entering regional gay swim meets.

As for David's days in Vancouver, there of course remained the matter of Jim, the man who only communicated through phone booths and beepers. Halfway through the games, David and Jim had failed to arrange more than coffee on the run. But Skywalker, never foresaking his role as cruise adviser, kept up the moral support.

One afternoon, as he tells it, he pushes David up to an open pay phone and directs him to dial Jim's beeper. Then they wait for the callback.

"Hi, it's me. Did you still want to get together tonight?" David asks.

. . .

"Well, we're planning to go to one of the events, nothing really formal yet. How 'bout you?"

. . .

"It's, uh, it's *David*."

. . .

"Jim? Who is this?"

Telling the story, Skywalker rolls his eyes. "They had reshuffled beepers among all the volunteers. This other guy—who knows who he is?—is getting a call from some guy who wants to go out. He's not really concerned exactly who it is. It doesn't really matter."

Skywalker saw the games as a dual opportunity: "I went to Vancouver looking for a hunk. I wanted an international hunk for a boyfriend." Shortly before the opening ceremony, he found what he wanted. His find was named—what else?—Scott; he was a swimmer from Los Angeles, and he came to be known as Speedo. They met in the pool, had lunch together with David and Skinny-dipper, repaired to private quarters for hot and heavy athletics, and parted. The next day, just before his first triathlete competition, Skywalker spotted Speedo at the pool, sassy and confident.

"You want to do dinner tonight?" he asks.

"I'm busy with the team tonight."

"Tomorrow, maybe?"

"Well, let's talk. I'll give you a call."

"Okay, but I don't have a phone. I'll have to call you, or we could just pick a date, to streamline it."

"Oh, we'll run into each other."

I'm not single for nothing, Skywalker thinks to himself. He lays it out: "Are you even interested in getting together again?"

Speedo smiles, blond and boyish: "Umm, no. Not really."

At which point Skywalker walks around the side of the pool, steps up to the starting block, clenches his toes over the edge, dives into the water, and swims one of his best races that week.

It was a great race, he says, remembering it all. "I went for hunk—and I got asshole."

Moments after he wins his race, however, as he stands, wet and dripping, at poolside, a new hunk appears. Alan, a swimmer from Team Washington, D.C., makes no secret of his interest in Skywalker. They cruise, they chat, Skywalker remounts the starting block and swims his next heat. At the finish line, he looks up to see Alan waving pom-poms. (The whole Washington team has brought pom-poms, and they never hesitate to wave them.) He shakes himself dry, walks over to Alan, and says: "I'm looking for a boyfriend for nine days."

"Fine," Alan answers, "but I'm not interested in pursuing a sexual relationship."

"Fine, I can do the no sex thing."

Result: "We do Mickey Rooney–Judy Garland for the rest of the Gay Games. We would hold hands, kiss, snuggle, make dates, have lunch, spend the afternoons together—just be each other's boyfriend."

Only once did Skywalker lose his clothes with Alan. He was bike training in nothing but shoes and shorts, clipped his handlebar on a utility pole, and was tossed into the road. Bloodied but largely undamaged, he showed up at Alan's door and was shuffled into the shower.

"I come out of the shower. Alan is napping. I lay down next to him, and it's so nice just to be lying down. He takes a pair of gym shorts and says, 'Here, put these on. I have a reputation to maintain.' "

A little later, David drops by. Eventually, the whole D.C. swim team is packed into the room. José, "a superstud with features to drool over," announces, "All right! Everybody out!" He points at David. "I've got this one."

The other men file toward the door. "Where you from?" José asks.

"I'm from Berkeley," David answers.

José slumps in dismay. "Oh, forget it. I'm a Republican."

Miss Charlie Brown, who bills himself as "The Bitch of the South" and performs every weekend at the Backstreet Cabaret on Peachtree Street in Atlanta, was born a pudgy little redneck boy in Lafayette (pronounced "La-*fett*"), Tennessee, near the Kentucky border. He is tall, about six feet two inches, and his weight is somewhere in the zone of two hundred pounds. There isn't much hair above his once sun-reddened neck, but that's just as well for a fellow who collects beautiful wigs and makes his living as the grande dame of southern drag—which, as anyone in Atlanta will tell you, is the biggest, finest, highest drag scene in America.

I met Charlie at about twilight time on a sticky August Saturday of the Hotlanta River Expo weekend. Hotlanta, as anyone in Atlanta will also tell you, is the biggest gay party in the world. It began in 1979 as a swank summer raft party on the Chattahoochee River. Some three hundred gym-crafted young men would take over the river for five hours of water fights and rowing, then repair to an array of "A-gay" parties where they would finish the weekend gorging, drinking, and carousing. A big ole southern frat bash *in pink.* By 1991, the number of rafters had grown to fourteen thousand, and the bash had swept through nearly every bar, restaurant, and hotel in Midtown, the toniest district in Atlanta. Unlike the older gay ghettos of the West Village or the Castro, Midtown embraces everyone and everything that's not poor. It contains the city's best corporate architecture (a series of pyramid-topped, postmodern, and neo-Deco office towers inhabited by IBM, AT&T and Bell South), the symphony hall, many theaters, the botanical gardens, Margaret Mitchell's dilapidated but soon-to-be-restored clapboard house, and a grand park—Piedmont—where cruisers in the bushes can peer out onto soccer fields filled with ruddy-cheeked schoolboys and their yuppie parents. Midtown *is* the New South.

Hotlanta weekend starts on Thursday and finishes with hangover parties the following Monday. The big race, which is more accurately described as a competition to see who can bomb his rivals with the most buckets of river water during a leisurely five-hour float, takes place on Sunday, about sermon time. Revelers converge from all over the Southeast and Midwest together with a fair number of fly-ins from New York and California and a handful from Europe and Australia. The Midtown Sheraton Colony is packed with scantily clad muscle boys patting one another's behinds, all eagerly courted by the management, which makes more on this weekend than on any other in the year. For Miss Charlie Brown, "a little old country cocksucker who couldn't wait to get away to the city," it's Heaven, Nirvana, and Shangri-La combined.

To say that Charlie Brown and Hotlanta are the South, or even the gay male South, wouldn't be quite right. Most southern gay men are not drag queens, and most don't have the money it costs to do Hotlanta. Hotlanta is also an overwhelmingly whiteboy party in a city whose population is 69 percent black. Atlanta is said to be the capital of black drag in America, but that's not got much to do with the Hotlanta River Expo. Black gay bars don't advertise in the Hotlanta program book, and Hotlanta revelers are expressly requested in the program and from the event stages not to patronize establishments that haven't supported the event. For all of that, however, Hotlanta does exude the honeyed-up fragrance of all things southern, at once randy and dandy, genteel and rude, reactionary and militant, brawny and delicate: the Fiesta Bowl of gay extravaganzas.

You start with Charlie Brown the way Charlie starts each show.

"YO-O-O-O Bitch!"

He cocks an ear, slaps his right hand on one sleek, satined hip, and clutches his left hand to the mike.

"I ca-an't he-ar ya."

Fred, Charlie's sound and light man (and husband), cranks up the reverb effect, and Charlie lowers his voice an octave.

"YO-O-O-O BITCH-bitch-bitch-bitch."

"YO BITCH!!!" the boys in the audience answer back, louder.

Charlie tosses his tush, satisfied that the crowd is awake. It has never occurred to Charlie, he tells me, that some people might be offended by the word *bitch,* that a man in drag might seem to be denigrating women when he says it. Drag queens are not women. They are send-ups of the "bitchy" person who's hiding out inside all men (the "inner bitch"?), especially gay men. Anyway, Charlie insists, the straight women who regularly come to the show—there seem to be half a dozen the night I'm there—never complain, even when he does his "straight pussy" routine. (A loud sniffing sound in the mike, a search around the cabaret tables, then hands on hips and a question to the crowd: "What do I smell?" The gay men in the audience murmur, hesitantly, "Straight pussy." Charlie, with his sound system back on reverb, calls out, "Stra-a-a-a-a-a-aight Puss-y-y-y-y-y!!! I smell Str-a-a-a-a-ight Pussy." At which point he stops at a table where he's been told a straight woman is sitting, interviews her, and asks how she could possibly stand to look at her poor straight husband now that she's seen all this gorgeous gay meat.)

It's been decades since shows like Charlie's played to packed halls in New York or San Francisco. So why are they so big here, in the heart of conservative Dixie, far from the studied stylistics of urban coastal life? There are drag and transvestite bars in the recognized gay districts, but they don't, as a rule, draw the butch river-rafting set. There are also punkish gender-fuck bars where performers *don't* shave their décolletage and *do* wear water-bag breasts meant to fall out. *They* certainly don't pull in the frat-ish gay jocks. Here in Atlanta, however, Charlie Brown is "the bitch of the South," or, as I recollect the intonation of introduction, *the* bitch of the South, the Queen Bitch.

A young gay activist who grew up in Kansas tried to explain it to me. Duncan is an umber-skinned man, medium height, thin and sinewy, who keeps his hair straightened and combed to the right. He assures me that his Scarlett is the grandest I should ever hope to hear—if I'm lucky enough to be around at the right time— and that Scarlett is the consummate bitch queen of southern fable. She is the icon of feminine toughness who's watched generation after generation of butch raft boys and dandies prattle away their time and energy while she kept the farm/house/family/household alive. Overwhelmed, surrounded, and finally unimpressed by the obtuse, puffed-up rhetoric of three centuries of bubbas who have sneered at them as brainless bitches, these Southern Women have taken on the word, embraced the denigration it implies, and transformed it into a monument of guileful determination; they have reinvented themselves as bitch queens, Scarletts all. And the drag queens? They are not so much female impersonators as men who know from within the universal effeminacy that is stomped on, kicked, and abused wherever it surfaces, and which in the minds of countless bubbas has added womanish men to the lot of uppity bitches. They are not bitches because they mimic women; they are bitches because they have been tough enough to probe at and display the femininity that resides within their maleness. And for that, toughness is required. Most have had to prove themselves in street brawls. If the raft boys howl at and love the act, Duncan tells me, it may well be because it forces them to admit (albeit silently) that they are not nearly tough enough to display the effeminacy that resides within *them*.

Duncan describes himself as an effeminate man, but when he does so, he looks straight at you with the eyes of a panther. In an instant, he can draw the fingers of his left hand softly down the side of his neck, lower his eyelids, and slip into his seductress kitten act. Panther-kitten. Kitten-panther. Back and forth, a dance of mutual disarmament. Inside is the anger and cunning ambition of an uncommonly talented, intimidatingly bright man.

"Effeminate men are still the outcasts!" he lectures me. We are sitting in the mezzanine café of the Westin Hotel, just below the signature Portman atrium of spun mauve masonry. We nibble at a very late supper—a skinny, bald, middle-aged white man and his angry black instructor.

"Effeminate men are still the outcasts," he repeats, more softly. "But you got to remember that just because you're effeminate doesn't mean you're gay. There are lots of effeminate straight men and lots of butch gay men." His voice rises again, this time both militant and coquettish.

"It's this whole way the so-called gay movement got taken over by men who want to be butch in order to cast out effeminate men, as though we're not 'real men.' "

A long pause, and then he looks at me with seductress eyes: "Honey, I've been a real man for a long time."

Duncan is not sticking around for the Sunday raft race. He works for one of the nation's few federally funded minority AIDS-prevention organizations, and his job requires him to fly out to the West Coast the next day. But he doesn't generally take part in the river rafting, in part because it's such an overwhelmingly white gay affair, and in part because Hotlanta is the epitome of that butch gay roustabout that has little room for effeminate men.

I ask him why it is that if the butch queers are always excluding the fems, they also flock to see Charlie Brown. He doesn't answer my question. Instead, he returns to body language, giving me another of those panther-kitten smiles, as though to say that maybe those pumped-up butches on their pumped-up rafts aren't sure what a real man is.

The official butch version of what makes a real man arrives

Friday night, when fourteen hunks from all over the country strut their stuff to vie for the title of Mr. Hotlanta 1991. The Miss Hotlanta drag show filled the Colony Square ballroom the previous night—a goofy burlesque event playing off that year's Hotlanta theme, "Birds of a Feather—The Wilder Side of Pink." The Mr. Hotlanta pageant fills the six-thousand-seat auditorium of the Civic Center. This is a Big Show: multitrack sound and light boards, hired TV crews, and enormous video-projection screens mounted on either side of the stage (but no signers for the hearing impaired—this is not San Francisco). The price tag for this night of steamy glitz tops out at slightly more than sixty thousand dollars.

The lights fade. A voice is heard, not altogether unlike that of Bert Parks in an earlier decade.

"Every year, all around the world, there is a celebration of life. In Rio de Janeiro, it is called Carnival. In New Orleans, it's called Mardi Gras . . ." Wild sounds rise from the hall. "But in Atlanta, *it's called Party Gras!*"

Screams fill the hall, lights go up, samba rhythms pour out of the sound system, and the "one hundred twenty toes" of the Doris Russell Dancers—a women's precision team in Rockette-style tights and red plumes—take the stage. All the Hotlanta organizers are done up in tuxedos. The contest judges, who have flown in from distant galaxies of the gay universe, are seated in the front of the hall, all of them men of a certain age except for one striking woman with long blond hair who sits in their midst. She directs Atlanta's largest AIDS service organization.

The hall of boys hoots as the dancers' act reaches its climax and hundreds of red and blue balloons rain down from net baskets near the ceiling.

Lights illuminate a semicircle of risers upstage.

One by one, hunks in tuxes walk to a center stairway, where each is met by a Doris Russell dancer and escorted, arm in elbow, almost to stage center front. Alone, each steps up to a microphone.

"Hi, everybody!" says Hunk One. "I'm Tim Thompson,

representing your host city of Atlanta." Cheers and super-roars as Thompson parts his lips into a big ole Georgia watermelon smile, then pivots and exits with his leggy escort, to be succeeded by the next tux hunk.

This is the formal-wear competition. There are two others, swim-wear and fantasy. There are also interviews and declarations. Keeping with the "Birds of a Feather" motif, each contestant must name his favorite bird. Tim, who by day is an assistant dean at Emory University, and whose parents and sister are in the hall cheering him on, chooses the eagle—symbol of honor and strength, he explains. Hunk Two, who's from Atlantic City, also likes eagles: They symbolize his country. The eagle gets two more votes on the power, freedom, and patriotism ticket, but one man chooses the falcon—in tribute to the fierce cunning of General Norman Schwarzkopf. Hummingbirds, ravens, mockingbirds—peacocks, of course—and even a penguin get their due.

Tim begins in a new, steam-creased, grease-monkey uniform, moves center stage, where his family and six thousand screaming Hotlantans can see, and slowly draws his zipper down to the pubic zone. Raising an oil can to his left pec, he squirts, then rubs the oil in ever so slowly. Then the right pec. Then all the way down the washboards, almost to the curlies. And another flash of that smile.

There follows a hard hat wearing a tool belt over his cutoffs, a state trooper, a farm boy with a hoe, a bare-chested G.I., a convict on a chain gang, a cowboy (the only black contestant) in boots and a pink scarf, a troglodyte, another hard hat, a California highway patrolman, another G.I., a marine, Tarzan, and Huck Finn. As they strut, the announcer tells us who their heroes are—most of them have chosen Terminator Arnold Schwarzenegger or Desert Storm general Norman Schwarzkopf.

We're not in Queer Nation anymore. Nothing makes that plainer than the preintermission display, as the lights once again fade and a diorama settles into place, filling the entire stage. Bright, crisp, and crepey, it is surely the biggest, the most expensive, the most dazzling American flag that has ever been displayed in Atlanta. On either side of the stage, the video screens light up with sunset vistas of America the exquisite, as into the pinpoint spot-light walks a baritone crooner.

"Glory . . . Glory . . . Hallelujah . . ."

The voice rolls out of a matinée-idol face above a black, satin-fronted dinner jacket. Whether it is really as deep and rich and resonant as it seems—at least the equivalent of Billy Graham's old gospel crooner George Beverly Shea—or whether it's only being equalized, modulated, and otherwise ultraprocessed by the sound-board console in midauditorium, this voice so thoroughly penetrates the hall and everyone seated in it that not even the most anarchist Queer National could doubt that the spirit of the Lord *and* General Schwarzkopf are palpably present. Just to be certain that doubters won't miss the point, the video-screen images have been cross-faded into pictures of the sands of Saudi Arabia and the sun-dazzled brows of our Desert Storm brothers. All the while, the crooner's face, his eyes uplifted, is superimposed into the midst of the butch soldier boys on maneuvers.

Any doubt in my mind over how this red-white-and-blue spectacular is playing to the crowd evaporates when the crooner segues into the very anthem of the Desert Storm domestic campaign, country singer Lee Greenwood's "God Bless the U.S.A." Half the house is clapping time, cheering themselves crazy in collective butch buddydom at a hyperventilating sound-and-light orgy of patriotism, while it's plain for all to see that the real but altogether ordinary-looking G.I.s on video have never had and likely never will have the oiled-up, sculpted bodies of the hunk-drag G.I.s we're watching in the fantasy show.

So this is Georgia, the state that fought all the way to the United States Supreme Court to affirm that sodomy really is a felony. Later, when I talk with Charlie Brown and his cowboy husband, Fred, I ask for guidance in understanding these rather confusing contradictions. Charlie, however, isn't in the guidance business. "Just enjoy it," he advises. And he hands me a four-page vellum photo spread entitled *Queen*. There's Charlie in a head shot, Charlie in denim shirt and jeans holding a cowboy hat, Charlie in a ragged-mousse blond wig, jewels, feathers, and makeup, Charlie in a double contact-print strip painting his lips.

Three quotes accompany the photos:

"I'm a bitch all the time. I don't feel really different after being made up."

"I enjoy it more than people enjoy me. I can feel like hell when I walk out there, and if I make people smile, you know, because the world's such a downer outside, if I make them forget the bullshit they've gone through all day, their worries, and I send them away smiling, I've really achieved what I went out there for."

"So many times I really hate to do my makeup, but I'd rather get it on and get out there. What I hate most is pantyhose. I have to put on three pair of pantyhose to cover the hair on my legs, and it's a chore."

eight

The
Terror
of
Touching

Bill Fotti, a tobacco farmer and artist who lives halfway between Lexington and Cincinnati, tells a story about losing his
virginity. It begins on a football field at Morehead State University, a small mountain college in the Appalachian foothills.

Bill has always loved to tell stories, and his move slowly, the
way an old wagon rolls across a hay field, pausing for a rut,
lurching slightly from side to side, but, in the end, proceeding
steadily and reliably. Careful storytelling, Bill says, goes with the
territory he grew up in, with the kind of parents he had (his father
was an Italian-American Baptist and all-around trader; his mother
was a rambunctious farm child who as a young girl hopped one
day onto the back of a truck headed for the excitement of Cincinnati), and with the kind of neighbors he has (plainspoken, God-
fearing farmers who've worked side by side with him and his
citified gay friends in the tobacco fields).

Bill's house sits at the foot of a twisting gravel driveway. It is a gabled one-story building, sided with white clapboard and weathered pine. Bill burns wood for winter heat. His paintings, some of which have been shown in New York galleries, hang all over the house. They are at once representational and flat, almost like icons. Many display an off-balance use of perspective. His colors are often raw, chromatic. One painting, of the inside of a bar, is suffused with erotic tension, and might just as likely be a cowboy saloon or an East Side New York pub as a gay bar. A pool table seems tipsy, ready to dump its colored balls right into your lap. Another painting, hanging in the entryway, shows two college basketball players embracing on the court. It was inspired by a photograph in a Louisville newspaper; Bill was struck by the tenderness these two young men showed each other in front of thousands of fans.

Bill's studio, reached by a ladder that leads up through a hatch, is in the gabled peak of the house. During the winter, he places one of his large canvases over the hatch to conserve heat.

"I had been at Morehead State about two weeks when I met some rather radical people," he tells me. "I had joined the debate team, the Baptist student union, and the drama club, and all three were hotbeds of activism against the draft and the Vietnam War." He digresses. "You know, Dionne Warwick came to Morehead that fall. She stood there on the stage and looked out to us all and said, 'Morehead. More Head? I can't believe it.'

"Anyway, oh yes, I met this nice guy, Doug. Such a nice guy. He was a leader of the student mobilization against the war." Almost twenty years after the fact, Bill slips into a dreamy tone when he speaks of Doug, who is still a friend.

"We went to each other's homes, we ate together, and we slept together often." He stops.

"It was not a sexual thing. I'd spend a weekend at his house; he'd spend a weekend at mine. We'd sleep in the same bed. Well, you wanted to do that—sleep in a bed with your buddy. I never had a taboo about that, always slept in bed with all my buddies. Boy Scouts slept in the same sleeping bags. All my friends came home with me during high school. We were straight, but we slept together. It was all an innocent and sweet thing, as far as I was concerned.

"One night, Doug and I were taking a walk around campus. We'd often take long walks, talk about what was going on, how we were going to escape being drafted. Out of the blue, Doug told me he loved me.

" 'Well, I love you too,' I said.

"He said, 'No, you don't know what I mean.'

" 'Well, maybe I do know what you mean,' I said.

"He said, 'I think maybe this is the end of our friendship.'

"I said, 'Well, we'll see.'

"We were on the football field. We sat there for a long time. He reached over and touched my hand. I didn't pull away. I was scheduled to spend the weekend with him at my family's home. That was my very first actual encounter with a man, that weekend, at my house, and it was exciting and terrifying. . . . And I wanted more of it."

It is a late October evening that is chilly enough to make you shiver when you crawl between the sheets. I am staying the night at Bill's house, which is down on the valley fields of the family farm, near the creek. His parents live in a bigger, two-story house up on the ridge. His ex-lover (they were together twelve years), an actor who works in commercials and industrial films, lives in a house two pastures away. Bill's parents have come to regard Bill's ex as a son.

The next morning, Bill shows me around the farm. Up at his parents' house, his ex, who is probably his closest friend, is helping Bill's mother start her car.

We walk to a pasture where about a hundred head of cattle are loping around. I meet the two horses, Ribbon and Victoria. Several cows amble over to where we're standing. "These are the young heifers," Bill explains. "We keep 'em away from the bull, until Christmas, I think. Then they get a little present. One of them's interested now. There's the bull.

"The girls seem to enjoy each other's company. I see them

being sexual toward one another. Of course, steers and young bulls, they don't care. A warm body's a warm body. They get excited. When someone's excited in a herd, they all get excited. It's contagious. Look over there. There's one girl mounting the other. Basically, it's because there's some sort of hormone in the air. Must be a turn-on."

On the way back down the hill to his house, Bill tells me about the first time he heard men talking about having sex with one another. "I was working on a farm outside Lexington when I was in high school. There were five guys up in the barn, on the tier rails [from which tobacco plants are hung to dry]. They were handing tobacco up from one tier to the next, which means it's a mighty tall barn. The third guy up was sort of quiet all day, and you know how conversations in tobacco barns can be pretty raunchy. Somebody said something about some 'dirty cocksucker,' and suddenly this guy on the third tier spoke up.

" 'Well, I don't know what you're talking about, 'cause I like sucking cock.'

"The place was just quiet for a long time. Nobody else said anything derogatory or raunchy, but I was knocked off my feet by this farmhand saying that."

As best as he can recollect, that hot summer day was the first time Bill focused on the image of an erect penis meeting a man's mouth. It had nothing to do with being gay. It was only a recognition of an act that two men could undertake to give each other pleasure. The plainness of the declaration by the man on the third tier rail disarmed all the men in the barn, stole away their slurs, and left them unable to say or do anything except to acknowledge that, yes, sucking cock is one of life's many ordinary pleasures. Those who enjoy it do it. Those who don't enjoy it don't. The third-tier man's casual courage and the other men's response affirmed a basic rule of Kentucky country life: People should be left alone to lead the lives they want (as long as they harm no one else) and be respected for it. By the time he was falling in love with Doug at Morehead State, Bill saw male-male sexuality as nothing more than the natural consequence of affection. He possessed no political, psychological, or stylistic overlay of what *being gay* was all about; he had no gay ghetto in which to live, no camp lingo or clothing code through which to communicate. All that came a year or two after college, when he had begun painting seriously and found his way to New York to meet gallery owners who would show his work.

Bill was, he says, something of a prodigy, or so he supposed at first. More than one Village gallery owner seemed ready to take him on, be his mentor, and, of course, squire him around the discos, showing off this young, talented, work-muscled man with the country accent and the beguiling stories. Too quickly, though, came the advice on how to paint. Earth tones, bring in more earth tones, one told him, explaining that earth tones were selling high that season. And some wanted more from the young man than his art.

"I drew my line, and I know it's unfair to associate the gay ghetto with people who disappointed me in my art career, but actually it was all one and the same," he says of the 1970s gay scene. He doesn't deny enjoying the exuberance, the bar and café life—the ready sex. But the time he spent in San Francisco, in the Castro, left a bad taste in his mouth. There, he felt too much like a physical commodity—a piece of young, beautiful meat, highly sought after but poorly valued. San Francisco seemed even cruder than New York. "I don't know what parts of the life in the gay ghetto I appreciate." Bill says. "I do appreciate that I'm free where I am now, but I didn't feel free there. I appreciate that I'm doing *exactly* what I want to do in my art instead of worrying about what color's important this year."

Only rarely does Bill show his work in galleries. At least 60 percent of it, he says, is never exhibited but goes directly to buyers who are part of the gay network. That fact speaks to his peculiar connection to what is called the gay community, or gay culture. His buyers are scattered throughout America. The men who have been his lovers have also found their way into his Kentucky valley from all over America—New York, Tucson, Columbus. Like most homosexual men, Bill does not live *in* gay America, even though he and his work are integral parts *of* it.

Bill Fotti's ambivalence toward what has become a national, even international, network of gay communities points out the dilemma of all gay Americans. The country's major cities may be the places where gay issues and fashions are defined, where gay men congregate for reassurance and celebration, but they often present a suffocatingly narrow, even racist, vision of gay life. A young Korean American man from Maine who settled in San Francisco in 1989, and who became active in queer activism and journalism, left for reasons not unlike Bill Fotti's for leaving New York in the early seventies. The mixture of barhopping and agitprop politics seemed banal and exclusionary; he found no place there to be who he was, no genuinely supportive community. A middle-aged African American man, prominent in both San Francisco's black political life and its gay community, quit patronizing most of the city's gay bars and clubs because he found little difference between today's hip, queer codes and the old macho-clone codes of the mid-seventies. Young white queers and middle-aged white gay men alike were eager to embrace his beautiful, powerful black body, but they were utterly uninterested in the life and sensibilities of a forty-seven-year-old African American.

And yet all three of these men have depended upon the country's urban gay communities to build their social and professional lives. From Castro Clone to Queer Clone, from poppers to ecstasy, from lumberjack flannels to the blousy "seventies retro" britches of the rave boys—body décor, language, sex fads, and techniques of political protest are generally fabricated in the gay ghettos and then almost instantaneously telegraphed to homosexual men all over America. Or, as a cabaret joke of the eighties had it, the three fastest means of modern communication are telephone, telegraph, and tele-fag. The blanket of sexual secrecy that once caused young boys to thumb through the sex words in Webster's Third International or to pull the abnormal psychology texts off the top shelf of the bookcase in search of self-definition has been replaced by an enormous, raucous homosexual image industry. If in the sixties there were few accessible images of what it might mean to be a homosexual adult, today a rural Kentuckian or a first-generation Asian American or a black man struggling toward a place in the middle class is likely to be bombarded, overwhelmed, suffocated, with options on how to live his life.

At first glance, the proliferation and replication of gay styles and attitudes throughout the American landscape seem to be a testament to how quickly change, once unleashed, affects mores and behaviors. No amount of Bible thumping by the Reverend Donald Wildmon, the Reverend Jerry Falwell, or Representative William Dannemeyer seems to hinder the campaign. Although AIDS promises to kill half the homosexual men in the metropolitan gay ghettos and Jesse Helms labors to turn art galleries into Presbyterian sacristies, the gay consumer market continues to expand by geometric proportions. By the end of 1991, even *Fortune* had decided it was time to feature a dashing gay man on its cover. Indeed, as *Fortune* reported, one of the reasons straight Americans have grown more accommodating to gay Americans is money. Gay men have emerged as one of the richest and least-tapped markets in America. Most don't have to pay for rearing children. They place a high premium on pleasure and spend lavishly on vacations, entertainment, and other personal comforts. And from sheets to silks to cock rings, they do care about fashion. It is hardly by accident that white-sale advertising inserts in the Sunday paper are just as likely to display a half-naked man twisted up in the percale as a leggy, airbrushed woman. Advertisers have learned that the right sexy male model will draw both male and female consumers. Even if they employ only covert homoerotic images, the nation's merchandisers (and their advertising agencies) understand full well how important the gay male consumer is to their profits.

The rub, however, lies in the nature of gay imagery in America. Subtle or blatant, the homoeroticism that now pervades ads for blue-jeans, underwear, whiskey, cologne, even milk, acknowledges unconventional desire—but only if the most conventionally beautiful bodies are used to display it. The irritant to my African American friend, my Korean American friend, or even to white men like Bill Fotti is that the boy in the sheets is always a gym-toned, blow-dried WASP from Central Casting, trendy urban division.

In the gay press, where homoerotic imagery is boisterously overt, the images are only somewhat more diverse. Over the last quarter century, scores of new publications have surfaced to serve a dizzying variety of interests and tastes. There are publications aimed at gay intellectuals, gay travelers, gay Latinos, gay African Americans, S&M aficionados, leather aficionados, S&M aficionados not into leather, transsexuals, latex fetishists, Faerie mystics, high-tech nerds, nature lovers, wolf cubs looking for daddy bears, and white boys in suits. And, of course, there are community newspapers that try to track everything from bashing statistics to drag queens and their courts to the underground market in experimental AIDS drugs. Collectively, these publications are the image guides to the myriad identities available to the homosexual man in late twentieth-century America. Most, however, have tiny circulations, and their success has depended upon their ability to saturate a tiny niche—mirroring the publishing successes of journals like *Crochet Fantasy* or *Juggler's World*.

Only one gay publication, *The Advocate,* has built any substantial national circulation. Since it was taken over by professional journalists in 1990, *The Advocate* has established itself as a serious magazine. Once devoted primarily to beefcake and community boosterism, it has recently broken important stories, secured interviews with major entertainment celebrities (gay and straight), and reported on scandals in which gay people have acted as nastily as straight people. Yet if in its editorial pages it fancies itself the *Newsweek* of gay journalism, *The Advocate*'s financial base—its personals and phone-sex ads—betrays a profile of gay America just as narrow as the bronzed white-man images in Calvin Klein's underwear ads. A typical issue, dated May 19, 1992, included a slick four-color beefcake-and-personals pull-out section. Forty-seven pumped up men were pictured selling either video or phone sex. All were white, all but one were clean-shaven, and nearly all lacked body hair. None appeared to have met his thirtieth birthday.

Just as balloon-breasted blondes made megamillions for the owners of *Playboy* and *Penthouse,* hairless white boys have been used by gay advertisers to sell their products and by gay publishers to sell their magazines. However, unlike *Playboy* and *Penthouse,* which are self-conscious sex books, *The Advocate, Frontiers* (in Los Angeles), the *New York Native,* and dozens of other papers that regularly wrap their covers in white beef are not essentially masturbation journals. They are, or claim to be, "whole life" papers that tell gay, mostly urban, male readers what it means to be gay in America. They set the paradigm on fashion from coupling rituals to facial hair to body piercing. And for general-interest newspapers, newsmagazines, and television news shows, even for sitcoms and films, they are the resource books that guide the straight coverage of gay life.

Carl Strange is a young black man who grew up in Texas, attended mostly white schools, went to Southern Methodist University, and won lots of prizes and awards. He is light coffee colored and wears shortish dreads, and aside from its color, his body is the sort regularly displayed in *The Advocate*'s ads. Sometimes he works as an activist, sometimes as a filmmaker, sometimes as a journalist.

We were colleagues at NPR; he was a producer of the Sunday-morning show. At the time, he was twenty-six and unsure about whether to commit himself to journalism or to gay activism—and if it was to be activism, activism for whom?

One evening after work, we are talking about his options. Inevitably, the conversation turns to how he, as a young, black, queer man has experienced the mostly white gay world.

"I always felt secure being gay, but I always felt iffy about being black," he says, and tells me that all the way through college, he had no contact with gay black men; his sex mates had been white.

"I was real ashamed of that," he says, "and it was a real sensitive point. I felt like a bigot, because I would only look at certain things—the things, the people, you're trained to look at." Carl wonders what his attractions would have been were it not for the "universal bombardment of white images and white values" that dominates American life. His gay white friends, however, seemed completely unaware of how thoroughly white the images of beauty are in film, television, and advertising.

One night during the summer after his graduation, Carl and a lesbian friend of his were at a dance club. A black man came up and started talking to them. Carl and his friend had often pretended to their classmates that they were dating, delighting in trickery, and they played that game with this stranger. He was not easily put off, though. Teasing led to flirtation, and flirtation led to Carl's first affair with another African American.

"It was like being approached by a woman. I felt really off balance," he says, for it was the first time in his life that desire and racial self-acknowledgment had come together. "It was very nice. When we got back to my place, I remember making a conscious effort to leave the lights on. It was so neat, when we were in bed, just seeing my skin next to his. It made me very, very happy."

But Carl couldn't tell the man why he was so happy. He felt too exposed, too vulnerable, to confess that until that night he had never admitted desire for black men. "I didn't know how to express it," he says.

Growing up in New Orleans, Carl had been an exemplar of what W.E.B. Du Bois called "the talented tenth"—the elite of African Americans, for whom every sacrifice should be made and who would then become the race's leaders and liberators. But though Carl's parents, recognizing his abilities, pushed him to excel in the largely white schools he attended, they also warned him that because he was not a "whitey," he couldn't expect to be honored for his achievements when he was an adult.

At home, Carl was black. But at school, he was, for all practical purposes, white: "I grew up with a certain set of kids, and you all conform to a certain set of values and outlooks. I'd have that when I went to school, and then I'd have to shift into another thing when I went home. Back and forth."

Carl carried that duality to college, but on campus, there was no black home for him to return to. At gay bars he frequented, everyone else was white; at first, he supposed they wouldn't be attracted to him. "I was acutely aware that I was different. You turn on the TV and all the images of beauty you see are of blond, blue-eyed males, moneyed, and I didn't have any of those things. So I said, I'll be smarter, I'll be funnier, I'll be wittier."

And it worked. All the way through college, he blended in so thoroughly with his white gay friends that sexuality barriers seemed far worse to him than race barriers. At times, his white gay friends would have to remind him, jokingly, "Carl, you're black."

The change came after he left Texas to work in New York. "In New York, I became politicized as a black man. I had never been to a black bar or an Asian bar or any bar where white men were a minority.

"Finally, I felt really, really proud to be gay, because I saw representation. I saw people who looked like me. Now, I'm one hundred percent sure."

Carl had long been accustomed to playing the role of the charming exotic who was functionally assimilated into the white gay scene. But on a private level, he had always been watching himself move through that world, asking himself whether he could be gay and still be acknowledged as a black man by the African American community. Coming to New York brought him together with other African Americans wrestling with the same question. It happened first when he was working on a video documentary about being gay and black. One of the other black men involved came up to him after the shoot.

"I'd really like to get to know you," the man said. "I really don't have very many black friends."

"At first," Carl tells me, "I thought it was a sexual come-on, but he was really serious. This guy was in his thirties, and he had never had black gay friends. I told him I thought eighty-five percent of us could say that."

The whiteness of gay iconography is pervasive. Frustration over the white homogeneity of the American gay movement was cited in both the rise and the demise of Queer Nation chapters in New York and San Francisco. It has brought division over funding of AIDS education and prevention campaigns, which, until the end of the eighties, were overwhelmingly directed by white gay men—even as the disease was spreading most rapidly among Latinos and African Americans. As late as 1992, the AIDS Project Los Angeles, with a fourteen-million-dollar annual budget, had not yet run a major AIDS outreach campaign to Latinos in the city that houses the second-largest Mexican population in the world. At the same time, many conservative black leaders resisted AIDS safe-sex campaigns in their communities. In Washington, D.C., black church leaders blocked AIDS agencies from placing safe-sex posters on the city's buses and bus stops.

One of the most recent protests over the white dominance of gay life concerned the Broadway musical *Miss Saigon,* a rendering of *Madama Butterfly* in which, at the time of the show's opening, a white actor played a Eurasian procurer. Asian lesbians and gay men saw the play as racist stereotyping, and they were enraged when the Lambda Legal Defense and Education Fund contracted with the show's producers for a benefit performance. Many white gays—including several board members at Lambda—were stupefied at the protests and regarded them as an assault on the artistic freedom of the musical's creators.

Canadian videomaker and activist Richard Fung explored the issue of Asian sexual imagery in a fascinating essay called "Looking for My Penis" (published in the 1991 collection *How Do I Look?*). Fung surveyed images of Asian men in North American gay porno. Not surprisingly, there weren't many. The few Asian men who do appear in gay porno almost never dominate white men; instead, they appear as feminized bottoms who serve white studs with their asses in bed and as literal servants in the nonsex scenes. One Asian-produced video, *Asian Knights,* does confront the hierarchy of the races directly. In it, two Asian men, Brad and Rick, discuss with a white psychiatrist their troubled sex lives.

"We never have sex with other Asians," Rick complains. "We usually have sex with Caucasian guys."

"Have you had the opportunity to have sex together?" asks the therapist.

"Yes, a coupla times," says Rick, "but we never get going."

Sure enough, the strapping blond shrink has just the solution. Strip down and get to work on each other, he tells them from his authority chair. Suddenly hard and horny, Brad and Rick start working each other to a frenzy as the doctor looks on. It might seem that the psychiatrist, having enabled the couple to break through their intimacy barrier, would withdraw. But the North American video market is, after all, overwhelmingly white, and these Asian producers know what sells. Mere moments pass before the psychiatrist drops his togs, moves to center screen, and takes on both the Asians. Q.E.D., blonds do have more fun—and never forget who's really in charge.

One video Fung explores, *International Skin,* presents a genuine multiracial romp, involving an Asian, a Latin, a black, and several whites. The premise is promising, but alas, once the action gets steamy, the whites fuck the people of color, and none of the nonwhites ever touch one another; they relate only to the whites. As Fung observes, there is no room in the video for the erotic pleasure of nonwhite men—either as participants or as viewers. "I may find Sum Yung Mahn [the Vietnamese star] attractive, I may desire his body, but I am always aware that he is not meant for me. I may lust after Eric Stryker [the white porn star] and imagine myself as the Asian who is having sex with him, but the role the Asian plays in the scene with him is demeaning. It is not that there is anything wrong with the image of servitude *per se,* but rather that it is one of the few fantasy scenarios in which we figure, and we are always in the role of servant."

In his essay, Fung relates a bedroom dialogue that has recurred in his life time and again, when after orgasm his white partner rolls over and asks where—what country—he comes from. The question, Fung points out, reveals the white presumption that all Asians are foreigners or recent immigrants and that a white man is incapable of telling them apart. Fung also tells of having to prove his "queer credentials" when he and a group of Asian men attempted to enter a gay bar in Toronto. None felt he was stopped specifically because of a color barrier, but believed, rather, that the doorman simply could not imagine that Asian men might be genuine homos or, for that matter, sexual at all. So pervasive is the stereotype of Asians as cold, passive, desexualized ascetics.

Richard Fung asserts that even when the many cultures making up American life are represented in the image industry—gay or straight—they are presented only for the delectation and edification of the white center. They appear as exotic spices in California surfer cuisine—a touch of Thai, an aroma of Brazil, an undertone of Harlem, a piquant dash of Veracruz. What leaves Fung so exasperated is his dual exclusion from the gay erotic imagination—he can be neither performer nor serious consumer. Worse, because he is seen as not innately erotic, he is scarcely seen as human at all, incapable of performing or consuming without the intervention of a white man. The gay ghetto and its homogeneous WASP imagery may have provided Fung "a place of freedom and sexual identity," but he confesses that it has also been a "site of pain and humiliation" that can be even more alienating than straight society.

In his breakthrough film *Tongues Untied,* Marlon Riggs looked closely at the problems of being a black man in a gay community that is white-oriented, and a gay man in a black culture that has little time or space for gay people. Some white viewers were disturbed that Riggs dwelt on the troubles and aspirations of black men loving one another without the mediation or even the consideration of a white superego, but the director's object was not to keep black and white men apart—he has a white lover—but to explore the completeness and realization of identity to be found within a race rather than across the races. Such self-affirmation is what Carl Strange found when he moved from Texas to New York and discovered a deeper validity to his desire after he stopped dividing his blackness from his homosexuality. His new, fuller self-confidence even enabled him to form richer relations with nonblacks as he continued "to play the rainbow."

When PBS prepared to air *Tongues Untied* in August 1991, pandemonium erupted. Though gay documentaries had been broadcast before, outcry from conservatives—both black and white—reached unprecedented volume. For many black ministers who had long denied the existence of homosexuality in their own communities, the film represented a calumny against black people. Public television stations, almost exclusively run by liberalish whites, hardly knew what to do. White conservatives, especially those in Congress who were upset that the film had received a few thousand dollars from the National Endowment for the Arts, ranted about the filth that the "homosexual lobby" was producing with government money. Conservative whites were able to raise their verbal assaults because for once, many in the black establishment were willing to join them; thus, they could pit the gay and lesbian movement against blacks.

The most obvious source of the rancor is Riggs's straightforward credo: "Black men loving black men is the revolutionary act." For years, black urban politicians throughout the country had made alliances with white gays and lesbians, supporting their cause with the presumption that gay rights ordinances only concerned whites. Riggs, allied with a growing movement of black gay and AIDS activists, confronted the black leaders with the existence of black gay men and with the leaders' dismal lack of action against the epidemic. Riggs and his cohorts represented a challenge to the old guard in America's black communities.

Perhaps more disturbing to white conservatives, Riggs's film recalled a heritage of black rebellion as old as the slave revolts of Denmark Vesey and Toussaint L'Ouverture. Neither in the bedroom nor in the streets, neither at worship nor at the playground, Riggs's work suggests, is there a necessary place for the white man, the white mind, or the white ego. Black men are capable of love independently and without reference to white authority: White men can be disposable. So not only was Marlon Riggs a pervert; he was a pervert in the clear and threatening tradition of African American rebellion.

In one of his last interviews, James Baldwin, who terrified much of white intellectual America in the 1960s with *The Fire Next Time,* spoke about this country's dilemma of race and sexuality. Talking with writer Jere Real of *The Advocate,* Baldwin linked America's obsession with the threat of homosexuality to its historic anxiety over the mythic destiny of the authoritative white male hero. "Certainly, it's all bound up in the idea of eliminating other races' sexual threat—the Indian brave, the Negro stud, or buck. The myth of white supremacy." Europeans who did not emigrate may acknowledge the messiness of their heritages, but Europeans who came to America needed pure myths of giants whose authority and control were unassailable and whose clean sexuality went unchallenged. "It's a combination of a certain kind of New England Puritan virtue linked to a southern master-slave notion," Baldwin argued. "It's part of that pathfinder, frontier mystique: It makes the male into a hero, and by his being a hero, it also uplifts, creates, the myth of the sanctification of the white woman."

Baldwin never addressed how thoroughly the images of the white gay movement have recapitulated those older images of the heroic stud—from Daniel Boone and Davy Crockett to Gary Cooper in *High Noon* and Kevin Costner in *Dances with Wolves.* Instead, he articulated a lament that runs through most of his fiction: He who clings to safety instead of reaching out toward freedom ends up having no life at all. To succumb to the security of mythic images is to be left in an empty cell. At the root of the problem, Baldwin said, is an inability to love "because that inability masks a certain terror, and that terror is the terror of being touched. And if you can't be touched, you can't be changed. And if you can't be changed, you can't be alive. . . . There's something in the structure of this country and something in the nostalgia that's at the basis of the American personality, it seems to me, that prohibits a certain kind of maturity and entraps the person, or the people, in a kind of dream love that can never stand the weight of reality."

Baldwin spoke both as a black and as a person who thoroughly transcended race. There is no doubt about who he was, sexually or racially, but what seemed to drive him most was the necessity to touch another human, regardless of race or gender. "It's not important to be gay . . . or important to be white . . . or important to be black," he told *The Advocate*. "What's important is to be *you*."

While Baldwin was not directly confronting the white porcelain quality of the dominant gay imagery, his words touch the discontent that many men feel with the character of gay ghetto life. Moving from the social terrain of the fifties and sixties, in which there were almost no portrayals of men touching, to today's plethora of queer images, there still persists a "dream love that can never stand the weight of reality."

Now, thanks to the economy of desktop publishing, there is a magazine for every dream and fetish and, therefore, no longer a need for the cruiser's traditional third question: "What do you like to do?" The gay-identity media have applied the principle of multicultural diversity to the territory of coital acrobatics, underwriting it with demographics (white, pierced bottom under twenty-five looking for Latin bear over forty-five) and taking the guesswork out of hunting. Look, for example, at the cutting edge of contemporary media: gay computer bulletin boards.

One board calls itself "Station House" and organizes its user codes around the jargon of the police. Each member, identified as an "officer," is on "patrol" in a numbered "car," and chooses from several topical areas labeled as "squad rooms." Another bulletin board is called "Backdoor": On-line users slip into "glory holes" and choose among topical "stalls." Upon joining either system, one fills out a questionnaire with the standard descriptive details—height, weight, eye and hair color, race, work, and hobbies. Farther down the list is a query about where one has body hair and how one trims it and requests for "cock description" (beyond certain dimensions, the System Operator asserts the right of inspection), relationship status, normal tricking venues, age preference, "favorite way to cum" (and favorite way for one's partner to cum), and type of sex preferred: Vanilla, S&M, Kink, or Raunch.

Choose Vanilla, and you're asked to assign yourself as "top," "bottom," "versatile," or "voyeur," after which there are questions on cuddling, kissing, sucking, and fucking (the latter distinguished among fuckee on tummy—legs spread; fuckee on back—legs up; doggie style; fuckee sitting on cock of fucker on back; both standing). It's almost enough to send a fellow into Achievement Test panic. (The "Heavy-Duty Kink" choice leads to quizzes on foreskin delectation and tissue piercings.)

The bulletin-board questionnaires serve rather like a Consumers Union template for product evaluation, and for those users proficient in applying the matching functions, they may be highly efficient. However, the place of efficiency in desire is questionable. In love, it is absolutely antithetical. I tried a couple of the boards, and after several months of tapping away, I realized that their efficiency has to do neither with love nor desire but with fantasy. Only a small percentage of board users have the slightest interest in touching anything more than their PC keys. Most of those I encountered who proposed assignations canceled them beforehand, and of those who arrived, a remarkable number bore utterly no resemblance to the personas they had electronically inscribed. (One board, in fact, offers at a surcharge a 20-percent club for that proportion of men who genuinely want to meet and touch the flesh of another human being.)

As entertainment—and even as news sources about vice-squad patrols, gay-bashing incidents, and gay political campaigns—the boards are effective. They cost about the same, minute for minute, as rented video porn. And they can lead to previously unexplored performance options, as thousands of fingers type out personas they've never dared to share in public. More than all other gay media, they are the hot medium of identity formation, and their range is nationwide. Through them, gay people in the Shenandoah Valley can keep current on queer finger-snapping style in Eureka Valley, update their repertoire of kink technique, and learn how to participate in a gay rights campaign. They can even exchange phone numbers and embark on adventures to remake their erotic, emotional, and working lives. All of that can happen, but usually it doesn't.

Despite the arrival of serious gay and queer journalism—in the remade *Advocate,* in the short-lived, erratic, but rambunctious *Outweek* and its successor, *QW,* in the thoughtful, cosexual, queer quarterlies like *Out/Look* and *Out*—the most readily available images of what it means to be homosexual in America are commercial. They advertise clothes, cologne, condoms, contact, and coitus—more or less in that order. And almost always, they fall far short of addressing the issues that James Baldwin raises in his prose, that Marlon Riggs presents in his films, that Richard Fung identifies in his essays, that Bill Fotti portrays in his paintings. Each of these men, as an image artist and as a sexual being who has benefited from the gay liberation movement, has sought to touch and change other human beings across the boundaries of private fantasy, to let loose a passion that thrives on the dangerous weight of reality rather than to hide within the weightless confines of a calculated dream love. All too often, the gay image industry seems to leave its men trapped within their own homogeneous fantasy worlds, where the promise of human contact fails to pass through the celluloid curtain to meet the touch of a stranger's hand.

nine

Paradox
and
Perversity

◆

**"What the paradox was
to me in the sphere
of thought, perversity
became to me in
the sphere of passion."**

Some homosexual men say that they knew in early childhood of their desire for boys and men. More men speak of confusion in their first desire. My own recollections revert to a movie house in Lexington, Kentucky, in 1958, at what was one of the first films I ever saw, *South Pacific*. It was at once an enticing and confusing movie for boys of the fifties who were realizing they weren't quite right. There were exotic U.S.O. men dolled up in grass skirts and bras with coconut cups—my first peek into the world of drag. And there were the lyrics of Oscar Hammerstein's ironic anthem to racial acceptance, about children being taught "to hate all the people your relatives hate." But mostly, I recall the first man I ever had a crush on: lithe, lean John Kerr, who played a young lieutenant agonizingly separated from a beautiful island girl by his fear of racial difference. To a child who was just developing his first intimations of what his own differences and attractions might be, there was a terrible poignancy in the film's underwater ballet. Accompanied by the bouncy lyrics of "Happy Talk," Kerr and France Nuyen, as the island girl, entered into a liquid dance that could take place only where no one else might see it.

My inexplicable appetite for Kerr, Kerr's tortured appetite for an impossible love, the schmaltzy ballad ("Some Enchanted Evening") of the French planter's love for the hick Arkansan, Nellie Forbush: All these mixed-up bits from Navy life of World War II were emotional Tinkertoys for a proto-queer child of the fifties. Like all the postwar musicals, *South Pacific* portrayed an American tableau of goodness and normalcy, where regular people seemed well on the road to the promised life. Yet within that scheme there was also subversion. Beneath the placid surface of the tropical water, a heroic white boy could play with a different kind of dark-eyed girl, and so betray the rules of tribal purity. As subconsciously alluring as the young lieutenant's body itself may have been, equally exciting was his pursuit of a different and therefore forbidden body. That journey is what propelled him beyond simple hometown romance into the waters of dangerous desire. To those of us whose incipient attractions were not of the conventional romantic boy-girl sort, difference became inseparable from desire. Unable to take our own flesh for granted, unable to take our relation to it as natural, we increasingly experienced desire as the pursuit of the mysteriously *unnatural,* the examination of difference beyond us as a route to comprehending the difference within us.

Along with the young lieutenant's underwater ballet, I possess the recurring image of that real-life young man on a dock, his body extended for the dive into a lake, sunlight brilliantly reflected on the bristling black hairs of his ankle. Both images might have been born in my mind the same year, the same summer, perhaps the same week. To a psychotherapist, they might indicate signs of a stunted sense of self, an adolescent incapacity to integrate internal identity with the social world or, perhaps, a desire to *introject* those image men into a boy's psyche. To the gay activists of the 1970s and 1980s, the images might indicate early intimations of gay identity, as though the moment in a darkened movie house before a wraparound Todd-AO screen presaged the bold new gay culture soon to emerge. In fact, the images remain as elusive to me today as they were then. There is no doubt that they were sexual, though not really about having sex, and they were certainly not about *being* gay. They were about being queer, exploring and absorbing the perverse strangeness of desire, though, again, they had nothing to do with the formality of being queer in the way that my scornful high school cheerleader classmate had supposed.

As I have worked on this book, I've become fascinated with the connection between queer desire and the social movement to compose a culture of desire, a culture fabricated by people who say that their defining identity developed out of the intimation and experience of queer or dissident or, popularly, "gay" desire. Surprisingly, there seems to be a near universal readiness among liberal-minded heterosexuals to grant the existence of a gay culture. While I was visiting Bill Fotti's farm in Kentucky, the topic arose with two of his "in-laws," that is, relatives of his former lover. These men, both straight, had come for the day to go hunting. "Of course there's a gay culture," they said with absolute confidence, as though the question itself were absurd. Even to straight men in rural Kentucky, and quite readily among gay men, the fact of that culture is taken for granted. If gay people live together, have parties among themselves, advance candidates for political office, organize their own churches, and, thanks to AIDS, have come to learn how to tend to their sick and arrange for their own deaths, then they must have a culture, mustn't they? From the old subterranean dance of "unnatural" difference, gays have entered into a new, respectable, and increasingly ordinary world of "normal" difference. Cities and states pass laws outlawing discrimination on the basis of sexual orientation. Private companies and some public agencies include "sexual minorities" in their "diversity sensitivity" training and affirmative-action hiring policies. Communities pass ordinances sanctioning domestic partnerships in lieu of marriage. Gay men and lesbians have come to occupy their own car on the train of multiethnic, multicultural opportunity. To our friends—and to our hate-mongering enemies—we have become a describable, identifiable, locatable people.

Even since the opening of this decade, gay people have moved forward rapidly. While it is true that gay men are dying from AIDS in great numbers, gays have also scored unprecedented victories, giving them greater prominence and power: In New York and Seattle, gays have won their first city-council seats; the *New York Times* has published more intelligent column inches on the lives of gays and lesbians than ever before; the president of the National Organization for Women announced that she had not only a husband but a woman lover; Madonna promoted the delectable image of the happy pervert to tens of millions (and a small documentary about black and Latin drag balls called *Paris Is Burning* became a hit); Hawaii and Connecticut became the third and fourth states to enact gay-inclusive antidiscrimination laws; reactionary senator Jesse Helms was beaten down in his latest efforts to forbid federal funding of homo, hetero, or any other erotic art; police in Houston got themselves dolled up as decoy queer boys to entrap fag-bashers; and the Supreme Court of my own home state, Kentucky, struck down a sodomy statute on equal protection grounds stating that the law unfairly discriminated against homosexual people. At the same time, queer-bashing has also increased. But if fundamentalist rabbis, preachers, and bishops have intensified their campaigns, forming alliances with kindred politicians of hate, they rail not at individual perverts but at "the homosexual lobby," labeling it a special interest group, thereby (if inadvertently) contributing to the notion that gay people are a force in American life.

Because we exist in headlines and film clips, we exist in life.

There is, however, a forgery that lies at the foot of every font of headline type, a forgery that permits us to see the world as the news and the news as the world. As foreign visitors note repeatedly, one of the marvels of American life is the capacity of the media to invent new social phenomena almost instantaneously. The movement for homosexual civil rights, for example, progressed steadily from the end of World War II to the present. During the

1960s, there were repeated demonstrations in Washington, Philadelphia, and San Francisco; but it was a June 1969 mêlée with the police outside the Stonewall Inn in Greenwich Village that became through folklore and media declaration the birthplace of Gay Liberation. Throughout the 1980s, gay men worked aggressively to change federal policies concerning AIDS research funding and the release of experimental drugs, but when a thousand ACT UP–ers descended on the FDA on a crisp October day in 1988, "AIDS activists" were born in the public perception, instantly inheriting the mantle of nonviolent civil disobedience from black people. Never mind that unlike Martin Luther King, Jr., and his civil disobedience allies, who went to and stayed in jail, most AIDS activists, who carefully staged their die-ins and blockades for the TV cameras, almost never spent a single night in jail. Both black civil rights activism and AIDS activism relied on television coverage to secure change, but by 1988, media certification had become nearly the sole measure of political authenticity in America. More than ever, we are forced to acknowledge that what we accept as everyday facts are to a large degree collaborative fictions.

The tension between fraud and authenticity has preoccupied contemporary discourse in politics, philosophy, and art since the opening of the postwar era. Among gay intellectuals it has been the critical question, derived principally from Michel Foucault and Roland Barthes, and later from feminist theorists and literary deconstructionists. But nearly all the current writing on homosexual identities derives from the nineteenth-century Oscar Wilde. To Wilde, forgery in the matter of identity was at the essence of art. "To invent anything at all is an act of sheer genius, and in a commercial age like ours, shows considerable physical courage," Wilde wrote in *The Importance of Being Earnest,* adding, "On the other hand, to corroborate a falsehood is a distinctly cowardly act." To sort out the invention, which is a form of forgery, from the falsehood, which is a form of cowardice, is to begin to get at the core of what gay culture is nearly a century after the passing of Oscar Wilde.

More than any other figure, more than Gide, Whitman, Isherwood, Wittgenstein, or Genet, Wilde has set up the conundrum of the contemporary gay/queer project. Transcending all the subsets of gay diversity, Wilde himself remains the icon of the fabulous. Like his contemporary Roger Casement, he was a man admitted into the halls of the ruling order who damaged the authority of the order. Casement gave the Parliament and the Home Office a whiff of colonialism's torture chambers and was hanged because, as a man who had spent so much time in the cause of "savages," he had become a savage pervert. Wilde, the darling of drawing-room literary society, was revealed as a corrupter of mannered life when it became clear that his true nightlife was spent either in debauchery with a younger aristocratic gentleman or in poking and being poked by the hardy working-class toughs of the West End. Wilde and Casement, both Irish radicals, became intolerable, but not because they participated in the grand charade of daytime civility and nighttime prowling. What landed the one on the gallows and the other in prison was that their material—Casement's reports and essays, Wilde's poetry and plays—opened up and revealed the charade. It had become impossible in England to read Casement's accounts of Europeans disemboweling natives in Africa and South America and see in Europe a higher morality; when his diaries surfaced, showing his relish for sodomy with the same natives, he himself stood exposed as a savage suitable only for sacrifice. After Wilde's arrest, it had become impossible to deny that buggery was a regular and flagrant behavior in the salons of the stylish nobility. These men's lives were deemed inseparable from their works. As one newspaper editorialist wrote of Wilde, his work had itself become a perversion in that it intentionally challenged and subverted the "wholesome, manly, simple ideals of English life." Wilde's intention, like Casement's, was to undo the order of class relations, undo the very idea of "natural desire" that ordered the relations between men and women. Wilde's fictions were not only about unraveling the conventions and moral codes of the English bourgeoisie; he also saw the search for "the natural"—natural order, natural morality, natural authority, natural identity—as a grand human fiction. He made the point clearly in his long letter written from Reading Prison, later published as *De Profundis:* "What the paradox was to me in the sphere of thought, perversity became to me in the sphere of passion."

Unlike the early sexual radicals (or today's gay nationalists) who saw human beings as possessing an array of sexual natures, Wilde sought through elegance, costume, language, and endless veils of charade to reveal every self as a forgery. There could be no reliable self—only the drag show whose value is measured by the art of its deception. In the anthropologist's terms, it was to be the spirit trickster who is at one moment a coyote, at another a rabbit, at one moment an eagle, at another a reindeer—each real, each a symbol of larger meanings. Reason cannot order and reconcile the multiple and competing surfaces of identity. Passion cannot map and contain the myriad forces and fault lines of desire. Only the fleeting mask, not some illusory face of permanent inner nature, captures the real. Wilde's writing remains so powerful—and so dangerous—because he celebrates mask as reality, artifice as nature, just as modern gay culture does.

In the 1964 essay "Notes on Camp," the most famous essay ever published on gay cultural style, Susan Sontag wrote that "Jews and homosexuals are the outstanding creative minorities in contemporary urban culture. Creative, that is, in the truest sense: they are creators of sensibilities. The two pioneering forces of modern sensibility are Jewish moral seriousness and homosexual aestheticism and irony." Sontag's pronouncements have been challenged ever since, because nobody can figure out what gay sensibility is or even if it exists. Activists for "sexual minorities" usually dismiss outright the notion of any unifying gay sensibility. What, they ask, unifies black male professionals caring for an adopted child in Atlanta's Midtown with an extended fuck-buddy family in San Francisco's Castro with an S&M daddy walking his boy on a collar and chain during Chicago's Hellweek with the Radical Faeries who don skirts and run to the woods, offering thanks to the great androgynous Mother Goddess? Can the enormous dif-

ferences in class, race, ethnicity, desire, and affection all be re-
duced to a single gay identity, a single sensibility?

How you answer depends on what you emphasize. For those
whose implicit goal is to free "straight-acting, straight-looking"
males to have sex and emotional intimacy with one another, exaggerated and inverted gay stylistics are irrelevant or, more likely,
embarrassingly offensive. After all, the argument goes, since there
are far more heterosexual cross-dressers than homosexual ones,
and since S&M shopkeepers serve eight to ten times as many
straight people as they do gay people, why assume that drag or
S&M has any specific association with homosexual desire?

But might it not be that the culture question has been wrongly
framed? Rather than the outer garb of gay communities, perhaps
the thing that really matters as the measure of cultural identity is
the technique gay men use in creating the garb. More telling than
the artifacts are the aesthetic perceptions and social arrangements
people rely upon to create them. As variegated as the many gay
demimondes may be in their inversion or exaggeration of masculine and feminine display, what unifies them is an ironic sensibility
in the construction of mask and costume. If that wink of the
trickster individual derives from and reveals something about the
essence of desire, if it leads us to inquire into the perverse and
paradoxical nature of our physical and social selves, might it not
offer the key to understanding the trickster nature of a shared
homosexual culture? That culture may not be well described by
the panorama of throbbing, thumping, thrusting boys on Fire
Island and along the Castro. Instead it may reside in the techniques
of artifice we have all used in the invention of our lives—from the
Wall Street broker who chooses ties with an uncharacteristic stripe
of mauve to the tobacco farmer who celebrates his harvest with a
Sophie Tucker party to the gentle minister who sears his nipples
with hot wax at the Mr. Drummer pageant to the leatherman who
becomes a foster parent to AIDS babies.

All of us in the modern world of processed imagery are engaged, to some degree, in the self-conscious invention of our
identities. Résumé consultants show us not how to report on our

actual professional experiences; they teach us how to script our experiences to meet the needs of our potential employers. Town planners don't merely design streets, parks, and houses; they create ready-made communities in which, for a down payment, we may participate, thereby becoming an Irvine, California, person or a Reston, Virginia, person or a Leisureworld person or, for just a week, a Club Med person. Modern marketing tells us that we may become any identity we choose if we pay the money and fashion ourselves appropriately. Gay men, however, go further. For them, life is a continuous theater of multiple identities, where irony is constant. Fire Island Jared, for example, can never fully erase his flip-chart self when he's in the sex bushes and can never erase his ecstasy self in the health-planning lecture. Luna and Gilberto may easily slip into high camp, but their sex is better in traditional street Spanish—and they can't imagine forgetting Mother's Day. Jonathan, the queer theorist, withdraws from the barricades once he decides that his gay comrades' antiwar slogans could threaten support for his Israeli homeland.

We know that even if we buy a Reston identity, we are constantly and simultaneously also anti-Reston identities, and, what's more, we celebrate the fact. There lies the essence of camp sensibility, of *queer* sensibility: intimate acknowledgment that there is no centered, secure self, that the modern self is a fluid fiction. To that end, Susan Sontag argued, camp spoke most directly to the universal human condition. Little wonder that homosexuals stood in relation to art as post-Holocaust Jews stood to the modern moral abyss.

On December 17, 1963—about the time Sontag was completing her essay—the *New York Times* published an unusually long front-page report headlined "Growth of Overt Homosexuality in City Provokes Wide Concern." The story's thirty-five hundred words detailed the haunts, behaviors, and characteristics of New York's "invert" population. Reporter Robert C. Doty left no doubt about the ominous threat the inverts presented.

The city's most sensitive open secret—the presence of what is probably the greatest homosexual population in the world and its increasing openness—has become the subject of growing concern of psychiatrists, religious leaders and the police.

Doty described two clubs—"notorious congregating points for homosexuals and degenerates"—that state liquor-authority chairman Donald Hostetter had recently closed.

Mr. Hostetter said the Heights Supper Club had a signallight system that "warned the boys to stop dancing with one another" when a newcomer was suspected of being a policeman.

The Fawn has a back room to which an admission was charged and where as many as 70 to 80 deviates had parties on Friday and Saturday nights. Most of the patrons were males, but on occasion police found women dancing with women.

Further on, Doty described a "range of gay periodicals that is a kind of distorted mirror image of the straight publishing world . . . designed to appeal to inverted sexual tastes." He reported that "inverts" had "colonized" entire city neighborhoods, that the deviate had established "vacation spots frequented by his kind" and even developed occupations where "his clique is predominant," enabling him to "shape for himself a life almost exclusively in an inverted world from which the rough, unsympathetic edges of straight society can be almost totally excluded."

With enormous dismay, the *Times* announced to the world that homosexuals had transformed themselves from mere individual unfortunates into an organized and threatening community. Between 1960 and 1965, there appeared a flurry of such reports in general-circulation "family" journals—*Life, Look, Time,* and *Newsweek,* among others. Often, the tone was less hostile than Doty's ominous description of a shadow world in the *Times,* but the new "gay" denizens appeared, at best, as sad unfortunates.

By 1990, when *Newsweek* devoted a cover story to "The Future of Gay America," the editorial attitude had shifted dramatically. The cover art depicted two clasped male hands, their forearms forming a V, surrounding a cautionary subtitle: "Militants Versus the Mainstream—Testing the Limits of Tolerance." With an obligatory acknowledgment that curing AIDS was at the top of the gay agenda, the magazine told its readers that gay people had "begun fighting for a slate of family rights including Social Security, medical benefits, inheritance, child custody and even gay marriage" and that they they had accumulated sufficient political clout to elect fifty openly gay people to public offices around the country. Having noted these civil objectives and accomplishments, however, the magazine honed in on the matter of personal deportment: "Should gays pursue their own countercultural lifestyle in such urban ghettos as San Francisco's Castro district, or assimilate into the dominant straight culture? Should they continue—within the bounds of safe sex—to have multiple partners or emulate heterosexual monogamy?"

Newsweek's writers talked to gays and lesbians who passionately called for a separate queer culture and to those who claimed that gays and lesbians can only find peace and liberty through acceptance of heterosexual mores. The article concluded on what seemed to be an upbeat, supportive note: "As the rebirth of activism proves, gays won't let up in their quest for a more visible—and influential—place in American society." Most gay activists I know were pleased and reassured by the content of the article and by a publication of *Newsweek*'s stature having chosen to devote so much attention to gay concerns. The contrast with the *Times* report of only a generation earlier could not have been more stark. Gay people had come of age as a respectable, if troubled, American minority.

And yet I found something distressing about the clean, wellscrubbed presentation of all these fiercely proud, wholesome, socially successful homosexuals. Of the two accounts, *Newsweek*'s ebulliently supportive, the *Time*'s nasty and hateful, there seemed to me a deeper truth in the latter. Through all his ominous imagery and forthright disgust, Robert Doty found and reported to his readers a disturbing territory of desire that, like Oscar Wilde's forgeries and charades, presented a genuine threat to the polite, orderly daylight world of homogeneous civility. Unlike *Newsweek*'s earnest gloss, Doty drew his eye down sharply, clearly, on a critical issue in American life: what sort of desire is acceptable and where it should be expressed.

Probably nowhere are the charades over identity and desire more pointed than in the military, where authenticity provides the bedrock of authority. In a totally enclosed system of specified rules and roles, the controversy over lesbians' and gay men's place in military life opens up the very anxieties that Robert Doty described directly and that *Newsweek* sought to deflect.

The dangers of unpoliced desire were at the heart of a news story that emerged just before Christmas 1988, when a blond, boyish fellow from Minnesota booked a small room at the National Press Club in Washington and called a press conference. Flanked by lawyers from Lambda Legal Defense, the gay civil rights law project, Joseph Steffan, his manner quiet, reserved, and exuding the confidence of command, told a bank of reporters and television cameras that he was suing the United States Navy for having forced him to resign from the Naval Academy just two weeks before graduation. Steffan, one of the Academy's most highly decorated midshipmen, had spent a summer on a nuclear sub, traveled widely with the Navy chorus, and sung at the White House. He was a star athlete, maintained a high academic standing, and held key student officer positions. But he made a mistake. Midway through his final semester, he admitted to a friend that he believed himself to be homosexual. The friend spoke to an Academy officer, and soon Steffan was advised to resign or face expulsion.

For a year after leaving the Academy, Steffan remained quiet, having elected to spare his family the stress and embarrassment of making his case public. He finished his degree in engineering at North Dakota State University in Fargo and found his first boyfriend. Then he grew angry. His anger was not the spontaneous outrage that characterizes Queer Nation. It was anger tempered by the study of Clausewitz, as methodical as a battle plan. He researched the stories of other gay military men who had lost their careers, and through them he made his way to the lawyers at Lambda. After careful assessment, he filed his suit and went to the press. Almost immediately, Joe Steffan joined the lecture circuit, arranged press interviews and talk-show appearances, and signed a book contract.

"I'm kind of going through Gay 101," he told me in February 1989. He needed to learn the "gay system," he said, who the players were, which issues counted, how coming out could help him realize some of the ambitions that had led him to Annapolis. The Navy, he said, had been an opportunity to participate in everything the American dream offered, to go beyond the quiet life his father had had as a pharmacist in a small Lutheran town in Minnesota. As he came to know the gay lawyers, lobbyists, and activists whose names frequently appeared in the *New York Times* and the *Washington Post,* he realized that being queer might not be a mark against him, that it might offer him opportunities that his straight peers could never hope to achieve. Joe Steffan, would-be Naval hero, became Joe Steffan, gay civil rights hero.

Joe Steffan is in many ways the perfect example of individual courage versus bureaucratic bigotry—he is a talented, accomplished man, conservative in demeanor, whose contributions and education were being recklessly squandered. But Steffan vs. the Navy is more complicated than that. The case is a contest over the regulation of desire and the control of its images. Naval authorities saw Joseph Steffan as the *Times*'s Robert Doty saw the back-room dance clubs: as a threat of unrestrained desire that could lead to breakdowns of discipline and authority.

Consider, for example, a barracks where Joe Steffan might bunk if he were to reclaim his spot in the Navy. A military barracks is designed to restrict and sublimate men's pursuit of pleasure, on the assumption that "sex objects"—women—erode discipline and damage morale. What happens, however, when a hundred nearly naked men walking around in their skivvies are acknowledged by one of their fold as the fleshly equivalents of a Betty Grable pinup? What happens when these men no longer fulfill their assigned roles as sexual aggressors but are, in effect, feminized as the desired objects of other (homosexual) aggressors a bunk or two away? Could that barracks retain the same sort of esprit de corps, the same sense of *homosocial* bonding (or buddy love), that displaces desire with comradeship? Can the captain still be a captain if all the squad knows that he's being buggered by a handsome private? Can the private keep his cool when he knows that the private next door dreams about deflowering him?

Late in 1991, General Colin Powell, the chairman of the Joint Chiefs of Staff, appeared before Congress and explained his continued opposition to admitting homosexual people into the military. "It's difficult in a military setting where there is no privacy," he said, "to introduce a group of individuals—proud, brave, loyal, good Americans, but who favor a homosexual life-style—and put them in with heterosexuals who would prefer not to have somebody of the same sex find them sexually attractive." Possibly more dangerous to discipline is the impact of the homosexual 10 percent on the presumed hetero 90 percent who theoretically would never be sexually interested in anyone of their own sex. As any prison guard can testify, once desire is acknowledged to exist within any constrained living quarters, enormous numbers of otherwise straight people will seek homosexual fulfillment. Only by excluding the prospect of homosexuality in a homosocial setting is it possible to police and exclude desire, and even then it doesn't always work.

Midshipman Steffan was driven out of the military for confessing desire; he was not removed for having sex. Homosexual acts in the military are often ignored as long as the participants do not acknowledge homosexual desire. Loneliness, drunkenness, terror, confusion: All have been accepted as sufficient excuses for occasional homosexuality. As Allan Berube made clear in *Coming Out Under Fire,* an enormous amount of homosexual sex took place on ships and in foxholes, most of it ignored by officers who saw it as acceptable relief for their soldiers from the tension of combat. Relief, however, is utterly different from embracing the objects and images of desire within the sanctuary where desire must be suppressed. To have secret sex in a toilet stall, behind a gun turret, or in a foxhole may even reinforce the repression, because the secrecy supplies an added sanction to stated corps policy. To that extent, sex *acts* are forgivable. They even strengthen the charade by intensifying identification with the mask of heterosexual identity. The game was over for Midshipman Steffan when he forced his mates to see that the identity he had shown them—reserved, tough-guy commander—was only one of the masks that made up who he is. Before, even if they had caught him in full coitus with a man, Joe's buddies could have allowed themselves to accept the official mask he presented as the essentially straight Joe, a guy who just got lonely and horny sometimes, like anybody else.

To hear their commander speak proudly of his craving to lie with another man—to be possessed by another penetrating male ego like their own—would disorient soldiers. It would threaten the whole arrangement of masks by which the master/subordinate command structure works—not to mention the confusing impact it would have on intimate (and ostensibly chaste) devotion in the midst of battle. If an authentic hero is not necessarily a conventionally authentic male, then how can any of us be sure of his own male authenticity? Once we question who we are, can we be sure to whom we will subordinate ourselves? It is not that homosexual men—or women—are themselves less loyal, less reliable, less faithful. The problem that General Powell cites concerns all those putatively heterosexual people whose sense of place, role, and identity relies on the denial of forbidden desire. By shattering the charade, more than morale is at stake. The threat to the military's carefully constructed system of "authentic" identity subjects the whole structure of authority to risk. Wartime, so the logic goes, is no place to play with the masks and charades of authority.

Figuring out how to think about "sex deviants" and what to do with them has consumed a remarkable amount of this century's mental energy. Homosexuals, as Michel Foucault and his followers have demonstrated, are rather new creatures, inventions of the Victorian obsession to categorize every thing on earth. *Homosexual* as a noun only came into currency during the last quarter of the last century. Until then, a whole array of "perverse" acts—from sodomy to pedophilia, from lesbianism to masturbation—was considered "unnatural" sexual behavior. Almost never, however, were individuals integrally identified with their aberrations. Any man of weak character might commit sodomy, with either another man or with a woman; but only in legal terms, as a convict, would he be called a sodomite. The reframing of sexuality from a broad set of acts anyone might commit to a peculiar set of acts identified with people of specialized desire is a gift of the twentieth century. For the first time, a man committing sodomy with another man became a homosexual whereas a man committing sodomy with his wife ceased functionally to be a deviant. (That sodomy laws in many states still apply to both heterosexual and homosexual activity is a reminder of nineteenth-century definitions of sodomy. Nowadays, of course, such laws are almost never applied against either gay or straight people, but efforts to repeal them have been stalled by arguments that their elimination would constitute an endorsement of homosexuality.)

Gradually over the first decades of the twentieth century, and then rapidly during the 1970s and 1980s, public discussion of sex led to a sociology of gay and straight in which straight stood for natural and most of the rest either disappeared or fell under the gay umbrella. No matter how much lip service is paid to the notion that we all exist somewhere on the Kinsey continuum of straight-to-gay desire, popular supposition holds that those in the middle are suspect perverts better pressed into the gay camp than the straight one. If there was any doubt over the extent of the dichotomy between straight and not-straight, it surely disappeared when lesbians (the human beings least likely to be infected with HIV) found themselves attacked along with gay men as spreaders of AIDS. Disease, like perverse desire, was presumed to belong to a category of people. To isolate the minorities of disease and desire

219

was to inoculate and protect the majority. Only through massive public-health campaigns did the general population begin to understand that acts, not identities, spread viruses.

Thrown in with AIDS-spreading gays was an array of pleasure-seeking perverts, the whole dope-smoking–commie-faggot parade whose unnatural appetites led them to engage in unnatural uses of the body. The campaigns against recreational drug use and perverse sexuality have developed striking parallels: Take unsanctioned pleasures into your body and you'll die a grisly death, either as a junkie or as an "AIDS victim." Of course, shooting up drugs and engaging in unprotected anal intercourse can lead to death, but lost in the image campaigns is the fact that most people who have anal sex have learned how to avoid HIV infection, just as most people who have smoked marijuana or swallowed acid or popped ecstasy tabs have not become junkies—elsewise half the country's college-educated forty-five-year-olds would be dead or in detox centers. Control campaigns aim to equate actions with identity. People who use drugs are dopers; people who get fucked are gay.

What has changed through the course of the century is not the nature of sex acts or how they are condemned by civic and ecclesiastical authorities. What has changed is this: Having failed to suppress forbidden desire, modern society has elected to isolate and assign it to a distant category of "other" people. The delicious irony in this century's struggle with forbidden desire is that the institution most dedicated to its suppression—the military—became a critical agency in its liberation.

World War II dispatched millions of American men into the largest all-male theater ever known, where the bonding of buddies could and did turn daily into the love of comrades. "You'd get a buddy," sailor Maxwell Gordon told Allan Berube, "and you'd look out for each other and pretty soon you started exchanging clothes. And you ate together, usually bunked close together, went down to the head and showered together, and shared everything together. Went to the dentist together, for God's sake! A lot of friendships became intense and men were getting closer and closer. People ended up lovers. The ship was crawling with them." Not gay, not straight, they simply fell in love.

But there was more going on between men in the war years than battlefield passion. The war came at a time when Americans were finally relinquishing the dream of bucolic community life, when the promise of the modern city defined the future. It also came at a time when psychotherapy had finally moved beyond the intelligentsia and was taking its place as a generally applied tool of human management. At the outset of the war, military psychiatrists argued forcefully that the homosexual was not a criminal but simply a type of human being incapable of controlling his condition. It followed that since homosexuality could not be stopped, homosexuals should either be excluded or "managed." It was a turning point in America's reconceptualization of homosexuality. Though the sodomy laws did not disappear, the new mental-health movement transplanted homosexuals from the jail cell to the psychiatrist's couch and opened up the first broad discourse over what homosexuality is. Whether or not doctors could "cure" homosexuality mattered less than that they saw it as a *condition*, a state of being that described vast numbers of human beings.

World War II drove Americans out of the safety of their old lives and habitats, pressing men into all-male settings and women into all-female settings. Gender roles were confused: Men became cooks and seamsters; women became mechanics and bus drivers. And for the first time in modern history, large numbers of people who harbored homosexual impulses were able to find one another at work and in broad daylight.

Once tens of thousands of Americans realized how many others were like themselves, they found it nearly impossible after the war to revert to the pinched lives they had left behind. When they returned to the civilian world, they landed not as individuals but in networks. Those who had been given so-called Blue discharges, marking them as homosexuals and, usually, excluding them from veterans' benefits, developed their own special solidarity. A dozen gay men who had been rounded up in a wartime purge in French New Caledonia settled in Los Angeles and dubbed themselves the Daughters of the French Revolution—all puns intended. Another group banded together as the Blue Angels, appropriating the title of the famous Marlene Dietrich film. In the coastal cities, these men, as well as a good many lesbians, sought to reclaim in civilian life the camaraderie that the military had unintentionally fostered in them. Quietly they settled in the bohemian zones of New York, Los Angeles, and San Francisco, forming bridge clubs, throwing outrageous drag parties, opening leather bars, staking out their own semisubterranean turf—much as Irish, Jewish, and Chinese immigrants had done before them. Without trying to, they created something like a culture.

The combination of war and urbanization eliminated the secrecy of forbidden desires. Farm boys and sailors flooded into the metropolises, where they could easily spot one another in shadowy alleys. Prosecutions, bar raids, and railroadings did continue, fueled by the viciousness of Cold War witch-hunts, but the underground communities continued to grow and spread—to the South, to the Midwest, to the nation's capital. Their clandestine status helped to solidify their special character and strength. Men and women who had learned to survive in combat zones were toughened in their resolve to live the lives that fate had issued them. Like homosexuals before the war, they were forced into a world of furtive signals and contacts; unlike the prewar homosexuals, their furtive behavior was communal, not individual, and was positively reinforced by early civil rights organizations like the Mattachine Society, the Daughters of Bilitis, and the Society for Individual Rights. By the 1980s, the overt laws of oppression had become little more than symbols to conservatives fighting a rearguard battle against the steadily growing movement for minority rights. Though the Supreme Court might uphold Georgia's sodomy law, the city of Atlanta and its leading hotels would flagrantly ignore it, welcoming, celebrating, and promoting a national homosexual party drawing thousands.

But—to steal a Jewish American cliché—is it really good for the gays? Or, to put the question more pointedly, is it good for the perverts? If gays and straights alike agree that gay people have built a gay culture, does the existence of that culture serve the cause of liberated desire or has it confined desire to a self-made prison of labels?

For a parallel, consider the century's other mass forbidden pleasure: drug use. When it became clear late in the AIDS epidemic that the second wave of infected people were intravenous drug users—IVDUs—a new language emerged. Gay activists had been so successful in forcing medical institutions to involve gay community leaders in research and prevention campaigns that it had become unthinkable to launch a new initiative without "community" participation. Thus, AIDS activists concerned with stopping HIV transmission among drug users began to speak of bringing in the "IVDU community" to develop needle-cleansing and needle-exchange campaigns. Involving people in campaigns to help themselves has theoretical merit, yet the invention of a "community" of human beings whose living conditions nearly defined the concept of anti-community, who were frequently homeless and jobless, whose sometime mates often had no knowledge of their drug injections, was at best a naïve illusion, at worst an Orwellian hallucination. To speak to and protect people who use drugs is one thing. To reify them and their imagined community with an acronymic identity—IVDUs—irrespective of age, class, sex, sexual orientation, ethnicity, or drug choice, was to join the movement of categorization propounded by conservatives who call any drug user a "freak." The jargon of therapeutics and rehabilitation labels all users (including sherry drinkers and marijuana smokers) as "substance abusers"; police lingo dismisses them as "heads" and "junkies." The effect is to separate the *natural* desires of "straights" from the pitiful, demented, criminal, perverse desires of "others." The good, clean people who just say NO to their submerged appetites (and if such appetites weren't universal, why would anyone have to say NO?) will be spared from degenerating into IVDU creatures. The specter of the communalized, labeled Drug User reassures everybody else that they are clean and natural—just as the image of responsible, respectable gay communities helps reassure straight people that they are really straight and that the deviants live somewhere else.

As long as perverse desire remained forbidden, it also threatened to be universally alluring. If such tantalizing desires can not be eliminated, however, might they not be effectively neutralized by identifying them and locating them on a bright, sunny, but marginal hill of constant exposure? Rather than continue the manifestly ineffective campaigns of suppression, allot the dissidents their own special territories where, like "savages" on reservations, they can live safe from assault, and where visiting tourists can also be reassured that their own desires hold nothing in common with the desires of the dissidents.

Those who want security in the knowledge of their own desire, those who seek to normalize their own identity, may gain liberation in gay nationalism—legal, territorial, and cultural. It provides a respite, a retreat, from a hostile world. Yet in the drive to construct a new gay homestead—in the words of even some of the radical Queer Nationals, a "safe space"—what becomes of the multiple masks of perverse desire? Do they not risk melding into the single visage of social identity, which by its very nature captures, polices, and inoculates the part of pleasure that is perversity? Does it not, like religious dietary laws, threaten to limit the menu of its own socially acceptable perversions? What then becomes of the perverter, for whom desire is inseparable from paradox, for whom the mask of identity implodes and dissolves into a succession of surfaces, for whom internal and external difference is continuous?

No matter how clearly we may think we know our true selves, how confident we are in our gay identities, we contain multitudes—not only the socially recognized array of leather boys, Radical Faeries, and shiny-toothed mustache couples. The mosaic of fluid selves is richer than we know or can know. In the late 1980s, there developed a circuit of periodic parties called "Jack and Jills," which were modeled after the jack-off parties that gay men had organized when AIDS began closing the bathhouses. The difference was that both gay men and lesbians came to the Jack and

Jill parties, and as chance would have it, queer Jacks occasionally found themselves playing with dyke Jills. "Here's the thing," a young man said to me in describing the event. "If I'm screwing a dyke, if I'm having vaginal intercourse, is it gay sex or straight sex?"

The man in question in no way perceived himself as bisexual. He did not aver desire for women. It simply happened that in the midst of an orgy where both men and women were present, the sensation of body experiencing body without reference to male and female identities led him, seemingly by accident, into a woman's vagina. A standard-issue therapist might suggest that in a setting where sexual anxieties were relaxed, the innate procreative instinct took over, enabling these two homosexuals to find heterosexual pleasure that their neuroses had heretofore blocked. The man, however, proposed a variation. "The sex was so hot between us," he said, "because we had let loose of all the usual role expectations that shape how men and women think of each other. It was like being kids exploring each other without knowing all the stuff guys learn about being in control. All we had was pleasure."

The sex they had was, in effect, a double perversity. It was a descent into pure animal delight, or so the man said. Yet, as he also told me, the added excitement between them came in part from the violation of gay identity. It was about rending yet another self-constructed mask and being reminded of how mutable all our masks are. To that extent, it was a momentary recovery of childish make-believe. Like playing doctor, it was at once innocent and forbidden, doubly forbidden because it violated both conventional sexual taboos and threatened to sabotage the hard-won security of "normal" homosexuality. Of course, it was only because of the expansiveness and resilience of gay community life that these Jack and Jill parties could take place at all. Or, to confound Wilde's terms, they were the manifest evidence of "perversity" made "paradox."

I am drawn deeper into the apparent perversity of the Jack and Jill parties, not because they appeal to me personally, but because

225

they draw me back to those adolescent images of desire and identity—the underwater swimmer, the boy on the dock, the high
school cheerleader who knew I was queer before I did. Queer, for
her, was simple: all that stuff that isn't straight. And what was
straight? Anything that comes naturally, that comes without examination, without consideration of a possible alternative.

Unlike most of the kids in our school, she was a city girl,
from Cincinnati, a tough industrial town where you learn early to
talk back fast. Country boys and girls didn't loosely throw around
epithets out loud, especially not at good kids like me. Reticence
led them not to speak. They might slip into their respective rest
rooms for a surreptitious smoke and gossip about who was a
queer, but they wouldn't spit it out in public so easily. This city
girl, however, had somewhere learned about the power of public
naming.

As a male, as a native, as an A student, as a person from a
prominent if not rich family, I had advantages she lacked. By
hurling the epithet at me in a setting where others could hear it,
she could claim to be less of an outsider than I, to be more de-
serving by virtue of her own presumed straightness of community
membership. The community could know her—and be reassured
of its own unexamined straightness—through her brash, outsider's readiness to identify the queer in their midst.

When time came for our class's twenty-fifth reunion, I went,
with the usual misgivings. It was a convivial event, held in a motel
dining room in a county where liquor could be served. The
evening was warm-spirited, and far more generous than our adolescence. But the most startling thing to me was the enthusiasm
with which the women spoke of their divorces. Divorce, two
women at my table said, was the best thing that had ever happened
to them; it had given them new life. We had grown up in an era
when the term *divorcée* was only slightly less opprobrious than
queer. The transformation in how my former classmates saw themselves and one another, how they embraced their reconstructed
identities, was more remarkable than this urban sophisticate might
have imagined.

The same transformation had presumably not overtaken the term *queer,* and I chose not to press the matter. Yet, as the post-modernists would have it, the contemporary construction of identity is totally fluid. Despite years of Bible-thumping assault, divorcées had been resurrected from fallen Jezebels into radiant heroines. The ground of normalcy that had once so fixed their identification was no longer recognizable. Do I take it to mean that adolescent boys will now come forward in their country churches to celebrate their images of male swimmers poised on docks? Hardly. But the change I witnessed does suggest how transitory are the bases upon which communities of forbidden desire have constructed themselves. Just as the image of the black man in America is constructed of the relation between black and white people in America and is profoundly different from the images of black men in Nigeria or Brazil, so Queer as a disdained minority of forbidden desire exists only in its relation to the straight majority.

Many black writers have pointed out that what it means to be white is no longer clear. Similarly, the ad writers for Calvin Klein, Johnny Walker, and Levi Strauss have shown that what it means to be straight is no longer clear. If, as Colin Powell says, straight men are distressed that they could be sex objects in the barracks, how do straight men respond to the plainly homoerotic Calvin Klein underwear ads? Do they share the lustful point of view of the photographer or the leer of the boy looking for lust? It's not accurate to say that the ads are targeted exclusively at gay men; the overwhelming majority of men who buy and wear underpants are straight. And it is banal gay fantasy to suppose that all the straight men wearing Calvins are simply closeted homosexuals. All we know is that this ad campaign—and dozens of other cultural phenomena like it—shows that straight American men are responding to the ambiguity of desire. They are willing to allow their eyes to rest upon the images of male loins, lips, or pectorals in unmistakably sexual repose; they know that the subject and object of desire are unclear, diffuse, disturbing.

These modern images imply action. Unlike the static studio

portrayals of the old Brooks Brothers man, the men in contemporary fashion spreads look expectant. Men of uncertain desire are moving onto the dance floor, are beckoning a partner to join them, are about to enter an embrace, are about to give/get head. Because the action is open-ended, because we know neither what these men will do nor with whom they will do it, they are enticing, intriguing, queer. Even the respectable pages of the *New York Times Magazine* are not immune. The May 24, 1992, issue featured a sepia-toned photo spread of slinky, see-through clothing for both men and women. One photo shows a young man with tousled hair, his right arm raised over his head, his fingers resting on a rock. His left hand is also pressed against the rock. The man is muscular, yet the chiaroscuro makes his skin look soft. Over his torso he wears a cotton-and-lycra tank top. His eyes are in full shadow, his lips in half shadow, a little parted. Farther into the spread, the same man appears again. In one thoroughly androgynous pose, he has his dukes up ready to fight, but the cuffs of his sheer black blouse are tucked inside his fists. In another photo, shot from behind, his arms are raised and his hands grasp a rock; his face is buried in the stone as though he were eating it.

"After staring at pages and pages of randy advertisements," Hal Rubenstein writes in the accompanying copy, "people are more than ready to be seduced by a little mystery. The power of the blatant is increasingly giving way to innuendo. . . . These days, what you see is not necessarily what you get, but it sure is fun imagining."

Mystery, as Rubenstein says, is the thing that seduces us all. If the old Calvin Klein underwear ads were so blatant that they became passé, still, there was something both queer and mysterious about them. We may not all be queer consumers, but the queerness of the boy in the sheer rags intrigues us. In looking at him, we are carried back to the age of mystery and desire, whatever those mysteries and desires may have been. The fundamentalists are right to be worried: The images of forbidden and unnatural desire do surround us. They lead all who look at them to consider all the possibilities of who they and their mates might be. From back-room dance bars to gay-ghetto billboards to downtown bus stops, the discourse and disarray of forbidden desire is everywhere.

This, then, is the conundrum of a gay culture dedicated both to desire and community.

This, too, is the conundrum of desire and community in the dream of a gay culture. As much as the invention of gay urban communities is testament to the newfound worldliness of proudly gay people, these communities have also been open, celebratory, sexual territories whose success may also be the means of their demise. To the degree that gay culture subverts and transgresses the taboos of forbidden desire, to the degree that it disturbs and rearranges society's presumptions about the very meaning of straightness, to the degree that it encourages everyone to linger a while longer on the queerness within them, it also destroys its own distinctive place and its raison d'être. Only by curtailing perversity, by arranging and codifying its own images of desire, by erecting (forging?) its own rules of inclusion and exclusion, status and shame—as all established cultures do—can it hope to persist.

The paradox of queerness is that it survives by continually collapsing and recreating itself. Traditional cultural separatists—black nationalists, radical feminists, Latin chauvinists, Hassidic communalists—secure their tribal meaning through the immutability of their codes, rights, and rituals. Queer culturalists recognize and realize one another through disruption and sabotage of their inherited traditions. Employing wit and the critical parody of camp, they unravel the hidden forgeries of their own inherited cultures and then self-consciously construct new cultural forgeries that they know are destined to dissolve. That is the essence of desire in the queer paradox. To persevere is to disappear. The community of identity exists only in the state of transformation. In the culture of desire, there are no safe spaces.

Bibliography

Adam, Barry. *The Rise of a Gay and Lesbian Movement*. Boston: Twayne, 1987.

Barthes, Roland. *A Lover's Discourse*. New York: Farrar, Straus and Giroux, 1978.

————. *The Fashion System*. New York: Hill and Wang, 1983.

Bartlett, Neil. *Who Was That Man? A Present for Mr. Oscar Wilde*. London: Serpent's Tail, 1988.

Bataille, Georges. *Erotism: Death & Sensuality*. San Francisco: City Lights, 1986.

————. *The Tears of Eros*. San Francisco: City Lights, 1989.

Bayer, Ronald. *Homosexuality and American Psychiatry: The Politics of Diagnosis*. Princeton: Princeton University Press, 1987.

Bellah, Robert, et al. *Habits of the Heart: Individualism and Commitment in American Life*. Berkeley: University of California Press, 1985.

————. *The Good Society*. New York: Knopf, 1991.

Berube, Allan. *Coming Out Under Fire*. New York: Free Press, 1990.

Browning, Frank, and John Gerassi. *The American Way of Crime: From Salem to Watergate*. New York: G. P. Putnam's, 1980.

Castells, Manuel. *The City and the Grassroots*. Berkeley: University of California Press, 1983.

Crimp, Douglas, ed. *AIDS: Cultural Analysis, Cultural Activism*. Cambridge, Mass.: M.I.T. Press, 1988.

D'Emilio, John. *Sexual Politics, Sexual Communities*. Chicago: University of Chicago Press, 1983.

D'Emilio, John, and Estelle B. Freedman. *Intimate Matters: A History of Sexuality in America*. New York: Harper & Row, 1988.

Diebold, David. *Tribal Rites*. San Francisco: Audiosis, 1987.

Dollimore, Jonathan. *Sexual Dissidence: Augustine to Wilde, Freud to Foucault*. New York: Oxford University Press, 1991.

Evans, Arthur. *The God of Ecstasy: Sex Roles and the Madness of Dionysus*. New York: St. Martin's Press, 1988.

Ewen, Stuart. *All Consuming Images: The Politics of Style in Contemporary Culture*. New York: Basic Books, 1988.

Foucault, Michel. *Discipline and Punish: The Birth of the Prison*, trans. Alan Sheridan. New York: Pantheon, 1977.

————. *Politics, Philosophy, Culture: Interviews and Other Writings, 1977–1984*. New York: Routledge, 1988.

————. *The History of Sexuality, Vol. I: An Introduction*. New York: Vintage Books, 1980.

————. *The History of Sexuality, Vol. II: The Uses of Pleasure*. New York: Vintage, 1986.

Gide, Andre. *The Immoralist*. Harmondsworth: Penguin, 1960.

————. *If It Die*. London: Penguin, 1977.

Greenberg, David F. *The Construction of Homosexuality*. Chicago: University of Chicago Press, 1988.

Hebdidge, Dick. *Subculture: The Meaning of Style*. London: Methuen, 1979.

Hockenghem, Guy. *Homosexual Desire,* trans. Daniella Dangoor. London: Allison & Busby, 1978.

Holleran, Andrew. *Dancer from the Dance.* New York: New American Library, 1978.

——. *Ground Zero.* New York: New American Library, 1988.

Katz, Jonathan Ned, ed. *Gay American History: Lesbians and Gay Men in the U.S.A.* New York: Thomas Crowell, 1976.

Kleinberg, Seymour. *Alienated Affections: Being Gay in America.* New York: St. Martin's Press, 1980.

Lurie, Allison. *The Language of Clothes.* New York: Vintage, 1981.

Rechy, John. *The Sexual Outlaw.* New York: Dell, 1977.

Rofes, Eric. *Gay Life: Leisure, Love, and Living for the Contemporary Gay Male.* New York: Dolphin Doubleday, 1987.

Sedgwick, Eve Kosofsky. *Epistemology of the Closet.* Berkeley: University of California Press, 1990.

Sypher, Wylie. *Loss of the Self in Modern Literature.* New York: Vintage, 1962.

Taussig, Michael. *Shamanism, Colonialism and the Wildman.* Chicago: University of Chicago Press, 1987.

Tiger, Lionel. *The Pursuit of Pleasure.* Boston: Little, Brown, 1992.

Weeks, Jeffrey. *Sexuality and Its Discontents: Meaning, Myths and Modern Sexualities.* London: Routledge, 1985.

——. *Sexuality.* London: Tavistock, 1986.

Weston, Kath. *Families We Choose: Lesbians, Gays, Kinship.* New York: Columbia University Press, 1991.

White, Edmund. *States of Desire.* New York: Dutton, 1980.

Index